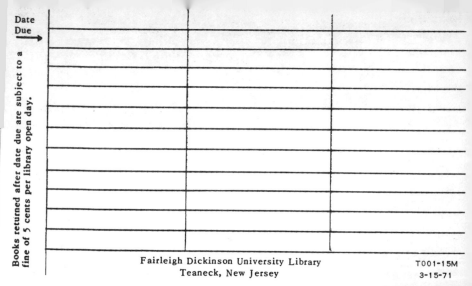

FORTITER ET SUAVITER

PR
3366
.A55

Congreve, William, 1670–1729.
    Letters & documents. Collected & edited by John C.
Hodges. [1st ed.] New York, Harcourt, Brace and World
[1964]

    xxii, 295 p. ports., facsim. 24 cm.

    Bibliography: p. 281–282.

    1. Authors—Correspondence, reminiscences, etc.   i. Hodges, John
Cunyus, 1892–   ed.   II. Title.   4/13/79

PR3366.A55   928.2   64—11528

*W*ILLIAM *C*ONGREVE: LETTERS & DOCUMENTS

William Congreve, the Young Dramatist

WILLIAM CONGREVE

Letters

&

Documents

collected & edited by

JOHN C. HODGES

HARCOURT, BRACE & WORLD, INC.

New York

first edition

Library of Congress Catalog Card Number: 64-11528
PRINTED IN THE UNITED STATES OF AMERICA

100145

To Cornelia Smartt Hodges

$\mathcal{P}$REFACE

WILLIAM CONGREVE (1670-1729) has been the subject of innumerable biographical sketches and of no fewer than seven full-length biographies. The first of these was a volume of more than three hundred pages published within a year of Congreve's death, and four belong to the present century. Yet the author of *The Way of the World* remains but a dim figure that has largely escaped us, as no one knows better than the present editor, who was also Congreve's last biographer.

Congreve was well known—enjoyed, loved, and esteemed—by the choicest men of his age. Dryden gave him his "entire Affection" (No. 56) and named him his literary successor. Pope dedicated his Homer to him as "a memorial of my friendship, with one of the most valuable men as well as finest writers, of my age and country" (No. 136). Swift wrote of "Congreve, whom I loved from my youth" (No. 141). And when Steele needed a judge of "known Humanity" in a literary controversy, he turned to Congreve as one with "Taste and Delicacy," with "Æquanimity, Candour and Benevolence," whose judgment he valued more than that of "any other Man living . . . one whom every wise and good Man looks upon with the greatest Affection and Veneration" (No. 139).

The urgent need to let Congreve speak for himself through his letters, and to see him through the eyes of his close associates, has prompted the editing of the materials brought together in this book. Through these the twentieth century can know something of Congreve as he was known to Dryden, Pope, Swift, and Steele. The letters and documents reveal a Congreve who had his share of human weakness but one who was astute and diplomatic. The very astuteness which helped to smooth his way during his lifetime has obscured some of his very human actions and has led to serious misinterpretations by later generations. If we forget Congreve as he has been misinterpreted by Johnson, Macaulay, and Thackeray, and, instead, look steadily at the contemporary evidence, we get a picture of him that has not been possible during the last two hundred years. Perhaps, with this truer picture, we can appreciate more fully the plays Congreve has left us.

The 157 letters and documents here assembled set forth Congreve's life and career—personal, business, literary. The first chapter contains the intimate personal correspondence with his closest friend and the family with which he lived in the Strand. The second chapter shows a warm personal element in Congreve's business and literary dealings with Dryden and Tonson, and it also touches upon his financial affairs and his long government service. The third, concerned primarily with literary matters, assembles for the first time all of Congreve's literary criticism. Congreve's famous letter to Dennis on humor in comedy (No. 110) has been printed many times. But his other ideas on comedy, in dedications to the plays and in letters to Dennis, are not so well known. The Appendix, concerned largely with events following Congreve's death, brings together letters and documents that help to clarify his puzzling will and his relations with Henrietta, Duchess of Marlborough.

Congreve prefixed the usual dedicatory letter to each of his major published works, sometimes with poetic epistles addressed to him by his friends, and he included with his collected *Works* in 1710 several verse letters to his patrons. Except for these, he made no effort to preserve his correspondence. He did not, like Addison, keep a letter book; nor did he, like Dennis and Pope, call in and edit letters that had passed between him and his friends. If he preserved among his personal papers any of the letters written to him, not one has thus far come to light. Letters either by or to him have been exceedingly difficult to find.

John Dennis, the critic, printed eight letters by or to Congreve in his *Letters on Several Occasions* (1696), and Pope edited four others in 1735 and 1737. More important were forty-three Congreve letters to Joseph Keally printed by George-Monck Berkeley in *Literary Relics* (1789). *The Gentleman's Magazine* printed three Congreve letters to Jacob Tonson in June, 1835; and five years later Leigh Hunt, in his *Dramatic Works of Wycherley, Congreve, Vanbrugh, and Farquhar*, printed six of the letters Congreve had written to Mr. and Mrs. Porter, with whom he lived in the Strand. These printed letters made the bulk of the fifty-nine collected by Montague Summers in his *Complete Works of William Congreve* (4 vols., Nonesuch Press, 1923, Vol. I, pp. 69-105) and of the sixty-four by Bonamy Dobrée in his *The Mourning Bride, Poems, & Miscellanies* (Oxford World's Classics, 1928, pp. 485-536). But neither Summers nor Dobrée made much effort to date or edit the letters collected, and each included only letters written by Congreve.

The present edition adds to earlier collections twenty-eight letters and documents *by* Congreve (including the important dedicatory letters), twenty-five directed *to* him, and forty *about* him. These ninety-three additional items, along with the sixty-four letters previously collected by Summers and Dobrée, make up the total of 157 letters and documents in this edition. This total excludes, as of lesser importance, the following:

1. Fifteen business notes or receipts signed by Congreve:
CONGREVE TO J. D. NARDVICE, 27 July 1710, MS. in Folger Shakespeare Library
CONGREVE TO BERNARD LINTOTT, 1 June 1715, Hodges, p. 106 (See Key to Abbreviations, p. xv)
CONGREVE TO MR. GRIGSBY, 14 August 1716, Hodges, p. 99
CONGREVE TO MR. GRIGSBY, 13 September 1716, Hodges, p. 99
CONGREVE TO MR. GRIGSBY, 30 March 1717, MS. in Huntington Library
AUTHORITY TO SELL STOCK, 6 April 1717, Bodleian MS. 25,427
CONGREVE TO MATHEW WYMONDSOLD, 26 April 1717, Bodleian MS. d. 1
CONGREVE TO WILLIAM LOWNDES, SR., 4 June 1719, MS. in William Andrews Clark Memorial Library, Los Angeles

CONGREVE TO MR. CRAIGGS, 18 June 1720, MS. in Folger Shakespeare Library

CONGREVE TO CHARLES LOCKYER, 16 November 1721, Evelyn Papers, Library of Christ Church, Oxford

CONGREVE TO JOHN WARNER, 21 November 1721, Widener Collection, Harvard

CONGREVE TO CHARLES LOCKYER, 15 February 1721/22, Hodges, p. 99

CONGREVE TO THOMAS SNOW AND JOHN PALTOCK, 14 October 1723, MS. in Huntington Library

CONGREVE TO THOMAS SNOW AND JOHN PALTOCK, 15 May 1724, MS. in Folger Shakespeare Library

CONGREVE TO JOHN WARNER AND COMPANY, December, 1724, MS. owned by Mr. Samuel Loveman, Bodley Book Shop, New York City

2. Sixteen verse letters by (*five*) *or* to (*eleven*) *Congreve:*

CONGREVE TO DRYDEN, October, 1692, Dobrée, pp. 252-253

BEVIL HIGGONS TO CONGREVE, March, 1693, Dobrée, *Comedies*, pp. 20-21

J. MARSH TO CONGREVE, March, 1693, Dobrée, *Comedies*, pp. 19-20

THOMAS SOUTHERNE TO CONGREVE, March, 1693, Dobrée, *Comedies*, pp. 18-19

THOMAS YALDEN TO CONGREVE, July, 1693, Dryden's *Examen Poeticum: being the third part of Poetical Miscellanies*, London, 1693, pp. 343-348

WILLIAM DOVE TO CONGREVE, November, 1693, *The Gentleman's Journal* for November, 1693

DRYDEN TO CONGREVE, November, 1693, Dobrée, *Comedies*, pp. 118-120

SWIFT TO CONGREVE, November, 1693, *The Poems of Jonathan Swift*, ed. by Harold Williams, Oxford, 1937, Vol. I, pp. 43-50

CHARLES GILDON TO CONGREVE, 1698-1699, Bodleian MS. 14,592

STEELE TO CONGREVE, March, 1700, *A New Miscellany of Original Poems, on Several Occasions*, London, 1701, pp. 335-339

STEELE TO CONGREVE, 1701, *A New Miscellany of Original Poems, on Several Occasions*, London, 1701, pp. 299-301

CONGREVE TO CHARLES MONTAGU, Lord Halifax, 1710, *Dobrée*, pp. 199-200

CONGREVE TO SIR GODFREY KNELLER, 1710, *Dobrée*, pp. 289-290

CONGREVE TO SIR RICHARD TEMPLE, 1710, *Dobrée*, pp. 323-326

WILLIAM DIAPER TO CONGREVE, 15 March 1711/12, Dedication to *Nereides: or Sea-Eclogues*, London, 1712

CONGREVE TO RICHARD TEMPLE, Viscount Cobham, 24 August 1728, *Dobrée*, pp. 400-402

3. Five items about *Congreve, besides many others mentioned in Chapter II:*

ADDISON ON DRYDEN AND CONGREVE, 3 April 1694, *The Miscellaneous Works of Joseph Addison*, ed. by A. C. Guthkelch, London, 1914, Vol. I, pp. 30-35

AGREEMENT FOR ADMISSION TO HAYMARKET THEATRE, 8 May 1704, Hist. MSS. Com., *Thirteenth Report*, London, 1893, Appendix, Vol. II, p. 185

More than half of the 157 items included are preserved in the original manuscripts, from which the letters and documents (with the few exceptions noted) have been edited—twenty of them for the first time. In general, the spelling, punctuation, and capitalization of the originals have been retained, except that sentences are regularly begun with capitals and ended with periods. (The manuscripts often leave the terminal punctuation uncertain; and, besides, sentences need to be clearly marked to insure easy reading.) Raised letters are brought down to the line, and most abbreviations in the text are expanded. Place and date of writing are placed uniformly at the upper right, where Congreve usually put them, with brackets around anything not supplied by the text. For letters by Congreve not edited from manuscripts, commas are omitted after the place name in the heading and after the salutation, in keeping with Congreve's common practice in his extant manuscript letters. For each letter or document, a footnote shows, first, the location of the manuscript (if extant) and, second, the first printed source (if any) and often one or more later editions.

One special detail requires notice here. Congreve's Irish friend Joseph Keally, to whom the dramatist wrote most of his extant personal letters, began spelling his name "Kelly" about 1702. The earlier, more commonly used spelling is followed throughout this edition except in transcribing the ten manuscript letters (Nos. 15, 16, 23, 29, 35, 37, 38, 43, 44, 46) in which the spelling is "Kelly."

ACKNOWLEDGMENTS

The editor is deeply grateful to the many keepers of books and manuscripts in Europe and America for generous assistance in the difficult search for Congreve materials; to the American Philosophical Society for a grant that made possible an extensive search through Europe; to the late Sir Geoffrey Congreve, Bart., and then to Major Christopher Congreve, for use of early Congreve family genealogy and other records; to Sir Ivone Kirkpatrick and to Ruth, Dowager Countess of Chichester, for kind permission to reproduce paintings of Congreve and Henrietta, Duchess of Marlborough; and to the University of Tennessee for substantial aid toward publication.

For the use of manuscript letters and documents, with permission to print or reprint, the editor is specifically indebted to the British Museum, the Scottish Record Office, the Middle Temple, Hoare's Bank in Fleet Street, the Bank of England, the Bodleian Library, the Cambridge University Library, the Library of the University of Edinburgh, the Earl of Home, and those in charge of records at Somerset House and the Public Record Office in London; to the Pennsylvania Historical Society, the Pierpont Morgan Library, the New York Public Library, the Folger Shakespeare Library, the Henry E. Huntington Library, the William Andrews Clark Memorial Library, the late Carl H. Pfortzheimer, and the libraries of Harvard, Yale, and the University of Texas.

Among others to whom I am particularly indebted are Professor Kathleen Lynch, Professor Robert Halsband, and E. S. de Beer, Esq., who have kindly allowed me to draw on their profound knowledge of Congreve's period; and my lifelong friend Alwin Thaler, whose fine scholarship and sound judgment have been my constant encouragement and guide.

ASTON   Anthony Aston, *A Brief Supplement to Colley Cibber, Esq; His Lives of the Famous Actors and Actresses,* printed in full in Cibber, II, 297-318.

BALL   *The Correspondence of Jonathan Swift,* ed. by F. Elrington Ball, 6 vols., London, 1910-1914.

BATESON   *The Works of Congreve,* ed. by F. W. Bateson, New York, 1930.

BERKELEY   George-Monck Berkeley, *Literary Relics,* London, 1789.

CIBBER   *An Apology for the Life of Mr. Colley Cibber, Written by Himself,* ed. by Robert W. Lowe, 2 vols., London, 1889.

DENNIS   *Letters Upon Several Occasions . . . Published by Mr. Dennis,* London, 1696.

DNB   *Dictionary of National Biography.*

DOBRÉE   William Congreve, *The Mourning Bride, Poems, and Miscellanies,* ed. by Bonamy Dobrée, London, 1928. (Letters, pp. 485-536.)

DOBRÉE, *Comedies*   *Comedies by William Congreve,* ed. by Bonamy Dobrée, London, 1925.

Erdswick Book   A manuscript genealogy of the Congreves begun by Sampson Erdswick about 1593 and continued since, generation by generation. Owned by Major Christopher Congreve.

Familiar Letters   *Familiar Letters of Love, Gallantry, and several Occasions, by the Wits of the last and present Age . . . ,* 2 vols., London, 1718.

GEC *Peerage*   G.E.C., *et al., The Complete Peerage,* 1910-   .

HODGES   John C. Hodges, *William Congreve the Man,* New York, 1941.

HOOKER   *The Critical Works of John Dennis,* ed. by Edward Niles Hooker, 2 vols., Baltimore: The Johns Hopkins Press, 1939-1943.

HUNT   Leigh Hunt, *The Dramatic Works of Wycherley, Congreve, Vanbrugh, and Farquhar*, London, 1840.

JOHNSON   Samuel Johnson, *Lives of the Poets*, ed. by George Birkbeck Hill, 3 vols., Oxford, 1905.

Library   John C. Hodges, *The Library of William Congreve*, New York: The New York Public Library, 1955.

LUTTRELL   Narcissus Luttrell, *A Brief Historical Relation of State Affairs*, 6 vols., Oxford, 1857.

LYNCH   Kathleen M. Lynch, *A Congreve Gallery*, Cambridge: Harvard University Press, 1951.

MALONE   Edmund Malone, *The Critical and Miscellaneous Prose Works of John Dryden*, 4 vols., London, 1800.

Memoirs   *Memoirs of the Life, Writings, and Amours of William Congreve Esq; . . .* by Charles Wilson Esq, London, 1730.

NICOLL   Allardyce Nicoll, *A History of English Drama, 1660-1900*, 4 vols., Cambridge: Cambridge University Press, 1955.

P.R.O.   Public Record Office, London.

SHERBURN   *The Correspondence of Alexander Pope*, ed. by George Sherburn, 5 vols., Oxford, 1956.

SUMMERS   *The Complete Works of William Congreve*, ed. by Montague Summers, 4 vols., London, 1923. (Letters, I, 69-105.)

WARD   *The Letters of John Dryden*, ed. by Charles E. Ward, Durham: Duke University Press, 1942.

Works (1710)   *The First [Second, Third] Volume of the Works of Mr. William Congreve*, 3 vols., London, 1710.

Works (1719)   *The Works of Mr. William Congreve: In Two Volumes. Consisting of His Plays and Poems*. The Third Edition, Revis'd by the Author. London, 1719. [The "Second Edition" was a reissue of the first with a title page dated 1717.]

CONTENTS

II *Dryden, Tonson, & Business Affairs*

III *Dennis, Addison, Pope, & Others: Chiefly Literary Criticism*

*W*ILLIAM *C*ONGREVE: LETTERS & DOCUMENTS

I JOSEPH KEALLY & THE PORTERS:

STRICTLY PERSONAL

Joseph Keally

Most of Congreve's known personal letters were written to Joseph Keally, a very dear friend in Ireland. Their friendship began, no doubt, when the two were thrown together as boys in the famous preparatory school at Kilkenny. Congreve had gone to live in Ireland when only four years old and had spent the next eight years in the busy seaports of Youghall and Carrickfergus, where his father was a lieutenant in the English garrison. Then when Congreve was twelve, just at the right age for preparatory school, his father was transferred to the regiment of the Duke of Ormonde at Kilkenny. The school there, sponsored by the Ormonde family since the days of Elizabeth, had recently been provided by the Duke with a commodious building and playing field adjoining the princely Kilkenny Castle, where the Duke of Ormonde held court as Lord Lieutenant of Ireland. The school was recognized as one of the best in the British Isles. Here was a golden opportunity for the son of a poor lieutenant, since the school charter provided that "children of all such as are attending in the service of the Duke of Ormond, shall at all times be admitted to the privileges and benefits of said school gratis."[1] Congreve was in his fourth year at Kilkenny when he was joined by an Irish lad three years his junior: Joseph Keally, the oldest son of a family that had lived for generations near Kilkenny. The two boys were together for eleven months before Congreve went on to Trinity College, Dublin, in April, 1686.[2]

Three years later, the English Revolution drove both Congreve and Keally away to England, where they were brought together again as students of the law at the Middle Temple in London.[3] Both had lodgings, perhaps together, in the vicinity of Arundel Street, a few minutes' walk from the Temple westward along the Thames River. This little street was about equally distant from the Middle Temple, to the east, and the Drury Lane Theatre, to the north. And while Keally was giving his attention to the law with a keen ambition to rise in his profession, Congreve was thinking first of the theatre and of his translations from the Greek and Latin that were calling him to the attention of Dryden's literary circle at Will's Coffee-house. The one was destined to become a vigorous, ambitious man of the world; the other, a writer and scholar who wanted a quiet life and a few very close friends.

Congreve's first letter to Keally was written on 28 September 1697, after Keally had gone away to promote his affairs in Ireland. He had sailed from England before King William ended the long war with France by the Treaty of Ryswick and while the French privateers were still seizing English vessels and bringing them captive into the northern French port of St. Malo. Congreve had reason to worry until he got word of his friend's safe arrival in Ireland. It may be that Keally soon returned to London for a period of sev-

---

[1] The charter is printed in full by Edward Ledwich, *Collectanea de Rebus Hibernicis*, Dublin, 1781, Vol. II, pp. 507-517.

[2] For Joseph Keally's life see Lynch, pp. 23-36. For Congreve's life in Ireland, see Hodges, pp. 9-29.

[3] For Congreve's admission to the Middle Temple, see No. 55.

eral years, since Congreve's next extant letter to him was dated
nearly three years later on 2 July 1700. From then until his untimely death in 1713, Keally resided chiefly in Ireland but returned to
London for occasional visits. He received at least one or two letters
from Congreve every year, and one year as many as nine. A total
of forty-four are known to us. Possibly many others have been lost.
Not a single letter from Keally to Congreve has been preserved.

Most of Congreve's letters to Keally are plain and homely, without any effort at style. They answer questions raised by Keally,
comment on the activities of the Whigs (the party with which the
two friends had aligned themselves), give information about their
acquaintances in London (particularly about their intimate acquaintances in the vicinity of Arundel Street), and follow with keen interest the fortunes of Keally in Ireland. The tone of the letters is
always one of full confidence and understanding. If Congreve re-
vealed his true self to anyone, no doubt it was to Joseph Keally.

The Porters

Of all Congreve's letters, the most friendly, intimate, and unre-
strained are the forty-four known letters to Joseph Keally and the
seven he wrote to the Porters. Keally was Congreve's friend from
boyhood, and the Porters became close friends to Congreve and
Keally during their earliest years in London. Edward Porter was,
according to a marginal note on his will, "formerly of the Inner
Temple, London," [4] and both Congreve and Keally were members
of the adjoining Middle Temple. A common interest in the law
may partly explain the friendship. Before Congreve began the study
of the law at the Middle Temple in 1691, to be joined by Keally
two years later, Edward Porter was already a householder in Arundel Street, a few minutes' walk along the Thames to the west. In
Arundel Street, or nearby, Congreve and Keally took lodgings.
When Congreve wrote from the country to Keally in London, he
ended his letter with "Pray remember me to my very good friends

[4] Lynch, pp. 18, 145.

and neighbors in Arundel-street" (No. 21). And after Keally completed his legal training and returned to Ireland, Congreve's letters reminded him that "the family in Arundel-street" (No. 6), or "our friends in Arundel-street" (No. 7), "are very much yours." On 4 December 1702, Congreve urged Keally to celebrate the approaching Christmas "in Arundel Street" (No. 11). Next year, after the terrible storm on 27 November 1703, Congreve reported in detail the damage "at Mr. Porter's" and the adjoining "Blue Ball" (No. 12). We know from the address of letter No. 4, dated 11 August 1700, that Mr. Porter lived "At His house in Arundel street against the blew-ball."

After 1703, there is no reference in Congreve's letters to Arundel Street. The Porters had moved back to a house in neighboring Surrey Street, where they had lived most of 1692. Since Edward Porter owned the houses in which he lived, the rate (assessment) books still preserved at Westminster make it possible to determine his different places of residence. On 26 June 1706, Congreve wrote Keally that he had "removed to Mr. Porter's in Surry-street." There he kept his lodgings for nearly twenty-three years, until his death on 19 January 1728/9. At these lodgings in Surrey Street, Congreve continued to build the fine library which his old friend and publisher Jacob Tonson would later describe as "genteel and wel chosen." Tonson was astute enough to know, as he wrote his nephew just after Congreve's death (No. 99), that everything of Congreve's would be valuable, and suggested that the nephew buy the library.

Congreve had begun to collect books at least as early as his schooldays at Kilkenny. One of his books still preserved bears Congreve's inscription and the dates 1682 and 1683.[5] About 1726, after Congreve had lived in Surrey Street for twenty years, he made a careful forty-four-page list of his books showing the placing of each book on one of thirty-three shelves.[6] In spite of trouble with his eyes, Congreve stayed much at home and made reading his chief

[5] See No. 2, note 8.

[6] See *Library*, p. 9.

diversion, using a magnifying glass to aid his defective eyesight (No. 41).

One bond between Congreve and the Porters was the fact that Mrs. Porter, born Frances Bracegirdle, was the sister of Anne Bracegirdle,[7] the beautiful and gifted actress who created the part of the heroine in each of Congreve's plays, and in whom Congreve was deeply interested. Anne Bracegirdle also played the part of Venus in Congreve's masque *The Judgment of Paris,* causing Congreve's note to Keally: "Our friend Venus performed to a miracle" (No. 8). Anne Bracegirdle lived with her mother in Howard Street, the short connecting link between Arundel and Surrey Streets.

From the repeated references in Congreve's letters to Joseph Keally, we know that the Porters and the Bracegirdles took a special interest in Congreve's Irish friend. Congreve wrote him how they inquired after him (No. 25), how "The ladies had all the concern imaginable" on hearing of his accident (No. 24), and how "The ladies here are much your servants; but some of them think your remembrance of them too general" (No. 30). Mrs. Porter took great pains to make linen shirts for Keally (Nos. 46, 47, 48), and seemed almost as interested as Congreve in his visits to London. She "went up to Bath," so Congreve wrote Keally in 1712, "almost on purpose to meet you and bring you up [to London] with her" (No. 50).

The seven Congreve letters to the Porters (five to Edward and two to Frances) cover about twenty-five of Congreve's forty years in London. The first of these is Congreve's earliest known familiar letter, written in 1692 at the age of twenty-two, about the time when he was making the final revision of his first comedy. He certainly wrote the letter from the very spot that was pointed out to Boswell and Johnson fifty years after Congreve's death as the place where *The Old Bachelor* had been written.[8]

---

[7] Mrs. Porter was long supposed to be the famous actress Mary Porter (see Hunt, p. xliii), until Professor Kathleen Lynch discovered her true identity by consulting the will of Edward Porter. See Lynch, p. 19.

[8] See John C. Hodges, "The Composition of Congreve's First Play," *PMLA,* LVIII (1943), pp. 971-976.

I   CONGREVE TO EDWARD PORTER

Ilam [1] *[August 21, 1692]* [2]

SIR

I am forced to Borrow Ladies paper [3] but I think it will contain all
that I can tell you from this place which is so much out of the
world that nothing but the last great news could have reacht it. I
have a little tried, what solitude and retirement can afford, which
are here in perfection. I am now writing to you from before a black
mountain nodding over me and a whole river in cascade falling so
near me that even I can distinctly see it. [4] I can onely tell you of
the situation I am in, which would be better expressed by Mr: Grace
if he were here. I hope all our friends are well both at Salisbury
and windsor—where I suppose you spent the last week. Pray when
ever you write to them give them my humble service. I think to go
the next week to Mansfield [5] race where I am told I shall see all
the Country. If I see any of your acquaintance I will do you right
to them. I hope Mr. Longuevilles [6] picture has been well finishd.
I am dear Sir

Your most humble
Servant

Ilam near Ashbourn   *Will: Congreve.*
in Derbyshire.
between 6 and 7 in the morning
birds singing Jolly breezes whistling and [   ]

Address: *To Mr. Edward Porter At his house in*
Surrey Street in the Strand

Postmark: *AV/21*

MANUSCRIPT: British Museum Add. 4293, f. 56. EDITIONS: Hunt, p. xliv; Summers, Vol. I, p. 98; Dobrée, pp. 522-523.

[1] The little village of Ilam is in Dovedale about five miles north of Ashbourne
in Derbyshire. This county is just east of Staffordshire, where the Congreve
family had been settled for many generations at Stretton Hall and where Congreve's father was born. The old manor house in which Congreve was staying
in 1692 is still standing. The modern Ilam Hall, built in 1816, is nearby.

[2] The year 1692 is determined by the address to Edward Porter "At his house in Surrey Street" combined with the youthfulness of Congreve's signature. Edward Porter lived in Surrey Street, as shown by the rate books at Westminster, for only the single year 1692 before moving there permanently some years after 1700. The youthful flourishes in the signature were long discontinued by Congreve before Edward Porter moved back to Surrey Street. The postmark shows the month and the day: August 21.

[3] The extant manuscript on which Congreve was writing measures slightly less than four by six inches, distinctly smaller than the page on which he usually wrote.

[4] This is the first reference to Congreve's defective eyesight. A rocky ledge near the old Ilam manor house is still placarded as the spot where Congreve wrote *The Old Bachelor*. Anyone standing at this spot can see just below him the waterfall on the Manifold River that Congreve describes as "a whole river in cascade" and also the "black mountain nodding over" him from the opposite bank. This site was shown to Johnson and Boswell in 1777 as the place where "Congreve wrote his 'Old Bachelor.' " See Boswell's *Life of Johnson*, ed. by G. B. Hill and L. F. Powell, Oxford, 1934, Vol. III, p. 187.

[5] Mansfield is in the adjoining county about twenty-five miles east of Ilam.

[6] William Longueville (1639-1721) had been, like Edward Porter, a member of the Inner Temple and had continued his association with the Inner Temple as reader or treasurer as late as 1695. He lived in Covent Garden in Bow Street near Will's Coffee-house, where young Congreve was a favored member in the circle of Dryden. See *DNB*.

2   CONGREVE TO JOSEPH KEALLY

London September 28: 1697.

DEAR JO:

I thought you were either drownd or a prisoner at St Malloes, which would have been a worse thing if not for you, at least for your acquaintance, for I would not willingly hear any more of St: Malloes.[1] You must not wonder if the Peace which affects all Europe should in some measure influence me; it has indeed put a stop to my intended pilgrimage for St Patricks.[2] I am sorry you are like to have no better an effect of your own. Maybe I may stay in England to as little purpose as you left it; but I am advised to try. My Lord Duke of Ormond [3] whom I waited on yesterday talks of going for Ireland on Monday next. I would not miss such an opportunity if it were not thought absolutely necessary for me to stay here. I believe my Lady Duchesse and the Good Bishop [4] will have their books at that time. I have no news of any kind to send you. I have not seen Bottom [5] since I received your letter but Amory [6] I just now parted with who is yours. Jerry Marsh [7] is here. As for Luther [8] I find him both by your account and his own proceeding unalterable. And I hope Champ and you will come over together. Pray give my hearty service to my Cosen Congreve.[9] Tell the Good Bishop I must have very good fortune before I am reconciled to the necessity of my staying in England at a time when I promised my selfe the Happinesse of seeing him at Kilkenny. I would say something very devout to the Dutchesse but you are a prophane dog and would spoil it. If the Bishop would sanctifie my Duty to her I would requite him in my way. Prithee Keally distribute my service in a most particular manner and make me popular amongst those acquaintance whom I have forgott. Let me hear when I may expect you and make haste to your

W: Congreve

Pray lett me know if you did not receive some letters from your brother [10] because I sent such a pacquett after you to Ireland. I did not write because I concluded you would know my seal.[11]

Postmark: *SE/28*

MANUSCRIPT: Berg Collection, The New York Public Library. EDITIONS: Berkeley, pp. 352-354; Summers, Vol. I, p. 83; Dobrée, pp. 503-504.

[1] Raids on English shipping from the northern French port of St. Malo continued. Keally could hardly have received Congreve's letter before Luttrell reported (9 October 1697) "that 3 English homeward bound Barbadoes ships were taken, and carried into St. Maloes."

[2] Apparently Congreve stayed in England to help celebrate the peace that was expected with the Treaty of Ryswick. Eight days after he wrote to Keally, he was reported "engaged in a poem on occasion of the peace, and all who are

acquainted with the performance of this gentleman expect something very extraordinary" (*Diary and Correspondence of John Evelyn*, ed. by John Forster, London, 1852, Vol. III, p. 369). This poem, entitled "The Birth of the Muse," was advertised by Jacob Tonson in *The London Gazette* for 18-22 November 1697.

[3] James Butler, second Duke of Ormonde (1665-1745), was the grandson of the first Duke, who had provided so generously for the famous preparatory school at Kilkenny attended by Congreve and Keally. The second Duke was preparing to return to his duties as Lord Lieutenant of Ireland. The Duchess had preceded the Duke by more than five months, as we learn from Luttrell, 22 April 1697: "The dutchesse of Ormond, with several persons of quality, are gone hence for Ireland."

[4] John Hartsonge (1654-1717), chaplain to the first Duke of Ormonde while Congreve and Keally were schoolboys at Kilkenny. In 1693 he was appointed Bishop of Ossary with his residence in Kilkenny (Lynch, p. 148). The books for the Duchess and the Bishop were probably copies of Congreve's *The Mourning Bride*, which had been acted with great success earlier in the year.

[5] Possibly Joseph Bottom, who died in the Barbadoes 23 November 1732. See the *Gentleman's Magazine* for 1732, p. 1083. Congreve referred to Bottom again in No. 18.

[6] Thomas Amory, a graduate of Trinity College, Dublin (1681), was one of the Irish Protestants who, along with Congreve, fled to England in 1688. He died in Ireland in 1728. See Lynch, p. 17.

[7] Probably the "J." Marsh who had written commendatory verses published with *The Old Bachelor* in 1693.

[8] Henry Luther, son of the mayor of Youghal, where Congreve spent his first years in Ireland, received his legal training with Congreve at the Middle Temple. See Lynch, p. 17. Apparently Luther and Congreve were together also at Kilkenny during 1682 and 1683 since those dates in Congreve's hand appear in one of his books preserved in the Yale Library along with the note, "Gulielmus Congreve est verus Possessor hajus Libri ex Dono Henrici Luther." See *Library*, No. 236.

[9] This cousin was probably Colonel William Congreve (1671-1746), of Highgate. See p. 82 and No. 93, note 4.

[10] Keally's brother John, then living in Portugal, is mentioned also in Nos. 11, 26, 47, and 48.

[11] Congreve's seal, showing the distinctive family coat of arms with three battle axes, is preserved with the original letter in The New York Public Library. Near the seal is the postmark, "SE/28." Along with this letter of 1697 is filed a separate sheet that is clearly the cover to No. 11, dated 4 December 1702.

This sheet carries the address, in Congreve's hand, "To Joseph Keally Esqre: to be left at the post office in Dublin," the postmark "DE/4," and the later manuscript note, "Congreve 1702."

3   CONGREVE TO JOSEPH KEALLY

London July 2. 1700.

DEAR KEALLY

By your last from Dublin I may guess this will find you at Kilkenny; where I hope you will settle your affairs, so that in a little time it may not be inconvenient for you to see your friends here, who very much regret your absence. I need not tell you that I do; who am not apt to care for many acquaintance, and never intend to make many friendships. You know I need not be very much alone; but I choose it, rather than to conform myself to the manners of my court or chocolate-house acquaintance. My neighbours [1] are very much yours; and, if you drink not their healths daily, are before hand with you in a kind remembrance. You have failed in your commission to Holywell; answer it as you can. The inclosed I received a week since; but could not venture to direct them at large to Dublin. The king goes on Thursday to Holland.[2] Eccles [3] is made master of his music, which was an employment void by the death of Dr Staggins; [4] it is worth L.300 *per annum*. Mein [5] is well, and yours. I am glad to hear from you. Pray don't grow rusty; and remember sometimes to write to me when you have idle hours. I am yours,

Will. Congreve.

I have not yet seen Dandridge; [6] but will, in my next, give you an account of that affair.

EDITIONS: Berkeley, pp. 320-321; Summers, Vol. I, p. 70; Dobrée, pp. 486-487.

[1] Congreve's neighbors included Edward Porter, his wife, Frances, her sister Anne Bracegirdle, the actress, and the mother of Frances and Anne. The Porters

then lived in Arundel Street and Anne lived with her mother in tiny Howard Street, just off Arundel. When Keally was in London, he lodged with or near Congreve in Arundel Street.

[2] Luttrell, 4 July 1700: "This morning, about 6, his majestie . . . went from Hampton Court for Holland. . . ."

[3] John Eccles (1650?-1735) composed music for songs in many plays, including Congreve's *Love for Love* and *Way of the World*, and also for Congreve's "Hymn to Harmony" in honor of St. Cecilia's Day (1703). Congreve reported that Eccles' music for his *Judgment of Paris* (1701) was "universally admired." See No. 8. In 1707, Eccles composed music for Congreve's *Semele*.

[4] Nicholas Staggins (1650?-1700) was master of "his majesty's musick" under Charles II, James II, and William III. Luttrell reported (on June 15) that he was found dead in his bed on 13 June 1700.

[5] In Berkeley, followed by Summers and Dobrée, this name appears as "Keir," evidently a misreading of "Mein." Charles Mein, a close friend to Congreve and Keally, was an Irishman employed at the Custom-house in London. Swift described him (*Journal to Stella*, 8 October 1710) as "an honest, goodnatured fellow, a thorough hearty laugher, mightily beloved by the men of wit"; and Gay, in "Mr. Pope's Welcome from Greece," called him "wond'ring Maine, so fat with laughing eyes." For Mein's letters to Keally, see Nos. 16 and 44. See Lynch, pp. 17-18.

[6] See another reference to Dandridge in No. 8.

4   CONGREVE TO EDWARD PORTER

Calais, [Sunday], August 11th: Old:Style, 1700

If any letters are left for me before
you receive this pray enclose them
to be left at the post house in Brussels.
For any that shall Come after your receipt
of this, I will trouble you with some
other direction.

Here is Admirable Champagn for twelve pence a Quart, as good Burgundy for 15 pence; and yet I have vertue enough to resolve

to leave this place to morrow for St Omers where the same wine
is halfe as dear again and may be not quite so good. (Dear Neighbour) Charles [1] and Jacob [2] and I have never faild drinking your
healths since we saw you, nor ever will till we see you again. We
had a long passage but delicate weather. We set sail from Dover
on Saturday morning 4 a clock and did not land here till 6 the
same evening; nor had we arrivd even in that time, if a french
open boat with Oars had not been stragling towards us when we
were not quite halfe-seas over, and rowd us hither from thence in
5 hours; for the packet boat came not till this morning; when I
come to Brussells I shall have more to write to you. Till then I am

> *most humbly*
> *and heartily your*
> *W: Congreve*

My humble service to my neighbour, your Mother,[3] Mrs: Anne:
Mr: Travers,[4] not forgetting the Alcayde who [I] hope in my Ab-
sence may be reconcild to Punch. Poor Charles is Just writing to
Mrs. Anne and striving very hard to send something besides the
Ballad, to please her much.

Address: *To Mr: Porter*
> *At His house in Arundel street*
> *against the blew-ball.*
> *London.*

Postmark: *AV/14*

MANUSCRIPT: British Museum Add. 4293, ff. 61, 62. EDITIONS: *Athenaeum*,
1831; Hunt, p. xlv; Summers, Vol. I, p. 100; Dobrée, pp. 525-526.

[1] Charles Mein (see No. 3) and Congreve, as this letter shows, had made the
passage from Dover to Calais on the preceding day to start a short Continental
tour. Congreve's next letter (No. 5) was written from Rotterdam nearly seven
weeks later at the end of September; and by 10 December 1700, Congreve was
back in London writing Keally about his "extremely agreeable" journey with
Mein (see No. 6). He probably got back about the middle of October as planned
in his letter from Rotterdam.

[2] Perhaps Jacob Tonson, Congreve's publisher. See pp. 76-80 and Nos. 57,
58, 62, 69, 75, 76, 91, 98-101.

[3] This may refer to Mr. Porter's mother (if there was such a person living with her son in Arundel Street), or, more probably, to Mrs. Porter's mother, Mrs. Bracegirdle, who was certainly living nearby in Howard Street with her famous actress-daughter Mrs. Anne Bracegirdle, twice mentioned in the letter as "Mrs. Anne."

[4] Perhaps Samuel Travers. See No. 9.

5   CONGREVE TO MRS. EDWARD PORTER

Rotterdam September 27: 1700

I leave you to Judge whither Holland can be said to be wanting in Gallantry, when it is Customary there to enclose a Billet doux to a Lady, in a letter to her husband.[1] I have not so much as made mention of this, to yours; and if you tell first, let the sin fall upon your head instead of his. For my part I keep the Commandments, I love my neighbour as my selfe, and to avoid Coveting my neighbours wife I desire to be coveted by her; which you know is quite another thing. About 5 weeks since, I wrote a very passionate letter to you from Antwerp which I believe you never receivd, for just now it is found, carefully put up by my Man, who has been drunk ever since. I understand you have not been in the Country. I am glad of it; for I should very much have aprehended the effects which solitude might have produced, joynd with the regrett which I know you feel for my absence. Take it for granted that I sigh extreamly: I would have written to the Alcayd, but that would make me reflect that I was at a distance from her, which is pain I cannot bear. I would have written to your Mother[2] but that I have changed my religion twice since I left england, and am at present so unsettled, that I think it fit to fix before I endeavour to Convert her to my opinion which I design to do as soon as I know what it is. I have discoursd with friers and monks of all orders, with zealots enthusiasts and all sectaries of the reformd churches. And I had the benefit to travel 12 leagues together in Guelderland with a mad Phanatick in a waggon, who preachd to me all the way things not to be written. Pray take care that Mr: Ebbub has good wine for I have much to say to you over a bottle underground: and I hope within 3 weeks to satisfie you that no man upon the face of the earth nor in the Cellar is more dear neighbour your Faithfull

and affectionate humble
servant than

W: C:

Address: *For Mrs: Porter.*

MANUSCRIPT: British Museum Add. 4293, ff. 59, 60. EDITIONS: *Athenaeum*, 1831; Hunt, pp. xliv-xlv; Summers, Vol. I, p. 99; Dobrée, pp. 524-525.

[1] Apparently Congreve enclosed the letter to Mrs. Porter with one addressed to the husband, but the letter to Mr. Porter has been lost.

[2] Mrs. Bracegirdle, who was living with Mrs. Porter's sister Anne in Howard Street.

6 CONGREVE TO JOSEPH KEALLY

London December 10. 1700.

DEAR KEALLY

I am very glad, if you are in earnest, when you find fault with not hearing from me; for by that you will know how justly I may reproach you for the same neglect. However, I was about writing to you when I received yours; but Sapho [1] being in labour, I was forced to hold my hand till her deliverance. Among other beauties which she has brought into the world, she has reserved one most like herself for you, if you can give us directions how to send it. I have not yet called for the Kerry stones; but your directions shall be observed. I am mighty sorry Amory [2] has been ill. I have preached as I ought to Mein,[3] and he has edified as he ought. Our journey [4] was extremely agreeable, though I think I had much the advantage, having seen French Flanders, which Mein missed for want of time, and yet lay at the Brill [4] almost as long (as I was making that tour) for a wind. One thing I must tell you which gave me much pleasure, and you may tell it to Amory and Robin.[5] Whenever we have seen any thing extremely surprising, chiefly in painting, though the picture has been the most solemn, the most devout, the most moving, both in the subject and the expressions of the passion; as soon as our Charles [3] began to be touched with it, he always burst out a laughing, which I like mightily; and so he did the first time he heard Abell [6] sing. Robin cannot be more the same than he is. Abell is here; has a cold at present, and is always whimsical; so that when he will sing, or whether he will sing or not upon the stage, are things very disputable: but he certainly sings beyond all creatures upon earth; and I have heard him very often both abroad and since he came over. I am very glad to hear you say you shall remember what you owe yourself. I wish you would think too what you owe your friends; who, though not able to engage your gratitude, ought to influence your good nature to think of seeing them, which you seem to give over even in your mind's eye. The family in Arundel-street are very much yours; so is Charles, and I am Robins. I have no news: It is none that Mr Montague is Lord Halifax,[7] and that I am entirely yours.

W. Congreve.

EDITIONS: Berkeley, pp. 322-324; Summers, Vol. I, pp. 70-71; Dobrée, pp. 487-488.

[1] A dog mentioned also in Nos. 7, 10, and 11.

[2] Thomas Amory. See No. 2.

[3] Charles Mein. See No. 3.

[4] For Congreve's journey to the Continent in company with Charles Mein, see Nos. 4 and 5. The Brill, or Brielle, near Rotterdam, was then much used as a port of embarkation for England.

[5] Robert Fitzgerald (1671-1725) was with Congreve in Dublin, at Trinity College, and later in London, where he studied law at the Inner Temple before he was called to the Irish Bar in Dublin about 1700. He returned to London for occasional visits. In 1708, he married Joseph Keally's younger sister. See Lynch, pp. 37-58.

[6] John Abell (1660?-1716?), a distinguished lutenist and alto singer greatly admired by John Evelyn. See *DNB*.

⁷ Charles Montagu (1661-1715), founder of the Bank of England, was created Baron Halifax in December, 1700, and Earl of Halifax in October, 1714. Congreve dedicated to him his *Double-Dealer*, 1693 (see No. 106), and his collected poems, 1710. See also No. 24.

7   CONGREVE TO JOSEPH KEALLY

London January 28. 1700 [*1701*].

The only letter which I received from you (Dear Keally) I immediately answered, though I was forced to direct to Dublin at large for want of better instructions. Whether you have received it or not I know not; for you take care to justify the character of the Irish seas. Since you have been so very silent, I am grown in charity with that brute Luther; ¹ have almost forgiven Fitzgerald; ² and, if I could ever have been angry with Tom Amory,³ should have been now reconciled to him. It is reported that you don't think fit to take notice of young Sapho,⁴ who is at a boarding-school accomplishing herself every day more and more, that she may one day find favour in your eyes; such as a certain necklace has done in the eyes of the whole town: for it has such a reputation of being right, that the lady is forced to declare very heartily to the contrary, least she should be thought to be wrong; so is forced to preserve her own reputation at the expence of the brilliants. I give you an account of it; because, as a haughty Spaniard, I know you expect it. Twenty-three beads grinding, cutting, polishing, setting, &c. come to four shillings each, and all together to four pound twelve. Talking of money, I must desire you to put Robin ² in mind, that his forgetfulness has like to have had an ill effect; for Charles has very narrowly escaped being arrested,⁵ and that near the custom-house, which might have had worse consequences than the arrest itself any where else. Maybe his modesty hinders him from writing about it; but I know he is forced to go out of town. We have had two new plays, a tragedy called the Ambitious Stepmother, written by Mr

Rowe of the Temple, and a very good one; another called the Lady's Visiting-day, written by Mr Burnaby; both acted at the new house.[6] The last is likely to have a run, and has something more in it relating to the title than the trip.[7] Poor Williams [8] the musician is dead. Sansom [9] has sent me a very beautiful mare, which should be at your service if you were here; but I hear you are going another way, and like to be married. Dick Steel is yours; so is Charles; so are our friends in Arundel-street, besides infinite thanks for the jewels, which I will not undertake to write down. I am just as I used to be, and as I always shall be, yours,

W. Congreve.

EDITIONS: Berkeley, pp. 317-319; Summers, Vol. I, p. 69; Dobrée, pp. 485-486.

[1] Henry Luther. See No. 2.

[2] Robert Fitzgerald. See No. 6.

[3] Thomas Amory. See No. 2.

[4] See No. 6.

[5] Apparently Charles Mein (see No. 3), a minor official at the custom-house, had been in danger of arrest because Robert Fitzgerald had forgotten to repay a loan.

[6] Lincoln's Inn Fields, opened by Thomas Betterton with Congreve's *Love for Love* on 30 April 1695, was called the "new house" to distinguish it from the older Theatre Royal in Drury Lane. *The Ambitious Stepmother*, by Nicholas Rowe (misread "Love" by Berkeley), published the next day after Congreve was writing, had been acted a few weeks earlier. *The Ladies Visiting-Day*, by William Burnaby (misread "Burnaly" by Berkeley), published nearly a month later on February 27, was evidently yet to be acted since it failed immediately on its production. Congreve's opinion that it "was likely to have a run" was probably based on what he had seen of the play in rehearsal at the theatre in which he had a share.

[7] "In allusion to Farquhar's comedy *The Constant Couple; or A Trip to the Jubilee*, Drury Lane, November, 1699, wherein the Jubilee is used as a mere catch-word." (Summers, Vol. I, p. 235.)

[8] Probably William Williams, known to have been one of the king's musicians about 1695-1699. See *Grove's Dictionary of Music and Musicians*, Fifth Edition, Vol. IX (1954), p. 308.

[9] John Sansom, schoolfellow of Addison and Steele at the Charterhouse, was a generous and obliging friend, as shown by the gift of the mare. In 1699, he

befriended Addison on his visit to Paris, and in 1702, loaned Steele £600. (See Walter Graham, *The Letters of Joseph Addison*, Oxford, 1941, pp. 5-6.) Congreve's interest in horses is suggested by his ownership of a volume entitled *The Gentleman's jockey, and approved farrier; instructing in the natures, causes, and cures of all diseases incident to horses*, London, 1717. See *Library*, No. 277. For other references to Sansom, see Nos. 30 and 34.

8   CONGREVE TO JOSEPH KEALLY

London March 26. 1701.

DEAR KEALLY

I should sooner have answered yours, and acknowledged the receipt of your bill; [1] but I have been something uneasy and unwell. I heard by a letter from James Hewsly [2] of your being gone into the country. I hope it is in order to take some care about an expedition hither. All your friends in this quarter are ever inquisitive about you, and nobody thinks your correspondence frequent enough. I wished particularly for you on Friday last, when Eccles [3] his music for the prize was performed in Dorset Garden, and universally admired. Mr Finger's [4] is to be to-morrow; and Purcell [5] and Weldon's [6] follow in their turn. The latter two I believe will not be before Easter. After all have been heard severally, they are all to be heard in one day, in order to a decision; and if you come at all this spring, you may come time enough to hear that. Indeed, I don't think any one place in the world can show such an assembly. The number of performers, besides the verse-singers, was 85. The front of the stage was all built into a concave with deal boards; all which was faced with tin, to increase and throw forwards the sound. It was all hung with sconces of wax-candles, besides the common branches of lights usual in the play-houses. The boxes and pit were all thrown into one; so that all sat in common: and the whole was crammed with beauties and beaux, not one scrub being admitted. The place where formerly the music used to play, between the pit and stage, was turned into White's chocolate-house; [7] the whole family being transplanted thither with chocolate, cool'd drinks, ratafia, Pontacq,[8] &c. which every body that would called for, the whole expence of every thing being defrayed by the subscribers. I think truly the whole thing better worth coming to see than the jubilee.[9] And so I remain yours,

W. Congreve.

Our friend Venus [10] performed to a miracle; so did Mrs Hodgson Juno. Mrs Boman [11] was not quite so well approved in Pallas. I have spoken to Dandridge; [12] but he does not mind me; so let him wait.

EDITIONS: Berkeley, pp. 324-327; Summers, Vol. I, pp. 71-72; Dobrée, pp. 488-489.

[1] Perhaps this bill was in settlement for the beads mentioned in No. 7. Congreve had very diplomatically, but carefully, mentioned the sum as "four pound twelve."

[2] James Hewsly, mentioned only here in Congreve's correspondence, has not been identified.

[3] John Eccles. See No. 3. Eccles was one of four distinguished composers competing for two hundred pounds in prizes to be awarded for the best music to accompany Congreve's masque, *The Judgment of Paris*, as announced in the *London Gazette* for 18-21 March 1699/1700. Eccles won the second prize of fifty pounds. John Weldon was first. The ornate old Dorset Garden Theatre on the Thames River was well suited to the performance of a masque requiring an elaborate setting.

[4] Godfrey Finger (in England *ca.* 1685-1701) was so humiliated by winning only the fourth prize of twenty pounds that he withdrew from England and returned to the Continent. On 3 December 1701, George Stepney, Envoy to Vienna, wrote to Lord Halifax: "I thank you for your Eccles his Musick, which I suppose is got by this time to Hamburgh and will shortly be here, where Finger will see it performed to the best advantage: He assures me notwithstanding the partiality which was shown by the Duke of Somersett and others in favor of Welding and Eccles, Mr. Purcell's Musick was the best (I mean after his own, for no Decision can destroy the Love we have for our selves)." Bodleian MS. 25,427, f. 67.

[5] Berkeley, followed by Summers and Dobrée, reads "Russel," which must be a misreading of "Purcel." Daniel Purcell (1660?-1717), brother of the late great Henry Purcell, composed music for Congreve's masque and won the third prize of thirty pounds. Purcell's music was performed on Friday, 11 April 1700 (see

the *London Post*). The fifty-four-page manuscript, apparently in the composer's handwriting, is preserved in the British Museum Add. MS. 29,398. See *DNB*.

[6] John Weldon (1676-1736), the young Oxford organist, won the first prize of one hundred pounds. See *DNB*.

[7] White's Chocolate House, established two years earlier in St. James's Street and immediately popular with the fashionable world, was probably the chocolate house Congreve had in mind for the opening scene of his *Way of the World*.

[8] A white or red wine, from the Basses Pyrénnées in southern France, that was frequently advertised in the contemporary *Daily Courant* as "perfectly neat, strong, deep, bright, and of the right delicious Flavour." Perhaps it was Pontacq that caused Swift to complain: "Congreve's nasty white wine has given me the heart-burn" (*Journal to Stella*, 16 February 1710/11). Instead of "Pontacq," Berkeley reads "portico," which is evidently a misreading since "portico" does not fit into the context.

[9] The last Jubilee in Rome, announced by Pope Innocent XII on 18 May 1699, had attracted great interest on the part of English tourists. Farquhar had capitalized on this interest by having his affected beau Clincher, in his *The Constant Couple; or, A Trip to the Jubilee* (Drury Lane Theatre, November, 1699), speak repeatedly of the Jubilee. See Summers, Vol. I, p. 236. Since Congreve had cast his lot with Betterton at Lincoln's Inn Fields Theatre, he might well have been jealous of Farquhar's success at the rival theatre.

[10] Anne Bracegirdle (1663?-1748) played the part of Venus in *The Judgment of Paris*.

[11] Mrs. Boman, or Bowman, was the adopted daughter of the famous actor Thomas Betterton and wife of the actor Boman. See Cibber, Vol. II, p. 211.

[12] See another reference to Dandridge in No. 2.

9   CONGREVE TO JOSEPH KEALLY

London June 7th: 1701.

DEAR KEALLY

Yours of the 15th: of may last was very wellcome to me, because it promises your presence here. I hope exchange will fall as low as you would have it, but should it continue as high as it is I hope you will get over it and lend a hand to poor Robin [1] for his gutts were not naturally made for mounting. You desire me to send you news and particulars concerning the impeached Lords [2] and say 'tis a banter to you; and truly 'tis just so to me. For tho they are impeached I believe they will never be tryd; for there is neither matter nor proof against them. Scaffolds are building in westminster hall; but however I should be sorry you should not come sooner than you need to take notes there at their tryall. All Arundell Street is much yours and hears of your designs with pleasure. Mr: Travers [3] in particular since you will have me name him to you. Pray send me word when you are just coming and make haste. Mein may write merrily or gravely, but I take the man to be moapd. I never saw a fellow so alterd.[4] I am, if you come this summer, still more yours.

W: Congreve

Address: *To Joseph Keally Esqre:*
       At Kilkenny
10 thro [5] *in Ireland*

Postmark: *IV/7*

MANUSCRIPT: Library of the Historical Society of Pennsylvania, Philadelphia. EDITIONS: Berkeley, pp. 327-328; Summers, Vol. I, p. 72; Dobrée, pp. 489-490.

[1] Robert Fitzgerald. See No. 6.

[2] Some twenty entries by Luttrell between 27 March 1701 and 28 June 1701 trace the efforts of the House of Commons to impeach the four lords (Halifax, Oxford, Portland, and Somers) for their part in "a treaty for dividing Spain, to the prejudice of our antient ally the emperor." On May 31, the House of Lords named June 9 as the day for the trial and ordered "that scaffolds may be erected in Westminster hall." But after the Commons boycotted the trial (Luttrell, 17 June), the Lords acquitted the four impeached peers (24 June), and the scaffolds in Westminster Hall were ordered torn down (28 June). Congreve was correct in believing there would be no real trial of the four lords in Westminster Hall.

[3] Berkeley, followed by Summers and Dobrée, reads "Fraser" for "Travers." But "Travers" is the correct reading as shown by comparison of the same name in the manuscript letter to Edward Porter (No. 4), written on 11 August 1700. This was probably Samuel Travers, a member of Parliament who had several government employments mentioned by Luttrell.

[4] For Charles Mein's narrow escape from arrest and forced withdrawal from London, see No. 7.

[5] This note in Congreve's handwriting just below the address showed that ten pence "thro" postage had been paid, sixpence from London to Dublin and four pence from Dublin to Kilkenny.

10   CONGREVE TO JOSEPH KEALLY

[*London, Summer, 1702*]

DEAR KEALLY

You are something slow both in your approaches and your answers; but I am glad to hear from you, and shall be glad to see you after having been so long tantalized. I had once thoughts of coming for Ireland this summer, but must defer it till spring. I hope you will keep your word of Michaelmas. Every body here wishes for you; but we are at present in great grief for the death of Sapho.[1] She has left some few orphans; one of which, if it can live, is designed for you. Nich. Bolton lives at Peckham,[2] somewhere beyond Camberwell, in a farmer's house, and follows the plough, and reads Homer at the same time; as Baker [3] the actor and paver used to pave with his part pin'd upon his sleeve, and hem [4] and rehearse alternately. Tell Robin [5] I thank him for his last kind letter. I am yours,

W. Congreve.

EDITIONS: Berkeley, pp. 328-329; Summers, Vol. I, p. 73; Dobrée, p. 490.

[1] This reference to the recent death of Congreve's dog Sapho, together with the mention of "this summer," places No. 10 almost certainly in the summer of 1702. The death of Sapho is referred to again in No. 11, dated 4 December 1702.

[2] About four miles southeast of Congreve's lodgings in Arundel Street.

[3] A Dublin comic actor and master street paver who would rehearse his parts while paving. See Baker, *Dramatic Miscellanies,* London, 1784, Vol. I, pp. 244-246.

[4] "The hem is the technical term for the outer edge of a millstone or a paving-stone, and to hem is to fit neatly paving-stones together and to join them." (Summers, Vol. I, p. 237.)

[5] Robert Fitzgerald. See No. 6.

11 CONGREVE TO JOSEPH KEALLY

December 4th: 1702

DEAR KEALLY

I had not time to answer yours before; but I carryd the enclosed for your brother [1] to the secretarys office the next morning and put it into the Portugall Pacquett. I have no great faith in your promises yet I am willing to expect your performance and hope you will celebrate the ensuing festivall in Arundell street. Great revolutions have been there since the Death of Sapho,[2] things not to be entrusted to frail paper and pacquett boats. My service to inhuman Robin [3] whose letters I allways punctually answered. An exactnesse I would not have you observe at this time, for—nil mihi rescribas attamen ipse veni.[4]—Jack: Allen. Epist: 3d:

Yours

Will: Congreve

Address: *To Joseph Keally Esqre:*
      to be left at the post office
        in Dublin

Postmark: *DE/4* [5]

MANUSCRIPT: The Bodley Book Shop, New York. EDITIONS: Berkeley, p. 330; Summers, Vol. I, p. 73; Dobrée, p. 491.

[1] Keally's brother John in Portugal. See No. 2.

[2] Congreve's dog, mentioned previously in Nos. 6, 7, and 10.

[3] Robert Fitzgerald. See No. 6.

[4] Ovid, *Heroides*, I (Penelope Ulixi), 2. Congreve's ascription of the quotation to the unidentified Jack Allen was apparently a joke that Keally would understand.

[5] Address and postmark taken from the manuscript in the Berg Collection, The New York Public Library. See No. 2, note 11.

12   CONGREVE TO JOSEPH KEALLY

London November 30. 1703.

DEAR KEALLY [1]

I think it a tedious while since I heard from you; and though, to the best of my remembrance, I answered your last, yet I write again to put you in mind of your old friends, every one of whom has very narrowly escaped the hurricane [2] on Friday night last. The public papers will be full of particulars. 'Tis certain, in the memory of man, never was any thing like it. Most of the tall trees in the Park are blown down; and the four trees that stood distinct before St James's, between the Mall and the Canal. The garden-wall of the priory, and the Queen's garden there, are both laid flat. Some great sash-windows of the banqueting-house have been torn from the frames, and blown so as they have never been found nor heard of. The leads of churches have some of them been rolled up as they were before they were laid on: others have been skimmed clear [3] off, and transported cross the street, where they have been laid on other houses, breaking the roofs. The news out of the country is equally terrible; the roads being obstructed by the trees which lie cross. Anwick, Coventry, and most of the towns that my acquaintance have heard of, are in great measure destroyed, as Bristol, where they say a church was blown down. It is endless to tell you all. Our neighbour [4] in Howard's-street 'scaped well, though frighted, only the ridge of the house being stripped; and a stack of chimneys in the next house fell luckily into the street. I lost nothing but a casement in my man's chamber, though the chimneys of the Blue Ball continued tumbling by piece-meal most part of the night at Mr Porter's.[5] The wind came down the little court behind the back parlour, and burst open that door, bolts and all, whirled round the room, and scattered all the prints; of which, together with the table and chairs, it mustered into one heap, and made a battery of them to break down the other door into the entry, whither it swept them; yet broke not one pane of the window which join'd to the back-court door. It took off the sky-light of the stairs, and did no more damage there. Many people have been killed. But the loss at sea is inconceivable, though the particulars are not many yet confirmed; and I am afraid poor Beaumont[6] is lost. Shovel, they say, and Fairborn,[7] are heard of. I hope you have been less sufferers. One should be glad to hear so from your own hands. Pray give my service to all friends. The King's-Bench walk buildings are just as before their roofs were covered. Tell that to Robin.[8] I am, dear Keally, yours,

W. Congreve.

EDITIONS: Berkeley, pp. 332-334; Summers, Vol. I, pp. 74-75; Dobrée, pp. 492-493.

[1] Berkeley here uses the spelling "Kelly," without the "a," perhaps indicating the spelling in the manuscript, which is now lost. See No. 15, note 1.

[2] Luttrell, 27 November 1703: "About one this morning a terrible storm arose, which continued till past 7, the wind south west; the like not known in the memory of man; blew down a vast number of the tops of houses, chimnies, &c.; the damage incredible, the lady Nicholas and a great many people killed, and many wounded; most of the boats and barges forced a shore; an East India ship cast away near Blackwell, besides several merchant ships and colliers; divers of the great trees in St. James Park, Temple, Grayes Inn, &c. blown down; and we are apprehensive we shal hear of great losses at sea."

[3] *Clear.* Berkeley, *clever;* Summers, *clean;* Dobrée, *clear.*

[4] Anne Bracegirdle was living with her mother in Howard Street, just around the corner from Congreve in Arundel Street. Congreve never mentions Anne Bracegirdle by name in any of the forty-four letters to Keally, but he repeatedly refers to her in a way that would be clear to Keally. See Nos. 8, 14, 24, 30, 31, and 34.

[5] Edward Porter's. See No. 3, note 1. Letter No. 4 was addressed "To Mr Porter At His house in Arundel street against the blew-ball."

6 On 30 November 1703, Luttrell reported many ships lost, including "the Mary, a 4th rate, with admiral Beaumont on board." For Rear-Admiral Basil Beaumont (1669-1703), see also *DNB*.

7 *Fairborn*, not *Fairholm*, as misread by Berkeley, followed by Summers and Dobrée. On 2 December 1703, Luttrell wrote: "We have yet no account of sir Clowdesly Shovell and admiral Fairborn." But Congreve was correct in reporting that they had escaped the storm. See *DNB* for Sir Clowdisley Shovell (1650-1707) and for Admiral Stafford Fairborne (knighted 1705 and died 1742).

8 Robert Fitzgerald would have a special interest in the King's Bench Walk Buildings since they were a part of the Inner Temple, where he had been a student of the law while Congreve and Keally were at the adjoining Middle Temple. See No. 6.

13   CONGREVE TO JOSEPH KEALLY

London February 12. 1703 [1704].

DEAR KEALLY

I forgot to thank you for the hint you gave me concerning a commissioner's place in your former letter, which you have repeated in your last. You may imagine I would not omit such an advantage if it were practicable; but I know it is vain, notwithstanding all the fair promises I have had; for I have not obtained a less matter which I ask'd for. I must have patience; and I think I have. Of my philosophy I make some use; but, by God, the greatest trial of it is, that I know not how to have the few people that I love as near me as I want. You will do me the justice to apply this as I intend it. I am yours,

W. Congreve.

My service to Robin 1 *and the rest.*

EDITIONS: Berkeley, p. 331; Summers, Vol. I, pp. 73-74; Dobrée, p. 491.

1 Robert Fitzgerald. See No. 6.

14   CONGREVE TO JOSEPH KEALLY

London May 20. 1704.

DEAR KEALLY

Last night I had yours of the 13th; and the first thing I do this morning is to answer it. I remember I told you I should soon write again, which was because I had not then seen the Duke of Ormond,[1] and did not imagine but I might have seen him before this time; but it is impossible, he is so often in private, and so often denied. I met him at court; and had an opportunity of telling him my unhappiness in not waiting of him. Lady Betty[2] and her sisters are very well, and your servants: so are all our neighbours. The ministry[3] is not so much altered as I find you have supposed. Mansell in the room of Sir Edward Seymour, and Harley in place of Lord Nottingam, is, as they say here, a change without an alteration. The timorous disposition of those at the helm occasions this seeming removal; but, in all probability, a little more time must produce something more barefaced, and it must either run openly in one or t'other channel. The translation[4] you speak of is not altogether mine; for Vanbrugh and Walsh had a part in it. Each did an act of a French farce. Mine, and I believe theirs, was done in two mornings; so there can be no great matter in it. It was a compliment made to the people of quality at their subscription music, without any design to have it acted or printer farther. It made people laugh; and somebody thought it worth his while to translate it again, and print it as it was acted: but if you meet such a thing, I assure you it was none of ours; which I don't think will appear again after next week, when our neighbour[5] is to have it acted for her benefit. Here is no manner of news but what the prints afford, the town being very dull. I am not much otherwise: but in dullness or mirth, dear Keally, always your

W. C.

EDITIONS: Berkeley, pp. 336-338; Summers, Vol. I, pp. 75-76; Dobrée, p. 494.

[1] See No. 2, note 3.

[2] Lady Elizabeth Cromwell, daughter of Vere-Essex, Baron Cromwell and Earl

of Ardglass in Ireland, married Edward Southwell, Secretary of State in Ireland, in October, 1703, and died on 31 March 1709. See *DNB* under Edward Southwell and Luttrell for 7 October 1703 and 2 April 1709. See No. 25 for the birth of a son to "Lady Betty" and No. 35 for a comment on her health when she came over from Ireland in November, 1708.

[3] Luttrell, 29 April 1704: "The earl of Kent, lord chamberlayn, Robert Harley, esq., speaker of the commons, and Thomas Mansell, esq., are sworn of the privy council; and the latter made comptroller of the household, in the room of sir Edward Seymour."

[4] This translation, from Molière's *Monsieur de Pourceaugnac*, was announced in *The Daily Courant* for 30 March 1704 as "a new Farce, never acted before, call'd *Squire Trelooby*," to be acted at Lincoln's Inn Fields Theatre along with the subscription music provided by the nobility. See Hodges, pp. 73-74.

[5] Anne Bracegirdle. See No. 12, note 3.

15 CONGREVE TO JOSEPH KEALLY

London June 20th: 1704

DEAR KELLY [1]

I had sooner thanked you for your dillask,[2] which is very good, had I not then been very lame of the gout when it came. The fit is pretty well over and I am at ease enough to write thus much to you. I wish you could keep your resolution of seeing the Bath. I should hope then by some means or other we might meet. All your Friends hereabouts are well and at your service. There is no news. The town is extream thin, rather thinner than usual at this time of year. Good wine scarcer than ever and Lemons very dear but I hope these things will mend by the time that I get abroad. Pray let me hear from you if I must not see you, for I am ever

your W. Congreve

Address: *To Joseph Kelly Esqr:*
in Dublin Ireland

MANUSCRIPT: The Earl of Home, The Hirsel, Scotland. EDITIONS: Berkeley, pp. 338-339; Summers, Vol. I, p. 76; Dobrée, p. 495.

[1] The spelling "Kelly" appears here and in all later manuscript letters directed to Joseph Keally (or Kelly). See Nos. 16, 23, 29, 35, 37, 38, 43, 44, and 46. All earlier manuscript letters (see Nos. 2, 9, and 11) have the spelling "Keally." Professor Kathleen Lynch (pp. 28-29) cites a letter written by Keally on 28 May 1702 and signed "Jos. Kelly," a spelling that she thinks Keally probably used from that date. This edition uses "Keally" throughout except in transcribing manuscript letters in which the name is spelled "Kelly."

[2] *Dillask* was misread *flask* when this letter was first published in 1789 and has since been followed by all editions until the present. The discovery of the original manuscript makes possible the corrected reading. *Dillask*, or *dillisk*, is a variant form for *dulse* or *dulce* (from the Gaelic *duileasg*), a seaweed used as food. In 1707 Sir Hans Sloane wrote of a "concretion . . . sticking to the leaves of the Delisk" from which "that plant is made delightful to the Irish palats" (*Oxford English Dictionary*, under *Dulse*). Perhaps we may think of *dillask* as an Irish delicacy enjoyed by both Congreve and Keally when they were schoolboys together at Kilkenny.

16   CHARLES MEIN TO JOSEPH KEALLY

Custom house London. October 10th. [*1704*]

DEAR KELLY

I received your letter which directs me to open your letter to Congreve in case he shou'd be out of town; [1] which accordingly I did, and deliver'd the enclosed letter with my own hand to the Duke of Ormond, whose answer was that he shou'd see you soon, and wou'd be very glad to serve you. As for your letters to St. Malo's, you must know, I have been upon a general survey of the Customs for above six months past, and received the letters you mention just upon my going away, and therefore intrusted them with Mr. Floyd who promis'd to take due care of them; of which matter Mr: Congreve who is just now arriv'd from the Country, tels me, he writt you word [2] as I desir'd him. I must now complain of you, as you do of me, for being so sparing of your Epistles, because you never write but upon business, tho in six months time; whereas if I had been here, I wou'd infallibly have troubled you with two or three in that time. It is now almost twelve a clock, and I can say no more than that I am heartyly

Yours

Cha: Mein.

Address: *For Joseph Kelly Esqr:*
at his house at Kilkenny Ireland

MANUSCRIPT: British Museum Add. 39,311, fols. 1, 2; summarized and partly quoted by Lynch, p. 29.

[1] Congreve was out of town. See No. 17.

[2] Evidently in a letter now lost.

17   CONGREVE TO JOSEPH KEALLY

London October 14. 1704.

DEAR KEALLY

I was in the country when your letter came with the inclosed to his Grace of Ormond; but Charles did it,[1] and I suppose has written to you. That which you mention by Mr Howard[2] I never received. This comes to you by a gentleman[3] desirous of your acquaintance; and Mr Porter[4] told me he had a mind, in order thereunto, to carry a letter from me to you. I have a multitude of affairs, being just come to town after nine weeks absence. I am grown fat; but you know I was born with somewhat a round belly. I find you are resolved to be a man of this world, which I am sorry for, because it will deprive me of you. However, think of me, as I am nothing extenuate.[5] My service to Robin, who would laugh to see me puzzled to buckle my shoe; but I'll fetch it down again. I am your

W. Congreve.

EDITIONS: Berkeley, pp. 339-340; Summers, Vol. I, p. 77; Dobrée, p. 495.

[1] That is, Charles Mein opened Keally's letter addressed to Congreve and deliv-

ered the enclosed letter to the Duke of Ormonde, as Mein stated in his letter to Keally dated 10 October 1704. See No. 16.

[2] Hugh Howard (1675-1737) was born in Dublin and came to England in 1688. After studying in Holland and Italy, he returned to Dublin for a few years before settling in London as a portrait painter. His acquaintance with Keally in Ireland led to the double commission of a portrait of Congreve for Keally and of Keally for Congreve (see Nos. 34 and 37). See *DNB*.

[3] Evidently the Mr. Mahun mentioned in No. 18.

[4] Edward Porter. See pp. 5-7.

[5] "*nothing extenuate*. This quotation from *Othello* has escaped the compilers of the *Shakespeare Allusion-Book*, 1909." (Summers, Vol. I, p. 238.)

18   CONGREVE TO JOSEPH KEALLY

London October 28. 1704.

DEAR KEALLY

I have at length received yours by Mr Howard,[1] who is one I like much at first sight. I will observe all your directions; but my father [2] has been so extremely ill, and yet continues ill, that I have had no leisure nor disposition to do it; but I hope the danger is past. I wrote to you by one Mr Mahun,[3] whom I am a stranger to, and to whom you are to be known. I gave your letter to Mein,[4] who has taken care to forward it for your picture. I am of your mind as to the Tale of a Tub.[5] I am not alone in the opinion, as you are there; but I am pretty near it, having but very few on my side; but those few are worth a million. However, I have never spoke my sentiments, not caring to contradict a multitude. Bottom [6] admires it, and cannot bear my saying, I confess I was diverted with several passages when I read it, but I should not care to read it again. That he thinks not commendation enough. You will let me hear from you sometimes. I am, my dear Keally, yours entirely,

W. Congreve.

EDITIONS: Berkeley, pp. 340-341; Summers, Vol. I, p. 77; Dobrée, p. 496.

¹ Hugh Howard. See No. 17.

² Since the father's illness had affected Congreve's leisure, apparently the father was then living somewhere near the dramatist, if not in the same lodgings with him. Perhaps he had taken up residence in London after retiring from his Irish post in 1702. A manuscript letter from the father to the Earl of Burlington in Ireland dated 6 July 1706 (Lismore Papers: Early Correspondence, National Library of Ireland) sends greetings to friends in Ireland and requests for himself and his wife "a chamber for one month at Chiswick [the Earl's country seat near London] . . . we being both of us in want of a little good Aire." The father asked that the reply be left for him at Burlington House in London, thus indicating that the dramatist's father and mother were then living in London. For other information about the father, see Nos. 31, 57, and 105; and Hodges, pp. 3-12, 29-34, 55-57, 129-130.

³ See No. 17.

⁴ Charles Mein. See No. 3.

⁵ Swift's *Tale of a Tub*, published during the Easter Term of 1704, had reached the "Third Edition Corrected" by June of that year. See *The Term Catalogues*, Vol. III, pp. 401, 418.

⁶ See No. 2.

19   CONGREVE TO JOSEPH KEALLY

London December 9. 1704.

DEAR KEALLY

I wrote to you some time since, upon receiving your letter by Mr Howard,¹ and another of a later date by the post. I thank you for his acquaintance. I like him very well. I have sat to him; and they say it will be a good picture. I wish I had yours; ² for I don't expect to see you much for the future. Here is nothing in town worth your knowledge; only I can tell you in general terms, that affairs begin to look as if they would mend. Rowe writ a foolish farce called the Biter,³ which was damned. Cibber has produced a play,⁴ consisting of fine gentlemen and fine conversation altogether; which the ridiculous town for the most part likes: but there are some that know better. My service to Robin.[5] I have a great cold, which makes writing uneasy to me. I am, dear Keally, yours ever,

W. C.

EDITIONS: Berkeley, pp. 342-343; Summers, Vol. I, p. 78; Dobrée, pp. 496-497.

[1] See No. 17.

[2] This hint probably led Keally to sit, during one of Howard's visits to Dublin, for the portrait mentioned in Nos. 34 and 37.

[3] Nicholas Rowe's *The Biter* was acted at Lincoln's Inn Fields Theatre 4 December 1704.

[4] Colley Cibber's *The Careless Husband*, acted on 7 December 1704, was just beginning a long run at Drury Lane Theatre with Mrs. Anne Oldfield in the lead. The reputation that Mrs. Oldfield gained in this play and increased during the next few years is said to have led to Anne Bracegirdle's retirement from the stage about 1707. Congreve naturally shows some disgust at the success of this mediocre sentimental play at the rival playhouse.

[5] Robert Fitzgerald. See No. 6.

20   CONGREVE TO JOSEPH KEALLY

London February 3. 1704 [1705].

DEAR KEALLY

I received yours of the 25th of January and am indebted to you one before that. I am glad you have received your picture, though I wish it had called on me by the way. Mine is not yet finished.[1] I have been so employed, and am still like to be so, that I have no time for any thing. I know not when the house[2] will open, nor what we shall begin withal; but I believe with no opera. There is nothing settled yet. All neighbours are well, and your servants. Mein[3] is now with me; and says, since your picture is come, he believes he shall never hear from you again; and for his own part, he knows not now about what to write to you. Some who have seen my picture since the third sitting, don't like it so well as I did after the first. I have not had time to see Mr Howard these six weeks. My service to Robin.[4] Tell him I shall want a fat box-keeper. I am yours,

W. Congreve.

EDITIONS: Berkeley, pp. 335-336; Summers, Vol. I, p. 75; Dobrée, p. 493.

[1] For portraits of Congreve and Keally painted by Hugh Howard, see Nos. 18, 19, 28, 34, and 37. The portrait of Keally mentioned in Nos. 34 and 37, apparently a second one, was being painted for Congreve.

[2] The fine new Queen's Theatre in the Haymarket, now nearing completion under Vanbrugh's direction, was to be managed jointly by Vanbrugh and Congreve "for the better Reforming the Abuses and Immorality of the Stage" (see *The London Gazette* for 21-25 December 1704).

[3] Charles Mein. See No. 3.

[4] Robert Fitzgerald. See No. 6. Congreve repeatedly refers to Fitzgerald's obesity. See especially No. 22. The reference to the need for a box-keeper at the new theatre is, of course, only a facetious remark to the successful young lawyer in Ireland.

21 CONGREVE TO JOSEPH KEALLY

Northall [1] *Friday morning,* [*October or November, 1705?*] [2]
I am very sorry to hear you have been so much out of order. I wish you may be well enough to come down this week. I fancy the air would do you good. For Amory,[3] I wish for him, but don't expect him. I thank you for sending the cargo, which is at last come safe. I sent my man to pay Mr Boddy [4] four pound, which was all that was due (discounting the money which I advanced to him) on the last quarter. His note, which I have for it, is in my escritoir; and if I had thought of it I would have sent you the key, that you might have given it him. It seems he durst not trust me in such an occasion, and would not give my man a full acquittance. I was by agreement to have six weeks warning. My quarter was up at Michaelmas or thereabouts, and he gave me warning on Bartholomew-day; which,

I believe upon computation, comes more short of what I ought to have had from him than my escritoir has transgressed by lying in his lodgings over and above the quarter-day. However, I told him before I left the town, that I would quit his lodgings at the quarter's end, having taken new, to commence from the same time; and therefore, if my few goods would be any trouble to him, desired him to let me know, that they might be removed in time, for I foresaw I should not be in town at that time myself. His answer was no civiler than barely became him; that if they remained there a fortnight there could be no damage; and if any new tenant should come that might have occasion for the room they took, he would send me timely notice. Notwithstanding all this, he has sent me word by my man, by word of mouth, that he hopes I will not let him lose a fortnight by me. Pray give yourself the trouble to let him know what I have writ, and charge him with the truth of every particular. If he can deny any one, I am sure I am much to blame. If he cannot, and I am sure he cannot honestly, I think modestly he has not paid me the civility nor the justice which belongs to me. You may assure him, when I come to town he shall have his note or notes, for I think I have two; and I think they are not more acknowledgements of his debt to me than they are testimonies of my civility to him. He says I have done him five pounds damage in his quilt. What he can make appear to be the real damage, I will satisfy him for it; but advise him to say no more than it is, or at least than the quilt is worth: for as I would not wrong him, so I will not be belied: of both which truths, when he gives me the occasion, I will convince him. This is what I think fit to say to Mr Boddy; and I ask your pardon for making you my proxy in such an affair, and with such a one. I heartily wish you your health, and here. Pray remember me to my very good friends and neighbours in Arundel-street. Yours,

Will. Congreve.

I live the life of a Carthusian, and am heartily sorry for Sanford.[5] The snuff you sent is excellent in both kinds.

EDITIONS: Berkeley, pp. 380-383; Summers, Vol. I, pp. 92-93; Dobrée, pp. 514-515.

[1] Northall is a hamlet some thirty miles north of London and about three and a half miles north of Ivinghoe. Congreve had apparently been spending vacations at Northall since his youth, for he speaks (No. 49) of jumping one-and-twenty feet on Northall Common. Swift mentions (No. 141) Congreve's excellent health in his earlier years.

[2] The date of this letter must be inferred from the contents. The reference to "neighbours in Arundel-street" indicates a date before 26 June 1706 (see No. 25), when Congreve moved permanently to Mr. Porter's in Surrey Street. The month was evidently October or November, soon after the Michaelmas (September 29) mentioned in the letter; and Keally was still in London. He had been there as late as November, 1705, for Congreve on 15 December 1705 (No. 22) had recently heard of Keally's "safe arrival" in Ireland.

[3] Thomas Amory. See No. 2.

[4] Probably Richard Boddy, who was assessed in 1698-1699 and also in 1699-1700 one pound ten shillings as a householder in Norfolk Street (the little street between Arundel and Surrey) at the same time that Edward Porter was assessed for one pound in Arundel Street. See the Rate Books, City Hall, Westminster.

[5] This might be Berkeley's misreading of "Sansom," who is mentioned in Nos. 7, 30, and 34. "Sanford" is mentioned only here by Congreve.

22   CONGREVE TO JOSEPH KEALLY

London December 15. 1705.

DEAR KEALLY

I thank you for your letter of congratulation,[1] and more for the account it brought me of your safe arrival. Robin [2] talks of going every day. I would have him stay till the weather is a little settled; for if he should be cast away, you know your water swells a man; and what a thing were he if he were swelled? I know he sends you all the news from the Smyrna; [3] so I have nothing to add but only that I have quitted the affair of the Hay-market.[4] You may imagine I got nothing by it: but when I was dipt, and asked myself, *Quid agam?* replies Terence, *Quid, nisi ut te redimas captum, quam queas minimo, si nequeas paululo, et quanti queas.*[5] I think I cannot end a letter better than with a smart quotation. I am, dear Recorder [6] and Judge *in futuro*, already in wisdom, gravity, and understanding, yours, and so is all the neighbourhood,

W. Congreve.

EDITIONS: Berkeley, p. 366 (misdated 1708); Summers, Vol. I, p. 87; Dobrée, p. 508.

[1] Keally had probably congratulated Congreve on his appointment as one of the five commissioners for licensing wine, with a yearly salary of £200, just double the salary he had received during the preceding ten years as commissioner for licensing hackney coaches. The office for wine licensing was located on the Thames River at the foot of Arundel Street, in which Congreve was then living, and could not have been more than a two-minute walk away. The business of the office was conducted by ten assistants, but Congreve must have spent some time there since he signed a document, now preserved in the Folger Shakespeare Library, granting an individual the right to sell wine. See also Hodges, p. 84.

[2] Robert Fitzgerald. See No. 6.

[3] The Smyrna Coffee-house on the north side of Pall Mall near St. James's Square was a center for political talk in which Keally was interested.

[4] The management of the Haymarket Theatre in collaboration with Vanbrugh. See No. 20.

[5]
> *Quid agas? nisi ut te redimas captum quam queas*
> *Minumo; si nequeas, paululo, at quanti queas.*
> *Eunuchus*, I, 1, 29-30.

"What should you do? Why, just redeem yourself from captivity as cheaply as possible? If you can't do it for a little bit, then pay what you must."

[6] Keally had been Recorder of Kilkenny since 2 June 1705. See Lynch, p. 29.

23   CONGREVE TO JOSEPH KEALLY

London April; 30th: 1706

DEAR KELLY

I am allways glad to hear from you whether there be any news or buisinesse in your letters or not. I have heard you had some thoughts of coming again [1] for England. I wish it were true. I think there is no doubt of your Governors ² returning to you again. I have been pretty free from the gout since the fit at Xmas. I have neither too much nor too little buisinesse and if I have the spleen it is because this town affords not one drop of wine out of a private house. All your friends hereabouts are well and at your service. I believe the Play house ³ cannot go on another Winter. Have heard there is to be a Union of the two houses ⁴ as well as Kingdoms. My service to Robin, Luther, Amory.⁵ I am

> *Yours*
> *Will: Congreve*

MANUSCRIPT: Bought by Maggs at the Sotheby sale, Lot 479, 16 March 1937. See a photostat of this letter in the Sotheby catalogue. EDITIONS: Berkeley, pp. 343-344; Summers, Vol. I, p. 78; Dobrée, p. 497.

¹ Keally had been in England late in 1705, as shown by No. 22.

² The Duke of Ormonde, who was continued as Lord Lieutenant of Ireland for another year. See Luttrell for 16 April 1706 and 12 April 1707.

³ The Haymarket Theatre, the joint management of which Congreve had given up about the end of 1705. See No. 22.

⁴ The Haymarket Theatre and Drury Lane (sometimes called Covent Garden) Theatre. Of this period in theatrical history, Colley Cibber wrote: "It was now the Town-talk that nothing but a Union of the two Companies could recover the Stage to its former Reputation, which Opinion was certainly true." See Cibber, Vol. I, pp. 327-328. The union of England and Scotland, then being negotiated, was accomplished in 1707.

⁵ Henry Luther and Thomas Amory. See No. 2.

24   CONGREVE TO JOSEPH KEALLY

London June 8. 1706.

DEAR KEALLY

I received yours with great surprise and concern; and the more because I had some hopes, about that time, of hearing you designed for England. I am sure you know me enough to know I feel very sensibly and silently for those whom I love; but the great escape you have had of your life is a reflection that alleviates the misfortune which you met withal. I hope this letter will find you perfectly free from pain and weakness; but have a care of stirring too soon.[1] I am sorry Robin Fitzgerald continues in so ill a state of health. I must be plain with you on his account: He did not live at a rate in this town to hope otherwise. Nothing but an absolute and continued regularity, and that with very good prescriptions, can recover so ill a habit of body. I wish he would take care of himself, or rather that he could. I was out of town when Lord Halifax[2] undertook his expedition. If you had been here, and inclined to such a ramble, I should not have avoided it; though, excepting the Court of Hanover, I have seen all that such a journey can show. The news is so general every post, that the public letters tell you all that can be told you. The ladies had all the concern imaginable at hearing of your ill accident. I have not seen Mein since I received your letter; but I expect that he should hang or stab himself when I tell him. I think he ought to do no less who affected to fast upon the news of Lord Donnegal's[3] death, and got drunk the night following. All here are your servants. Pray let me hear of your recovery, which cannot be more welcome to you than to your

Will. Congreve.

EDITIONS: Berkeley, pp. 344-346; Summers, Vol. I, p. 79; Dobrée, pp. 497-498.

[1] Keally had broken his leg. See Lynch, p. 30. See also No. 26.

[2] Berkeley reads "Dr." Halifax, evidently his (or the printer's) misreading of "Ld." Halifax. In the Preface, Berkeley noted that his "distance from the press" made "correcting the errata utterly impossible." Congreve might well have thought favorably of a Continental trip with Lord Halifax—a good friend, patron, and fellow member of the Kit-Cat Club. Lord Halifax was then at the Court of Hanover, having been sent the preceding April on a special mission for the Queen (see Luttrell 6 and 13 April 1706). His return was reported by Luttrell on Tuesday, 20 August 1706: "On Sunday the lord Hallifax arrived here from Hanover, convoyed by the men of war which brought over our 7 East India ships from Holland." See also No. 6, note 7.

[3] Arthur Chichester, third Earl of Donegal (1666-1706), was first reported as taken prisoner (Luttrell, 2 May 1706) and later as killed in the battle before the fort of Montjoui on 10 April 1706.

25   CONGREVE TO JOSEPH KEALLY

London June 26. 1706.

DEAR KEALLY

I have really thought it tedious not to have heard from you. That I have not written has been, as you imagine, from business; but business no more profitable than mine uses to be—full of vexation, and without any good consequence. Mein has succeeded better, which I suppose he has told you of. How my friends, as you call them, mean to proceed in relation to me, I know not yet. They speak as they used to do, and may consequently do as they use to do.[1] I am glad you give me hopes of seeing you: I wish you may persevere. Pray wish Lady Betty [2] joy from me of her boy. I am removed to Mr Porter's [3] in Surry-street, where I shall be glad to hear from you till I may hope to see you; which, believe me, is one of the things I wish the most heartily for in the world. Your neighbours enquire after you, though you don't remember them. Yours,

W. Congreve.

EDITIONS: Berkeley, pp. 346-347; Summers, Vol. I, pp. 79-80; Dobrée, pp. 498-499.

[1] Congreve had apparently been led to expect come lucrative political appointment such as he finally received at the end of 1714. See No. 82.

[2] Lady Elizabeth Cromwell. See Nos. 14 and 35.

[3] Edward Porter, at whose house in Surrey Street Congreve had lodgings for the remainder of his life. See pp. 5-7 and Nos. 1, 4, 51, 52, and 54 (Congreve's letters to Porter).

26 CONGREVE TO JOSEPH KEALLY

London September 10. 1706.

DEAR KEALLY

I have of late forborne writing to you till I could see your brother; [1] which having done, *liberavi animam meam;* though I hope to meet him more than once before he sets forwards for Ireland. I could have wished his affairs had obliged him to stay here, that you might have been obliged to come hither as you once hinted; but I think the least you can do is to set him so far on of his way back again. I hope your leg is so well [2] that it makes not any unnecessary addition to the gravity of your walk. The play-houses have undergone another revolution; [3] and Swinny, with Wilks, Mrs Olfield, Pinkethman, Bullock, and Dicky, are come over to the Hay-Market. Vanbrugh resigns his authority to Swinny, which occasioned the revolt. Mr Rich [4] complains and rails like Volpone when counterplotted by Mosca. My Lord Chamberlain [5] approves and ratifies the desertion; and the design is, to have plays only at the Hay-Market, and operas only at Covent Garden. I think the design right to restore acting; but the houses are misapplied, which time may change. I have written an ode [6] which I presented to the Queen, who received it very graciously. Though you may have seen it, yet I will send you one by your brother. My service to Robin. I am, dear Keally, your

W. Congreve.

EDITIONS: Berkeley, pp. 347-349; Summers, Vol. I, p. 80; Dobrée, p. 499.

[1] John Kelly. See No. 2.

[2] See No. 24 for the accident in which Keally had broken his leg.

[3] The "revolution," involving Vanbrugh's giving up the management of the Haymarket to Owen Swinny, is explained in some detail by Colley Cibber (Vol. I, pp. 328-337). The actors who, according to Congreve, came over from Drury Lane (Covent Garden) with Swinny were apparently Robert Wilks (Cibber, Vol. I, pp. 235-256), Mrs. Anne Oldfield (Vol. I, pp. 305-312), William Penkethman (Vol. I, pp. 149-152), William Bullock (Vol. II, pp. 361-362), and Richard Estcourt (Vol. II, pp. 331-333), called "Dicky." Estcourt and Congreve were close friends. Swift tells how, on 16 February 1710/11, he

"called at Congreve's, and dined with him and Eastcourt, and laughed till six."
See No. 41.

[4] Christopher Rich, the avaricious and oppressive manager of Drury Lane
Theatre, had refused to unite directly with Vanbrugh but was outwitted by
Swinny as an agent for Vanbrugh. See Cibber, Vol. I, pp. 327-331. See also
No. 71.

[5] Henry Grey, first Duke of Kent (1664?-1740), was Lord Chamberlain from
1704 till 1710. On 14 December 1704 he signed the license authorizing Vanbrugh and Congreve to manage the new theatre soon to be opened in the Haymarket. See No. 70.

[6] "A Pindarique Ode, Humbly Offer'd to the Queen, on the Victorious Progress
of Her Majesty's Arms, under the Conduct of the Duke of Marlborough. To
which is prefix'd, A Discourse on the Pindarique Ode," published in folio, 1706.
See Dobrée, pp. 327-341, and No. 125.

27   CONGREVE TO JOSEPH KEALLY

London July 12. 1707.

DEAR KEALLY

I must congratulate you on report, since you have not been so kind
to give me any more agreeable notice, of your changing your condition so much for the better. I, with all your friends here, have
drank your health and prosperity ever since the news [1] has been
confirmed to us. They all give you their service and good wishes;
and though I long to hear from you, yet I hope you will be so
much taken up with joy, that you will not very soon find time to
excuse your neglecting to inform me of an adventure so important
to you. I would give my service to Robin; but this is intended only
to wish you joy, and must not be profaned with the name of any
bachelor. I am, Dear Keally, yours,

W. Congreve.

EDITIONS: Berkeley, pp. 354-355; Summers, Vol. I, p. 82; Dobrée, p. 502.

[1] The news was Keally's marriage to Elizabeth Monck in Dublin on 5 June
1707.

28   CONGREVE TO JOSEPH KEALLY

London January 29. 1707 [*1708*].

DEAR KEALLY

I have yours of the 5th instant; but have not yet heard any thing of Mr Howard [1] or the picture. If I committed any mistake in relation to it, it was impossible for me to do otherwise. I remember at one time of his coming for England, I had a letter from you (I think too he brought it), in which you recommended me to his acquaintance, and told me he had promised to draw my picture for you. He said something to the same effect himself. He came afterwards to see me more than once, to remind me of sitting; and at last appointed a time. He almost finished one picture; and not liking it, pressed me to sit again for a new one. I was willing, because I understood he took all that care for you in friendship; and besides, I thought it might be of consequence to him to have my picture seen in his house well done, as being a face known by most of them whose approbation might be of use to him. These two considerations apart, sitting for my picture is not a thing very agreeable to me; but most certainly, had I had the least ground to apprehend that he expected me to have paid him, I would have done it. Nay, I knew not of his going for Ireland; nor indeed did I apprehend that the picture was finished: for, if I do not misremember, I heard him speak yet of another sitting. So that if chance had put it into my head to have mumelled something to him about being obliged— and making amends—and pray tell me—nay be free, &c. I had not the opportunity. The thing of most consequence is our liking, and the likeness of the pictures. I have made your compliments to Mr Addison, having seen him once by accident. It is not so familiar a thing to see him as it was ten years ago. [2] My service to Robin and all friends. I have written to Luther. [3] I directed it to Dublin, taking it to be term-time. All here are your servants. I am your

W. Congreve.

EDITIONS: Berkeley, pp. 349-351; Summers, Vol. I, pp. 80-81; Dobrée, pp. 500-501.

[1] Hugh Howard. See No. 17.

[2] This refers to the period before Addison's extensive foreign travel, 1699-1703, during which Addison wrote three letters to Congreve (Nos. 120, 121, and 123). Perhaps Addison came to Congreve's attention as early as 1694 through his *Account of the Greatest English Poets*. Steele said (see No. 139) that Congreve, by introducing Addison to Charles Montagu, caused Addison to enter upon a literary career.

[3] Henry Luther. See No. 2.

29   CONGREVE TO JOSEPH KEALLY

London. February 7th: 1707 [*1708*]

DEAR KELLY

You are better at Observing the remissnesse than pursuing the strictnesse of a correspondence; or else the pacquett boats are too blame. I have written twice since you found fault with my silence. I write now to know how you do for I have nothing to send you worth knowing. There is a mighty fraction in all parties, Whigs and Torys promiscuously joyning and opposing each other. When the present commotions are likly to subside I'll tell you which I think will go [to] the bottom. I believe I told you the Duke of Richmond [1] had been long before preengaged; but if he had not I could have relyed much on any answer I might have had from him. My service to Robin. I am yours

W. *Congreve.*

(All here are well and your servants.)

Address: *To*
    Joseph Kelly Esqr
        in Dublin
Postmark: *FE/7*

MANUSCRIPT: The Earl of Home, The Hirsel, Scotland. EDITIONS: Berkeley, pp. 357-358; Summers, Vol. I, p. 81; Dobrée, p. 501.

[1] Charles Lennon, first Duke of Richmond (1672-1723), was the natural son of Charles II by the Duchess of Portsmouth.

30   CONGREVE TO JOSEPH KEALLY

London March 2. 1707 [1708].

DEAR KEALLY

I thank you for your letter, and for the usquebaugh, though not received; for I believe the ship was gone before it came to the port. I have had two letters this and the last week from Mr Sansom,[1] and he makes no mention of it. Whenever it comes to him I am sure he will take care of it. There is nothing of news, but that the pretended Prince of Wales is arrived at Dunkirk, 'tis thought in order to embark for Scotland.[2] As for domestic affairs, they are yet in very whimsical circumstances, and I don't care to write my own conjectures. The ladies here are much your servants; but some of them think your remembrance of them too general. I wish you could give me some hopes of seeing you. I am very much concerned Robin has not better health. Our fat friends have suffered. King of the Royal Oak died last week, and poor Cornigh the taylor this week; so there is once more a widow and a well customed house for Robin, if he be in condition to venture. I hear a paper crying now in the street, of taking six French men of war before Dunkirk, but it sounds too like Grubstreet to send it you. Besides, this being general post night, if there is any public news arrived, you will have it with the packet. I am, Dear Keally, yours,

W. Congreve.

EDITIONS: Berkeley, pp. 355-357; Summers, Vol. I, p. 82; Dobrée, pp. 501-502.

[1] John Sansom, collector of customs at Bristol. See Nos. 7 and 34.

[2] Luttrell, Thursday, 4 March 1707/8: "This morning came an expresse from Ostend, with letters from major general Cadogan and others to the duke of Marlborough, &c., advising that the French were embarking 18 batallions at Dunkirk, with 200 English, Scotch, and Irish officers, and great store of arms,

where the pretended prince of Wales, with some Scotch peers, were arrived; and designed to be ready to sail by next Saturday, as they gave out, for Scotland."

31   CONGREVE TO JOSEPH KEALLY

London May 12. 1708.

DEAR KEALLY

I have yours this day of the 6th instant for which I thank you, and most particularly for your friendly sense of my loss.[1] I know you are no stranger to sentiments of tender and natural affection, which will make my concern very intelligible to you, though it may seem unaccountable to the generality, who are of another make. I am pretty well recovered of a very severe fit, which has lasted a month. I think to go abroad for air to-morrow; and by degrees depend upon time to cure what reasoning and reflection seldom effect. I had written to you sooner than any body; but the fulness and violence of my fit was such, that it disabled me. I thank you for your usquebaugh, whether ever it arrives or not, but am more pleased that you give me hopes of seeing you this summer: I hope your resolution will continue. All here are always inquisitive after you, and desirous to be remembered to you. The legacy you have heard of is in part true, being one thousand pounds.[2] I can write you nothing of news nor politics, but could tell you something if you were here; for the intricacy and variable posture of things is such, that it does not admit of any account which might not be contradicted, or at least altered in the next post. In the main, there is no doubt of a Whig parliament. My service to Robin, Amory, and Luther. I am, Dear Keally, yours,

W. Congreve.

EDITIONS: Berkeley, pp. 358-359; Summers, Vol. I, pp. 83-84; Dobrée, pp. 504-505.

[1] Possibly a reference to the death of Congreve's father, who had retired from

his stewardship of the Burlington estates in Ireland about 1702 and was still living as late as 6 July 1706. See No. 18.

[2] Probably a reference to the £1,000 left to Anne Bracegirdle in the will of Robert Leake, third Earl of Scarsdale, who had died 27 December 1707. See the will, proved 2 January 1707/8, at Somerset House, London, P.C.C., Barrett 20. See also Hodges, p. 87.

32 CONGREVE TO JOSEPH KEALLY

London August 2. 1708.

DEAR KEALLY

I have your letter just on my coming from the country, and have time only to answer it before my going to the bath. I will thank you for it at more leisure; but no leisure will ever afford me time enough to acknowledge the goodness of that lady [1] (who has not her equal), in remembering one, only considerable in being her creature. I am sure she means the usquebaugh [2] should do me good; and in order to that, I am sure it will be more a cordial, and consequently more effectual, by coming with her, than if sent by any thing alive. You will not fail to do me right in my service and thanks to her. I am, Dear Keally, yours,

W. Congreve.

P. S. Every body is your servant; but the old gentlewoman [3] is gone to God.

EDITIONS: Berkeley, p. 360; Summers, Vol. I, p. 84; Dobrée, p. 505.

[1] Perhaps Lady Elizabeth Cromwell, the "Lady Betty" mentioned by Congreve in No. 35 as having arrived from Ireland.

[2] This usquebaugh, or Irish whiskey, which Keally was sending to Congreve, is mentioned also in Nos. 30 and 31.

[3] This "old gentlewoman" was probably the mother of Anne Bracegirdle and Mrs. Porter, who lived with Anne in Howard Street. Congreve mentioned her in writing to Mrs. Porter from Rotterdam on 27 September 1700. See No. 5.

33　CONGREVE TO JOSEPH KEALLY

London August 3. 1708.

DEAR KEALLY

This is the third letter I have written in answer to the last I had from you; and I hear so much of privateers, and the taking of packet-boats, that I imagine neither of the other have come to your hands.[1] I hope the subject of congratulation will always belong to you, though the contrary has been too lately a theme for me. I hear you have encreased your family by two. I wish you joy, both of the fruit of your own planting,[2] and the engrafting of Robin,[3] to whom I wish much happiness with your sister. You are close husbands of your pleasures in Ireland; and we old friends must always know the first news of you from common fame. All here are your servants, and wish you joy. I am unalterably [4] yours,

W. Congreve.

EDITIONS: Berkeley, p. 361; Summers, Vol. I, p. 85; Dobrée, pp. 505-506.

[1] If Keally's last letter was written May 6 (mentioned in No. 31), then Nos. 31 and 32 account for the two letters that Congreve feared lost.

[2] This was Keally's first child, Elizabeth, who lived to the age of seventy-eight and preserved the letters Congreve had written to her father. She died in 1783, and six years later her kinsman George-Monck Berkeley published forty-three of the forty-four known letters of Congreve to Keally. See Lynch, pp. 23, 24, and Berkeley, p. xi.

[3] Robert Fitzgerald (see No. 6) married Keally's youngest sister, Ellen, on 10 July 1708. See Lynch, p. 56.

[4] Perhaps Congreve used "unalterably" to suggest that even though Keally had neglected his old friend by failing to notify him directly of the birth and marriage in his family, his friendship was too deeply rooted to be affected.

34 CONGREVE TO JOSEPH KEALLY

London October 9. 1708.

DEAR KEALLY

I had been in the country [1] for six weeks, and at my coming to town received both your letters at the same time. My last day's journey I rode very hard; which shook me so much, that [it] disturbed the gout which was in repose. I have been confined a week; but I hope, as it was a forced fit, it will be a short one. I can walk about; and this is the first letter I write. I congratulate Robin's gout, but he must practice patience. I am glad you like Mr Howard's picture: [2] many do, though I always thought it too chuffy; and you may safely make him take it down, for I shall never be so fat. I am glad to hope for yours. I think he has a fair occasion either to touch from Sir Godfrey [3] after you have sat, or to touch from you after he has copied the other. Mein is well, very fat, and yours. I am sorry from my soul for Sansom. [4] The neighbourhood are in health and your servants. I thank you cordially for all. I make use of my philosophy, and love you as ever. Yours,

W. Congreve.

EDITIONS: Berkeley, pp. 362-363; Summers, Vol. I, p. 85; Dobrée, p. 506.

[1] Apparently at Bath. See No. 32.

[2] The painting of Congreve's portrait for Keally by Hugh Howard is mentioned in Nos. 17, 18, 19, 20, and 28. Howard also painted Keally's portrait for Congreve, as shown later in this letter and also in No. 37.

[3] Evidently Sir Godfrey Kneller had painted a portrait of Keally which Howard could use in getting a true likeness of Keally.

[4] Luttrell, 12 August 1708: "Mr. Jacob Reynardson, a merchant of this citty, is made collector of the customes of Bristol, with 600l. per ann., in the room of Mr. Sanson, lately gone off for a considerable summ." Sanson's appointment to this position had been mentioned by Luttrell under 4 August 1698: "Mr. Sansons son, of the custome house here, succeeds sir Cornwall Bradshaw as comptroller of the customes at Bristoll." Perhaps Sanson's liberality, as indicated by his gift of a mare to Congreve (No. 7), contributed to his defaulting in his account.

35   CONGREVE TO JOSEPH KEALLY

London November 9th: 1708

DEAR KELLY

I extreamly congratulate your recovery and thank you for letting me know it so soon. I am very well after my short fitt, which I hope has prevented any further visitations for this winter. I thank you for the Latin Ballad.[1] I think it is as well as the thing will bear, and so dos Mein [2] who continues of all men the hardest to be pleased with any modern essays. They talk warmly of Lord Pembroks [3] being High admirall, Lord Wharton [3] your Lord Lieutenant, and Lord Sommers [3] President of the Councill. I think it very likely to be as they talk. I am glad Robin [4] has got rid of his Urchins at any rate. My service to him and all who love you. All here are your servants and wellwishers. I am intirely yours

W. Congreve

Lady Betty [5] has brought a cold with her from Ireland that I think almost dangerous.

Address: *To*
        Joseph Kelly. Esqr
              in Dublin
Postmark: *NO/9*

MANUSCRIPT: The Earl of Home, The Hirsel, Scotland. EDITIONS: Berkeley, pp. 363-364; Summers, Vol. I, p. 86; Dobrée, pp. 506-507.

[1] A Latin version of Congreve's fourteen-stanza ballad beginning "Ye Commons and Peers." Congreve's poem and Keally's Latin version were published together in Tonson's *Poetical Miscellanies,* the Sixth Part (1709). See Dragosh Protopopesco, *William Congreve, a Sheaf of Poetical Scraps,* Second Edition Enlarged, [*ca.* 1924], p. 25.

[2] Charles Mein. See No. 3.

[3] Congreve's conjectures were correct, as shown by Luttrell, 16 November 1708: "Last night the lord Wharton kissed her majesties hand in order to be lord lieutenant of Ireland. As also the lord Somers to be president of the council; both which places the earl of Pembroke enjoyed, who is now to succeed the prince

[George, who had died October 28] as lord high admiral." Thomas Wharton, first Marquis of Wharton (1648-1715), and John Somers, first Baron Somers (1651-1716), were prominent Whigs and fellow members with Congreve in the Kit-Cat Club.

[4] Perhaps Robert Fitzgerald's marriage on the previous July 10 (see No. 33) had something to do with his getting rid of "his urchins."

[5] Lady Elizabeth Cromwell. See No. 14. The "almost dangerous" cold that Congreve here mentions was probably related to Lady Elizabeth's death from tuberculosis next year on 31 March 1709.

36 CONGREVE TO JOSEPH KEALLY

London November 29. 1708.

DEAR KEALLY

I am very glad to hear of your recovery; I can send you the same news of myself; I am very well. I fancy you had not received a letter from me before you writ your last; for in that I told you of the changes that were intended. The hint you give me is very kind, and need not seem unfeasible to any who does not know particular persons and circumstances as well as myself. There is no explaining such and so many particulars in a letter; but my views lie another way, which if I accomplish, they will more answer my purpose than the other in every respect, but the pleasure of seeing you.[1] Ease and quiet is what I hunt after. If I have not ambition, I have other passions more easily gratified. Believe me I find none more pleasing to me than my friendship for you. I am, yours,

W. Congreve.

All here are well at your service.

EDITIONS: Berkeley, pp. 364-365; Summers, Vol. I, p. 86; Dobrée, p. 507.

[1] Keally had evidently suggested that Congreve seek a position in the government service in Ireland. At about this time, Addison was appointed Secretary of State for Ireland.

37   CONGREVE TO JOSEPH KEALLY

London May 23 [*1709*]

DEAR KELLY

Your letter came just as I was intending to write to you. I had written long since but I have been troubled with several light indispositions and threatnings of the gout from ill weather and easterly winds. But I hope I shall rubb on, tho I have more frequent colds than ever. The preliminaries of the peace [1] were sent over here and are returnd yesterday again ratified by the Queene. They are not publickly known, but to be sure you will soon have them. I was 6 or 7 times to look for Mr: Howard [2] before I could find him. At last I saw him and your picture which is like you but too warmly painted as you hinted. I shall press him to make an end of it. Mr: Addison [3] surely knows Mr Tonson [4] to well to think he will come for Ireland for having said so, unlesse some considerable subscription may be set afoot to induce him. Pray give my service to Mr: Addison and Tidcomb: [5] not forgetting Robin, whom I should be glad to see strutt about the hall as great as the Prince of Conde. [6] Mein is as you hope fatt rich and mellancolly very variable when awake and nothing but his sleepynesse makes him tollerable. Amory looks well. I drink your health with him, and wish to see you. I am glad his excellency [7] pleases so well. No body knows better how to do it. You say nothing of my Lady. [8] I am Dear Kelly your

W Congreve.

Address: *To Joseph Kelly Esqr*
            in Dublin

Postmark: *MA/24*

MANUSCRIPT: The New York Public Library. EDITIONS: Berkeley, pp. 368-369; Summers, Vol. I, pp. 87-88; Dobrée, pp. 508-509.

[1] Although Congreve gives only the month and day for this letter, the year is unmistakably shown by the reference to the peace preliminaries. On the next day, Tuesday, 24 May 1709, Luttrell wrote: "Saturday night Mr. Walpole,

secretary to the lord Townsend, arrived here from Holland with the preliminaries for a general peace; Sunday evening they were read before the queen
. . . and Monday morning sent back by him to the Hague."

[2] Hugh Howard was then finishing for Congreve the portrait of Keally mentioned in No. 34.

[3] Joseph Addison, then Secretary of State in Ireland.

[4] Jacob Tonson, Congreve's publisher, was the first Englishman to popularize
publication by subscription.

[5] Tidcomb, misread "Aidcomb" by Berkeley and followed by Summers and
Dobrée. Lieutenant General John Tidcomb (1642-1713) had an army assignment in Ireland. He and Congreve were fellow members of the famous Kit-Cat
Club presided over by Jacob Tonson.

[6] The Prince of Condé was well known for his haughtiness, which was to be
expected of a "first prince" of the pompous court of Louis XIV. Perhaps this
haughty prince had been called to Congreve's attention by his recent death,
reported about two months before (29 March 1709) by Luttrell.

[7] Thomas Wharton, first Earl and later Marquis of Wharton, then Lord Lieutenant of Ireland. See No. 35.

[8] Lady Wharton, through whom Keally secured an appointment in 1710. See
No. 38.

38   CONGREVE TO JOSEPH KEALLY

[*London, March or April, 1710*] [1]
I sent to you by 9 a clock this morning but you were gon out. I
went and made your Compliment to Lady Wharton and she will be
glad to see you when you please. I fasted till 3 in hope you might
have come this way. Pray let me know how you are disposed to
morrow.

Yours
W Congreve

thursday afternoone

Address: *To Mr Kelly*

MANUSCRIPT: Pierpont Morgan Library, New York. EDITIONS: Berkeley, p. 367; Summers, Vol. I, p. 87; Dobrée, p. 508.

¹ Both the approximate date of this note and the purpose of Keally's visit to Lady Wharton, wife of the Lord Lieutenant of Ireland, are indicated by a letter from Joseph Addison to Keally written from London on 13 April 1710: "I shall, I believe, be following you the latter end of this month, and shall defer giving you an account of any thing here, that I may have the pleasure of talking all when we meet. Lady Wharton was speaking to me two mornings ago with great esteem of you, and tells me that my Lord is fully determined to put you into the appeals when in Ireland, which I did not think fit to make the least doubt of." Berkeley, pp. 384-385. Keally's appointment as Commissioner of Appeals was made on 23 June 1710. See Lynch, p. 30.

39   CONGREVE TO JOSEPH KEALLY

Richmond ¹ *June 6.* [*1710*]

DEAR KEALLY

I am weary of the town and politics. I tell you truly, I have not cared to inform myself of the probabilities as to change or continuance of the ministry; and nobody who is in the secret can affect to be more ignorant than I really am. If you would have my own private sentiments, I will own I expect nothing that will please me.

I saw Mein last night. We remembered you and all friends. I find the air of this place and Spaw water ² does me much good. I believe I shall pass most of the summer here. It is impossible any change can be in the court and Mr Addison ³ not able to inform you. All your friends I left very well. My service to Robin and Amory. I am, dear Joe, yours ever,

W. C.

EDITIONS: Berkeley, pp. 371-372; Summers, Vol. I, p. 89; Dobrée, p. 510.

¹ Richmond is a suburb of London on the south bank of the Thames. Twickenham, to which Pope moved in 1719, is nearby on the north bank a little farther to the west. On 11 September 1722, when Congreve and Gay were at Bath, Pope wrote to Gay: "Pray put Mr. *Congreve* in mind that he has one on this

side of the World who loves him. . . . There are Ladies in and about *Rich-mond* that pretend to value him. . . ." See No. 140.

² The record of Congreve's purchases of "Spaw water" from Tom Twining's Coffee-House has been preserved in the original ledger. See Hodges, pp. 103-104. For Congreve's purchases of spa water through Pope, see No. 135.

³ Addison had evidently followed Keally to Ireland as planned in his letter to Keally dated 13 April 1710. See No. 38, note 1.

40   CONGREVE TO JOSEPH KEALLY

London August 10. 1710.

DEAR KEALLY

You will have all the news I can send you before this come to your hand; and I am afraid you will think that time enough. No man that I know (without exception of any) is able to make any con-jecture of what is intended by the proceedings at court. There are those who yet are of opinion the present parliament will meet again. If that should be, it can only be because the next, in all appearance, will not differ so extremely from it as some have believed. My service to all friends. Yours,

W. C.

Lord Rivers ¹ sets out on Monday for Hanover on some errand of importance and dispatch, not hard to guess.

EDITIONS: Berkeley, pp. 372-373; Summers, Vol. I, p. 89; Dobrée, pp. 510-511.

¹ Richard Savage, fourth Earl of Rivers (1662-1712), had served in the army under King William in Ireland and in Flanders. On Thursday, 10 August 1710, Luttrell reported: "Earl of Rivers is goeing to the court of Hanover, being sent by her majestie on some private message, some say, to offer the command of our army in Flanders to that prince." On 26 September 1710, Luttrell reported that Rivers had been made "general of the English horse in Flanders."

41   SWIFT TO STELLA

London, October 26, 1710

I was to-day to see Mr. Congreve, who is almost blind with cataracts growing on his eyes; and his case is, that he must wait two or
three years, until the cataracts are riper, and till he is quite blind,
and then he must have them couched; and besides he is never rid
of the gout, yet he looks young and fresh, and is as chearful as ever.
He is younger by three years or more than I, and I am twenty years
younger than he. He gave me a pain in the great toe, by mentioning
the gout. I find such suspicions frequently, but they go off again.

London, February 13, 1710/11

. . . then I went to visit poor Congreve, who is just getting out of
a severe fit of the gout, and I sat with him till near nine o'clock.
He gave me a *Tatler* he had written out, as blind as he is, for little
Harrison. 'Tis about a scoundrel that was grown rich, and went and
bought a Coat of Arms at the Herald's, and a set of ancestors at
Fleet-ditch; 'tis well enough, and shall be printed in two or three
days,[1] and if you read those kind of things, this will divert you.

London, February 16, 1710/11

. . . I went to-day into the city for a walk, but the person I designed to dine with was not at home; so I came back and called at
Congreve's, and dined with him and Eastcourt,[2] and laughed till
six, then went to Mr. Harley's. . . .[3] Congreve's nasty white wine
has given me the heart-burn.

Chelsea, July 2, 1711

. . . I called this morning to see Will Congreve, who lives much
by himself, is forced to read for amusement, and cannot do it without a magnifying-glass. I have set him very well with the ministry,
and I hope he is in no danger of losing his place. . . .

Chelsea, October 15, 1711

I sat at home till four this afternoon to-day writing, and ate a roll and butter; then visited Will Congreve an hour or two, and supped with lord treasurer, who came from Windsor to-day, and brought Prior with him. . . .

London, October 29, 1711

I was all this terrible rainy day with my friend Lewis [4] upon business of importance; and I dined with him, and came home about seven, and thought I would amuse myself a little after the pains I had taken. I saw a volume of Congreve's Plays in my room, that Patrick [5] had taken to read; and I looked into it, and in mere loitering read in it till twelve, like an owl and a fool: if ever I do so again; never saw the like. . . .

London, January 5, 1711/2

. . . Then I went and visited poor Will. Congreve, who had a French fellow tampering with one of his eyes; he is almost blind of both. . . .

EDITIONS: Jonathan Swift, *Journal to Stella*, ed. by Harold Williams, 2 vols., Oxford, 1948, pp. 69, 70, 191, 193, 305, 306, 384, 396, 455 (from Letters 7-38), based on the editions of Letters 2-40 by Deane Swift in 1768. The manuscript used for the edition of 1768 has been lost.

[1] Congreve's essay appeared on 17-20 February 1710/11 as No. 292 in the continuation of *The Tatler*, edited by the young poet William Harrison (1685-1713). See *DNB*.

[2] Richard Estcourt, or Eastcourt (1668-1712), an Irish actor, made his first appearance at Drury Lane Theatre in 1704. Congreve and Estcourt were possibly friends in Dublin while Congreve was a student at Trinity College (1686-1688) and Estcourt an actor at the Smock Alley Theatre. See No. 26.

[3] Swift's great influence with Robert Harley, the head of the Tory ministry, probably explains why Congreve, a staunch Whig, did not lose his place as Commissioner for Wine Licenses while the Tories were in power from 1710 to 1714. See Nos. 45, 77, 79, 81, and 89.

[4] Erasmus Lewis (1670-1754), Under-Secretary of State. See also No. 77.

[5] Swift's Irish servant.

42   CONGREVE TO JOSEPH KEALLY

London November 9. 1710

DEAR KEALLY

Si vales bene est, ego quidem valeo.[1] And what else can a man write
in these latter times, when false prophets arise, and so forth. I write
to you because I will write to you, and always must desire to hear
from you. I live entirely at home, see nobody, nor converse in any
manner. I would send you my books,[2] which will be published in a
month,[3] if I knew by whom. If you know any body coming your
way send me word. My service to Robin and Luther and all friends.
Excuse me to Luther and yourself for not writing oftener; 'tis very
painful to my eyes.[4] All here are well and your servants. Yours,

W. Congreve.

EDITIONS: Berkeley, pp. 373-374; Summers, Vol. I, pp. 89-90; Dobrée, p. 511.

[1] Addison used this same quotation from Cicero in a letter to Congreve written
in December, 1699. See No. 121.

[2] *The Works of Mr. William Congreve*, 3 vols., London: Printed for *Jacob
Tonson*, at *Shakespear*'s Head over-against *Catherine Street* in the *Strand*.
MDCCX. Congreve mentions his books again in Nos. 43 and 45 and finally
notes in No. 46 (5 July 1711) that they have just been sent to Keally. For
Congreve's copy of the collected *Works*, 1710, see *Library*, item No. 96.

[3] Congreve's books were advertised in the *London Gazette* for 5-7 December
1710.

[4] Congreve's deficient eyesight—apparently myopia—is suggested in one of his
early letters to Mr. Porter (No. 1), written 21 August 1692, about "a whole
river in cascade falling so near me that even I can distinctly see it." By 1710,
Congreve was troubled with cataracts which seriously limited his reading and
writing for a number of years. See also Nos. 41 and 49.

43 CONGREVE TO JOSEPH KEALLY

London December 15. 1710

DEAR KELLY

Tu, ne cede malis, sed, contra, audentior ito.[1] I told Lord Castle-comer,[2] Mr: Addison and Mr Dopping[3] with whom I drank your health last night that I would begin my letter to you like a Tatler with a latin sentence. The application of which I would leave to your selfe. I see mein[4] seldom, but if he would he could write you no news; for things happen like earthquakes suddain unusual and unforeseen. Mr: Addison, very well applyd a line out of Oedipus yesterday which will shew you how things go here—one but began

—To wonder, and strait fell a wonder too.[5]

I have sent to Harry Kelly to inform me by whom I may send you my books and the print done by Smith[6] which is generally liked. I have since I began this letter seen mein. I suppose you will hear soon from him. All the neighborhood are much yours. My service to Robin, Luther &c.

I am Dear Kelly

Yours

W C

Address: *To Joseph Kelly Esqr.*
in Dublin

Postmark: *DE/15*

MANUSCRIPT: The Carl H. Pforzheimer Library. EDITIONS: Berkeley, pp. 374-375; Summers, Vol. I, p. 90; Dobrée, pp. 511-512; *The Carl H. Pforzheimer Library* (New York: Privately Printed, 1940, 3 vols.), Vol. I, pp. 208-209, where Congreve's "15" is misread "17."

[1] Virgil's *Aeneid*, VI, 95. "Yield not to calamities, but on the contrary become bolder." The italics in the text are mine.

[2] Christopher Wandesford, second Viscount Castlecomber in the Irish peerage, was a Member of Parliament from 1710 to 1712 and a member of the privy council in Ireland. See *DNB*.

[3] Samuel Dopping, son of Bishop Anthony Dopping, had during the preceding months taken a very active part in the Irish Parliament, as reported in letters by

Addison. See the *Letters*, ed. by Walter Graham, Oxford, 1941, pp. 136, 141, 142, 147, 154, 169, 175, 177, 219, 222, 248.

[4] Charles Mein. See No. 3.

[5] *Oedipus*, Act I, Scene 1, ll. 28-29, by Dryden and Lee.

[6] John Smith (1652-1742) made a mezzotint engraving of the Kneller portrait of Congreve. A copy of "Mezzo Tinto Prints by J. Smith, Large Paper, Folio" is one of the items listed in Congreve's manuscript Book List. See *Library*, item No. 375. See also letters Nos. 45 and 101.

44   CHARLES MEIN TO JOSEPH KEALLY

Londn. December. 29th. 1710

I have seen a letter of yours to Mr. Congreve wherein there is some honourable mention made of me, and when you say (pleasantly enough) that you fancy these latter times make me look as if I had seen a serjeant, you little think how much you have exceeded your own conceit; for I have been kept in close durance for these six weeks, of and on, by an ugly hurt in my leg, which is not yet cured, and which makes me sympathize with poor Robin [1] in his gout, his temperance, and his impatience; and I am litter'd about, as he us'd, with a multitude of unread Books. I find you expect to be let into the mysterys of the Times, Intrigues of Partys &c. Know this for once, that you on the other side of the Water are all in the dark, and so are like to be for us here, who live in so pure a light, as— hurts the aking sight. You say you read [Hist]ory, by which, no doubt, you mean that you are Wise; but I say, Travel. [Thus] is it to behold in History, as it were in a Mirrour, the Face of antient [tim]es; to be able by a quick piercing and delicate Wit so to fit the Past with the Present that it may serve on all occasions as a most prudent and faithful Counsellor, neither to be awed by fear, nor corrupted and led aside by Interest; if at the same time you are acquainted with the humours and manners of the age you live in. Travel I say. But I beseech you, my dear, old, and bosome friend, be not inquisitive. Have the gout with FzGerald,[1] drink with Luther, and go powder'd among the Beau Monde like your Servant, but I entreat you, nay I conjure you (for the States sake) not to be inquisitive. Travel, I say again.

Your

C: M.

It is whisper'd about as if what I mention'd to you in my last pass'd some Careers.[2]

Address: *For Joseph Kelly Esqr   Dublin*

MANUSCRIPT: British Museum Add. 39,311, f. 3. EDITION: Lynch, p. 31.

[1] Robert Fitzgerald. See No. 6.

[2] In this postscript, which is added in Mein's hand on the verso of the folio, "the State" is crossed out so that it is barely legible and "what I mention'd to you in my last" is written above. Apparently Mein is reporting the rumor that recent party changes have passed over (neglected) some persons in office. Letters by Mein and Congreve at this period of political uncertainty are very cryptic. It is significant that the writers sign only with their initials.

45   CONGREVE TO JOSEPH KEALLY

London March 10. 1710 [*1711*].

DEAR KEALLY

I was not enough recovered from a very ill fit of the gout when I received yours to answer it sooner. I wish you and Robin joy of your olive-branches. I hear nothing of young Mr Harris[1] about your Holland. All here are ready to serve you; and bid me tell you so. I have books[2] ready for you, and three prints in a case; one for you and Robin and Luther, when I can get any body to carry them. Ossy Butler[3] says his brother will go next week, by whom I may send them.

The Marquis de Guiscard was examined on Thursday last by a committee of the cabinet-council about some treasonable correspondence with France. Mr St John,[4] after several questions, to which the prisoner answered very readily, at last produced a letter, the contents of which made him change colour; and on a sudden, with a pen-knife, he offered at Mr St John; but he being too far from him, he stabbed Mr Harley,[5] who sat nearer him. The penknife broke against his breast-bone or a rib, so that he is in no danger. Guiscard, not knowing it was broke, stabbed twice or thrice on. Several of them drew their swords and wounded him, but not mortally. The matter of the information against him is kept very secret. He is in Newgate.[6] I am, dear Keally, yours,

W. C.

EDITIONS: Berkeley, pp. 370-371; Summers, Vol. I, p. 88; Dobrée, pp. 509-510.

[1] Mr. Harris, Keally's cousin, was securing linens from Holland to be made into shirts by Mrs. Edward Porter for Keally. See Nos. 46, 47, and 48.

[2] The books were the three volumes of the collected works. See No. 42. The three prints were the engravings by Smith mentioned in No. 43. See also No. 101.

[3] Ossy Butler. Berkeley reads "Offy," followed by Dobrée. Summers reads "Ossy."

[4] Henry St. John (1678-1751), created Viscount Bolingbroke in 1712, was Secretary of State in the Tory government that came into power in 1710.

[5] Robert Harley (1661-1724), created Earl of Oxford in 1711, was Chancellor of the Exchequer 1710-1714. See also Nos. 41, 77, 79, 81, and 89.

[6] Luttrell reported the incident on 8 March 1710/11: "About noon count Guiscard, (brother to marshal Guiscard, governor of Namur,) who some time since came from the Cevennes, was taken into custody upon Mr. secretary St. Johns warrant for high treson, and being under examination at 4 a clock, before a committee of council at the Cockpit, and Mr. Harley, chancellor of the exchequer, putting some close questions to him, he pull'd out a penknife and stabb'd Mr. Harley; whereupon swords were drawn, and Guiscard wounded, and since carried under a strong guard to Newgate; Mr. Harley's stab happ'ning upon a rib, his surgeons are of opinion it is not dangerous." On 17 March, so Luttrell reported, Guiscard "died in Newgate of a mortification in his shoulder."

46 CONGREVE TO JOSEPH KEALLY

London July 5. 1711

DEAR KELLY

Yesterday at Garraways Coffeehouse [1] I met your Cosen Mr: Harris who payd me, on your account ten guinnes for which I gave him my receipt. I believe by the time you can send me directions what to do with it, their will come a new Cargo of linnen from holland to the person who is already well supplyd. The inhabitants of these buildings are redy to receive your commands [2] and all well at your service. I know no news. My service to Rob: [3] and all friends.

I sent you some prints   *Yours*
and books [4] *by Mr Buttler.* [5]   *W Congreve.*
Your Cos: Harris [6] *sayd he*
was to take post for Ireland yesterday afternoone.

Postmark: *IV/5*

MANUSCRIPT: British Museum Add. 39,311, f. 5. EDITION: D. Crane Taylor, *William Congreve*, London, 1931, p. 209.

[1] Garraway's Coffee-house in Exchange Alley was a meeting place for businessmen. It became especially prominent during the South Sea Bubble of 1720 and continued active till 1866.

[2] That is, Mrs. Edward Porter is ready to make shirts for Keally. See Nos. 45, 47, and 48.

[3] Robert Fitzgerald. See No. 6.

[4] Congreve had waited seven months to find someone to carry to Keally his collected works (see No. 42) and the engravings of his portrait (see No. 43).

[5] Brother of the Ossy Butler mentioned in No. 45.

[6] See No. 45, note 1.

47   CONGREVE TO JOSEPH KEALLY

London November 2. 1711.

DEAR KEALLY

I am well recovered of a fit of the gout, which has hindered my writing to you for some time past. It took me the day after my return from the country, and lasted five weeks; but was more favourable than usual as to the pain of it. Your brother [1] was so kind to come twice to see me; but I believe his journey towards you has prevented my returning his visit. Mrs Porter has sent you by him eleven shirts; a piece of holland ordinarily making ten, but her skill has produced eleven.[2] Inclosed is her account. She waits for an occasion to lay out the remainder of the money in something which may be acceptable. My service to Robin and all friends. I am, dear Keally, yours faithfully,

W. Congreve.

EDITIONS: Berkeley, p. 376; Summers, Vol. I, pp. 90-91; Dobrée, p. 512.

[1] John Keally. See No. 2.

[2] See No. 45, note 1.

48   CONGREVE TO JOSEPH KEALLY

December 11. 1711.

DEAR KEALLY

I hope long before this you have had the satisfaction of seeing your brother. Mrs Porter hopes you are pleased with your linen. She sent several times to inquire after your brother (who had promised to call again), in order to have paid him the remainder, or to have sent some odd thing, as she calls it, an apron or so, to the value of it. She is mighty scrupulous about it, and I write this by her direction; after which I will follow your direction, and drink your health down with her scruples. You have all public transactions in the public papers, so I pretend to write you no news. I generally give you some early conjectures. I think I see a glimpse, and that's all. My service to Robin and all friends. All here are faithfully yours, as I am entirely,

W. C.

EDITIONS: Berkeley, p. 377; Summers, Vol. I, p. 91; Dobrée, pp. 512-513.

49   CONGREVE TO JOSEPH KEALLY

May 6. 1712.

DEAR KEALLY

I have thought it long since I have either written to you or heard from you; and I write to you now without any other pretence than to ask you how you do, and to tell you how I am. As to my gout I am pretty well; but shall never jump one-and-twenty feet at one jump upon North-hall Common [1] again. I have an old conjuror who has been some time about my eyes,[2] and I hope will be able to keep them from being worse; and who, if I had met with him seven years ago, could have quite cured me. The commission of my office is changed; but I am continued.[3] This is all I can say, except that all here are much your servants. Pray let me know how it is with you and honest Robin; to whom give my love and service. I am ever yours,

W. C.

EDITIONS: Berkeley, p. 378; Summers, Vol. I, p. 91; Dobrée, p. 513.

[1] See No. 21, written from Northall, where Congreve spent some of his vacations.

[2] See No. 42, note 4.

[3] Congreve was greatly worried lest the change in government would result in the loss of his office as Commissioner of Wine Licenses. See Nos. 41, 77, 79, and 81.

50   CONGREVE TO JOSEPH KEALLY

London October 29. 1712.

DEAR KEALLY

I this instant received yours of the 22d, and the first thing I do is to answer it. You do very well to reproach me for my silence, after having made me expect to see you every day this summer, or at least this autumn. Mrs Porter went to the Bath almost on purpose to meet you and bring you up with her. She and all neighbours are very well, and very much your servants. Mein is well, and thrives prodigiously.[1] We can't sit on the same side of a coach, though I am no fatter than I use to be. If you design to come this winter, pray go on board the packet-boat, that you may not be liable to any uncertainty but that of the wind. I had not the happiness to see Sir Pierce at all the last time he was in London; so that he may come off well enough about saying that I could not see him, if he cares for an evasion; but I fancy he likes his own way of telling a thing better. News! No, Sir, no news, I thank you; nor no glimpse. But one thing I'll tell you, whenever it comes, it will be no longer a glimpse, but a glare:[2] and so my service to Robin and all friends. Ever your

W. C.

EDITIONS: Berkeley, pp. 379-380; Summers, Vol. I, p. 92; Dobrée, pp. 513-514.

[1] See No. 3, note 5, for Gay's reference to Charles Mein as "so fat with laughing eyes."

[2] This seems almost prophetic of the time two years hence when Congreve's party would come again to power and when he would be recognized adequately.

51 CONGREVE TO EDWARD PORTER

> [*Stowe, Buckinghamshire*], *new years day*, [*1714?*] [1]
> This is to wish you and Mrs: Porter and my friends in Howard street [2] a happy new year, and next to condole with you for the damnd weather. God knows when the snow will let me stirr; or if a thaw should come upon it when the flouds will be down. I am by a great fire yet my ink freezes so fast I cannot write. The Hautboys who playd to us last night had their breath froze in their instruments till it dropt of the ends of them in icicles. By god this is true. My service and sorrow to my friends for not being with them.
> > *I am your most obedient servant*
> > *W. Congreve.*

Address: *To Mr. Porter at his house in*
Surry Street in the Strand London

Frank: *R. Temple*

Postmark: *Buckinham, IA/4*

MANUSCRIPT: British Museum Add. 4293, ff. 57, 58. EDITIONS: Hunt, p. xliv; Summers, Vol. I, p. 98; Dobrée, pp. 523-524.

[1] The date 1714 is indicated by the small postmark, which was just coming into use at that time. A later date than New Year's Day, 1714, seems improbable because the frank "R. Temple" should have been "Cobham" after Sir Richard Temple was created Baron Cobham in 1714. The address to Mr. Porter "in Surry Street" in Congreve's mature hand indicates a year later than 1702. Congreve was evidently spending the Christmas Season with his good friend Sir Richard Temple at Stowe, Buckinghamshire. Congreve's fear that he would be snowed in for a time was apparently well founded: the letter was not postmarked till January 4.

[2] The friends in Howard Street were, of course, Anne Bracegirdle and her mother.

52   CONGREVE TO EDWARD PORTER

[*London, 1714?*]

SIR

If you see Mr Custis [1] to night pray know of him if it be possible for me to have a picture of Lord Rochester [2] which was Mrs: Barrys.[3] I think it is a head. I think it is not as a painting any very great matter. However I have a very particular reason why I would have it at any reasonable rate, at least the refusal of it. If this can be don, he will very much oblige his and

> *Your*
> *very humble servant*
> *Wm Congreve.*

fryday even:

Address: *To Mr Porter*

MANUSCRIPT: British Museum Add. 4293, f. 64. EDITIONS: Hunt, p. xlvi; Summers, Vol. I, p. 101; Dobrée, pp. 526-527.

[1] John Custis, Gent., who had inherited a part of Mrs. Barry's estate. See R. G. Ham, *Otway and Lee, Biography for a Baroque Age*, New Haven, Yale University Press, 1931, p. 239. The date of Congreve's letter No. 52 is very tentatively set as 1714, the year following Mrs. Barry's death, after Mr. Custis had inherited the picture of Lord Rochester and was in a position to sell it.

[2] John Wilmot, second Earl of Rochester (1647-1680), was the patron of Mrs. Barry and trained her carefully for the stage. She was said to have been his mistress.

[3] Elizabeth Barry (1658-1713), perhaps the most famous actress in Congreve's period, was especially successful in tragic parts. As Zara in Congreve's *Mourning Bride*, she won greater acclaim than Anne Bracegirdle as Almeria, supposedly the leading part. See John Harold Wilson, *All the King's Ladies*, Chicago, University of Chicago Press, 1958, pp. 110-117.

53   CONGREVE TO MRS. EDWARD PORTER? [1]

August 9th: [1717?]

I am very sorry to hear you are indisposed; tho I believe the season
is a great part of your distemper. I assure you it still keeps me back
and I have frequently vapours to that excesse, that if I had not some
free intervals, I should think my selfe rather impaird than improved
in my health. I dont tell you this by way of Complaint so much as
by way of Consolation for if good air, moderate exercise, temperate
living, perfect ease and plenty cannot resist the influence of this
miserable season; you may imagine what power it must necessarily
have over you in town, upon the remainder of your last years dis-
order. Your Cough is what I am most concerned for because it is
most troublesome to you tho I make no doubt of that being also va-
pourish or hysterick. I am only glad you have Dr: Robinson,[2] who
I make no question will set you quite right. Pray let me hear soon
that you are better. You must amuse your selfe any way no matter
how. I am just now as hot as the devil in my hands and it is but
between six and seaven in the morning and promises to be a fine
day. But I [3] can never be again imposed on by the dissimulation of
the weather. We live here like good middling sort of friars in a
pretty retirement onely we have no Nuns. I fancy a good friar would
do you no more harm than a good nun would me as [4] Dr: R———
or Dr: Dunny. I should take it for a prodigious favour if you would
let me hear from you and be overjoyd to have you tell me you were
better. If I could send you anything that would do you as much good
as such a letter would do me; you should have very little Cause,
and very little time longer to complain.

MANUSCRIPT: British Museum Add. 4293, f. 64. EDITIONS: Hunt, p. xlvi; Summers, Vol. I, p. 101; Dobrée, pp. 527-528.

[1] Since this letter is apparently addressed to a lady and since it is preserved
along with the manuscript letters to the Porters, it may very well have been
written to Mrs. Porter. Another possibility, less probable, is that the letter was
addressed to Lady Betty Cromwell, who returned from Ireland with a dangerous
cold in the autumn of 1708 and died with tuberculosis on March 31, 1709. See

No. 35. The date, only a very wild guess, is placed somewhat late because of the maturity of the handwriting.

[2] Possibly Dr. Tancred Robinson (d. 1748), who was knighted by George I, to whom he was physician-in-ordinary. If Dr. Tancred Robinson is the physician named, the use of "Dr." instead of "Sir" points to a date for the letter prior to the conferring of knighthood.

[3] Misread "you" by Dobrée.

[4] Congreve clearly wrote "as" but apparently meant "or."

54   CONGREVE TO EDWARD PORTER

Ashley [1] *thursday* [*1717-1719*]

SIR

I am glad Mrs Porter and you are better in health. I was two days (as usual) in hopes that I had been so too, but on Monday [2] was as ill as ever. I am again in hopes; but I can say little more till two or 3 days more shall be past. 'Tis a subject I am weary of. I am sorry the house is not done because if either health or buisinesse should call me to town I must be sadly inconvenienced. I make no doubt but you will know as soon as you can what resolution Mrs. Draper [3] or the executors will come to, for it is equally uneasy to us all to be at an uncertainty: in the mean time I hope you will let me know when so much of the house is don that if any accident should incline or oblige me to come to town I may have the satisfaction of knowing where I may be. As to the rest we must look forward as well as we can. I am with constant inclination and sincerity to Mrs. Porter and your selfe a very

Faithfull and humble servant.

Wm Congreve

Address: *To Mr Porter at his house in Surry Street.*

MANUSCRIPT: British Museum Add. 4293, ff. 54, 55. EDITIONS: Summers, Vol. I, p. 97; Dobrée, p. 522.

[1] This letter and Nos. 83, 131, and 133 were written from Ashley (Walton-on-Thames), the seat of Richard (Boyle), Viscount Shannon, not far from Pope's villa in Twickenham. In No. 83, dated 5 October 1717, Congreve mentioned his bad health, which prevented his going to London to look after business related to his secretaryship for Jamaica. Possibly No. 54 was written about the same time, for Congreve was still unwell and fearful that "buisinesse" might call him to London.

[2] Dobrée reads "on Monday I was," evidently thinking Congreve had written "I" where a blot occurs in the line. But the lower part of the "I" does not appear below the line, as it certainly would if Congreve had written "I."

[3] Probably the widow of William Draper, Esq., Surrey Street, who had the substantial assessment for two pounds in the Westminster City Rate Books for 1695-1696. In 1721-1722, his name fails to appear, and Mrs. Draper is assessed for two pounds five shillings ten pence as a householder in Surrey Street.

II DRYDEN, TONSON, &

BUSINESS AFFAIRS

Dryden

The Revolution of 1688 deprived Dryden of his laureateship and
turned him to translating for a livelihood. It also closed Trinity
College, Dublin, and brought Congreve to London. Perhaps young
Congreve, then nearly twenty, met Dryden, nearly sixty, as early
as 1689 or 1690. Congreve's scholarly grounding in Latin and
Greek—after four years at Kilkenny under Edward Hinton and
two or three at Dublin under St. George Ashe—at once commanded
the old poet's attention. By 1692, the younger man, both as poet
and as translator, had so gained the respect of Dryden that he used
Congreve's commendatory verses as sole preface to his translation
of the six satires of Persius and also enlisted him as one of the
"Eminent Hands" invited to aid in translating the sixteen satires of
Juvenal. Next year, as Dryden issued a volume of miscellaneous
poems, he included fragments from Homer translated by Congreve,
"whom I cannot mention without the honour which is due to his

excellent parts, and that entire affection which I bear him." Then he went on to commend Congreve as "more capable than any man I know" to translate the whole of Homer (No. 56). Four years later, with his translation of the *Virgil* completed, Dryden submitted his manuscript to Congreve for review and praised him warmly for the assistance given.

During the fall of 1692, when *Juvenal and Persius* was about to come from press, Dryden read the manuscript of Congreve's *Old Bachelor* and declared, according to Southerne, that "he never saw such a first play in his life, but the Author not being acquainted with the stage or the town, it woud be pity to have it miscarry for want of a little Assistance: the stuff was rich indeed, it wanted only the fashionable cutt of the town" (No. 102). So Dryden put the play in order, and it was acted with great acclaim. Probably Dryden's warm regard for the young poet, translator, and dramatist inspired Southerne to write the commendatory verses printed with the play, naming Congreve as Dryden's rightful literary successor. Certainly the idea pleased Dryden, for he used it a few months later in the famous lines prefixed to Congreve's second comedy, *The Double-Dealer*.

> *O that your Brows my Lawrel had sustain'd,*
> *Well had I been Depos'd if You had Reign'd!*
> *The Father had descended for the Son;*
> *For only You are lineal to the Throne.*

When *The Double-Dealer* failed to please the audience, Dryden stood staunchly by his high estimate of it. "My verses," he wrote William Walsh, "were written before the play was acted. But I neither altered them nor do I alter my opinion of the play" (No. 60). Soon afterwards, in "An Account of the Greatest English Poets," Joseph Addison joined in acclaiming Congreve as Dryden's true literary successor.

> Congreve *shall still preserve thy fame alive,*
> *And* Dryden's *Muse shall in his Friend survive.*

It is surprising that the newcomer could win so much praise from his contemporaries without arousing their envy. Perhaps, as Dryden wrote,

> *So much the Sweetness of your Manners move,*
> *We cannot Envy you, because we love.*

Dryden's sincere affection for young Congreve stands out not only in the verses he addressed to him, but also repeatedly in his letters to Jacob Tonson, where he writes, "I am Mr Congreve's true Lover and desire you to tell him, how kindly I take his often Remembrances of me . . . and hope I shall never lose his Affection" (No. 59).

Dryden made good use of Congreve's legal training in his contracts with Tonson. Congreve served as Dryden's witness in the contract for the *Virgil* (No. 61) and also in the contract for the *Fables* (No. 66). Since, as Dryden stated in a letter to Tonson (No. 59), Congreve represented Dryden in drawing up the Tonson-Dryden "Advertisement of Second Subscriptions" for *Virgil* (No. 63), the old poet probably depended also on Congreve in preparing contracts for the *Virgil* and the *Fables*. By the time the *Virgil* contract was drawn, Congreve had already been reading law at the Middle Temple for more than three years. It has been observed that this contract was "a shrewder document than one might expect from the poet." [1]

Congreve did not fail to return the affection that old Dryden lavished upon him. He never forgot Dryden's injunction to "Be kind to my Remains." Congreve edited Dryden's plays in six volumes and, in the Dedication to the Duke of Newcastle (No. 84), spoke of his "Happiness" in being "as intimately acquainted with Mr. Dryden as the great Disproportion in our Years could allow me to be. . . . I loved Mr. Dryden . . . indeed Mr. Dryden had Personal Qualities to challenge both Love and Esteem from all who were truly acquainted with him."

Tonson

Dryden and Congreve were fortunate in having Tonson as their publisher. Perhaps no English publisher has been so outstanding in

[1] See *Review of English Studies*, Vol. XIII (1937), p. 303.

his own age as was Jacob Tonson. He was old enough to start his apprenticeship four years before Milton died in 1674; and four years later, in 1678, the twenty-two-year-old Tonson set up his shop "at the *Judge's-Head* in *Chancery-Lane*, near *Fleetstreet*." [2] Within a few years he bought an interest in the publication rights of *Paradise Lost* and, as soon as he could, the full rights. In 1688, he brought out a fine edition of *Paradise Lost* by subscription. He evidently considered this one of the greatest achievements of his career, for many years later he sat with a copy of this edition in his right hand as Sir Godfrey Kneller painted his picture for the Kit-Cat Club.

Tonson was first to popularize the issuing of great literary works by subscription. Before Tonson, it has been pointed out,[3] only one work was published by subscription, but Tonson projected at least twenty-one such publications before his "retirement" in 1720. These included, in addition to *Paradise Lost,* such masterpieces as Dryden's *Virgil* (1697), the works of Horace (1699), Terence (1701), Saint Evremond (1705), Julius Caesar (1712), Spenser (6 vols., 1715), *The Spectator* (8 vols., 1712-1715), and the collected poems of Prior (1718), Gay (2 vols., 1720), and Milton (2 vols., 1720).

After twenty years in Chancery Lane or Fleet Street, Tonson moved his shop to "*Gray's-Inn-Gate* next *Gray's-Inn-Lane*," [4] where Tonson's older brother Richard had published books before his death in 1691. There Tonson kept his business from about November, 1698, until 1710, and took as partner his nephew Jacob Tonson II, son of Richard. In 1710, Tonson made a final move to the sign of "*Shakespear's* Head over-against *Catherine Street* in the

---

[2] From the title page of Dryden's *Juvenal*, 1693. Beginning with 1694, the address on Tonson's title pages reads "at the *Judge's-Head* near the *Inner-Temple-Gate*, in *Fleet-street*." If Tonson had moved his shop from Chancery Lane, he had not moved it far.

[3] Hale Sturges, "The Publishing Career of Jacob Tonson, the Elder, 1678-1720," unpublished dissertation, Yale University, 1936, pp. 14-15.

[4] From the title page of Congreve's *The Way of the World*, 1700.

Strand." [5] He accumulated a large fortune, partly from his great publishing business and partly from judicious investments. About 1720, he bought an estate in Herefordshire near Ledbury called "The Hazells," left his house at Barn Elms and his business in London to his nephew, and spent his remaining sixteen years developing fine apple and grape orchards and making cider and wine for his many friends. His mind was as keen as ever, his memory remarkably good, and he kept in close touch with affairs by reading, as they came out, the new books and periodicals—"The Prints," he called them—and by keeping up a voluminous correspondence with his nephew.[6] He never fully retired from his publishing business.

Tonson's close friends were chiefly Kit-Cats, members of the famous club that he founded about 1700 and held together for nearly twenty years. The club is said to have grown out of a weekly dinner meeting to which Tonson invited promising young poets, including Congreve. Their favorite meeting place was the pastry shop of Christopher Cat, from whose abbreviated name the club came to be called the Kit-Cat. Perhaps the astute publisher had in mind the financial benefits to come from publishing his guests' works. Sir Richard Blackmore hinted at this in his poem on "The Kit-Cats," 1709:

> *To him the Profit, and to them the Fame.*

Among the early members were Steele, Walsh, Addison, Congreve, and Vanbrugh. Later, many noblemen were elected, but only Whigs. One tie that bound them all was a common interest in the principles of the Revolution of 1688 and a determination to insure the Hanoverian succession on the death of Queen Anne. Among the nobles who made up the forty-odd members of the club were the dukes of Marlborough, Kingston, Somerset, Montagu, Dorset, Grafton,

[5] From the title page of Congreve's *Works*, 1710.

[6] For a helpful edition of eighty-five Tonson letters, most of them written from Ledbury to his nephew in London, see Lawrence Edwards, "The Letters of Jacob Tonson," unpublished dissertation, The University of Tennessee, Knoxville, 1956. Six of these eighty-five letters have been edited and published by Sarah Lewis Carol Clapp, *Jacob Tonson in Ten Letters by and About Him*, The University of Texas Press, 1948.

Richmond, Devonshire, Manchester, and Newcastle and the earls of Bath, Essex, Carlisle, Lincoln, Berkeley, Godolphin, Wilmington, Halifax, and Stanhope. Yet the founder, secretary, and leader of this aristocratic group was only a middle-class tradesman. Unquestionably, the "genial" Tonson combined rare tact and ability to lead; but even so, he could hardly have established an intimate relationship with so many men of quality if he had not first developed a club of such literary distinction that all felt honored to join.

About 1703, Tonson bought a home at Barn Elms on the outskirts of London and, while he was away on a business trip to Holland, had it made ready for the entertainment of the Kit-Cats. Congreve wrote (No. 69) of his eagerness to see the new house at Barn Elms. And Vanbrugh wrote on 15 June 1703:

> . . . the Kit-Cat wants you, much more than you ever can do them. Those who remain in towne, are in great desire of waiting on you at Barne-Elmes; not that they have finished their pictures neither; tho' to excuse them (as well as myself), Sir Godfrey has been most in fault. The fool has got a country house near Hampton Court, and is so busy about fitting it up (to receive nobody), that there is no getting him to work.[7]

The pictures mentioned by Vanbrugh were the portraits of the individual members that Sir Godfrey Kneller had been commissioned to paint for the special Kit-Cat room being prepared at Barn Elms. By 1720, Sir Godfrey had painted forty-three portraits that were destined to be carefully preserved by many generations of the Tonson family until the famous collection was bought in 1945 for the National Portrait Gallery in London. The old publisher thought so highly of the Kit-Cat portraits that he planned to move them to his country home at Ledbury, but he finally compromised by ordering inexpensive copies at a guinea each for the country place and left the fine Kneller originals with his nephew at Barn Elms.

The tone of all the Congreve letters to Tonson is that of warm friendship, without the least touch of the bickering that sometimes appears in the Dryden-Tonson letters. No doubt the letters from

[7] *The Complete Works of Sir John Vanbrugh*, ed. by Bonamy Dobrée and Geoffrey Webb, London, 1927-1928, 4 vols., Vol. IV, p. 7.

Tonson to Congreve were equally friendly, but these have all been lost, along with all other letters written *to* Congreve, except to the very limited extent that copies were kept by the writers. In letters written to his nephew (Nos. 98-101), Tonson mentioned Congreve repeatedly and showed clearly the fine feeling and high regard he had for him.

Theatrical and Business Management

Congreve cared little for business, especially for any phase of business that involved controversy. But he was not inept in handling his own affairs; indeed, his ability to make ends meet in spite of a modest income during his first twenty-five years in London speaks well for his management. Perhaps at that time, as Swift tells us in his "Libel on the Reverend Dr. Delaney,"

Congreve scarce cou'd spare
A Shilling to discharge his Chair,

but he always seemed to live within his means. After his income became ample during the last fourteen years of his life, he continued his simple way of living in Surrey Street, invested his money wisely, and left a substantial amount. Jacob Tonson knew Congreve's habits well enough to be confident, as he wrote his nephew (No. 99), that the poet had built up a considerable estate. Congreve was not a careless, easy-spending Steele or Gay. He was more like Addison, though his income from public office was never more than a small fraction of that enjoyed by Addison.

Our first records of Congreve's business affairs concern his joint management of the new theatre in the Haymarket. Vanbrugh had taken the lead, chiefly because as an architect he was interested in building a stately theatre. But in doing so, Colley Cibber tells us, he sacrificed all the qualities of a good playhouse "to shew the Spectator a vast triumphal Piece of Architecture! . . . scarce one Word in ten could be distinctly heard in it . . . the articulate Sounds of a speaking Voice were drown'd by the hollow Reverberations of one

Word upon another." [8] Worse still, the Haymarket was nearly a mile west of the established theatrical district of Drury Lane and Lincoln's Inn Fields and, as Cibber tells us, was surrounded by streets that "were then all but so many green Fields of Pasture, from whence [the Haymarket] could draw little or no Sustenance, unless it were that of a Milk-Diet." [9] Both the defects of the building and its location made failure of the company inevitable. Although the two managers worked together harmoniously enough, they could not hope to avoid controversy with Christopher Rich, the cantankerous old manager of the rival company at Drury Lane (see No. 71), nor did their slender receipts enable them to meet their obligations to expensive, and perhaps temperamental, opera singers (see Nos. 72, 73). Only a few months after the Haymarket opened, on 9 April 1705, Congreve was glad to make over his share to Vanbrugh, even though he had to buy himself out of the partnership, as suggested in his letter of 15 December 1705 to Joseph Keally (No. 22).

In another letter to Keally (No. 23), Congreve reported that he had "neither too much nor too little buisinesse." A limited amount, without the bickerings incident to theatrical management, he found tolerable. By this time Congreve had opened a small checking account with Hoare's Bank in Fleet Street (No. 74), and later began to make sizable investments in bank stock and annuities at the Bank of England (Nos. 78, 87, 90) and in South Sea Stock. His cousin Colonel Ralph Congreve thought well enough of the dramatist's business acumen to empower him "either to Buy in South Sea Stock, or to sell or dispose of any sum or sums which I now have or may have in the said Stock" (No. 80). This arrangement was made during Ralph's three-year period as Lieutenant Governor of Gibraltar (1713-1716), and evidently worked out to his satisfaction, since Ralph, shortly before his death in 1725, named his cousin William Congreve one of three persons to execute his last will and testament (No. 93).

[8] Cibber, Vol. I, pp. 321, 322.

[9] Cibber, Vol. I, p. 322.

Another executor named by Ralph Congreve was his brother Colonel William Congreve of Highgate. Ralph (1669-1725) was a year older and his brother William (1671-1746) a year younger than their cousin William Congreve the dramatist (1670-1729). The younger brother, William, was probably named for the dramatist's father, Colonel William Congreve (1637-1708?). About 1695, the dramatist stood godfather to William Congreve, son of Colonel William Congreve of Highgate. And in 1699, still another William Congreve was born to John Congreve, older brother of Ralph and William, in Staffordshire. Thus by 1700, there were living no fewer than five William Congreves, all descended from the dramatist's grandfather Richard Congreve (1609-1689), of Stretton Hall, Staffordshire.[10] Only the known handwriting of the dramatist enables us to distinguish his signature from that of the contemporary kinsmen who bore the same name. Particularly confusing have been documents signed by Colonel William Congreve of Highgate. Many of these have been catalogued by American libraries as documents signed by the dramatist, and even the Bank of England confused the two Williams and left in the dramatist's account for six months two sums amounting to over £245 that rightfully belonged to the Colonel (No. 87). Fortunately, we have one manuscript signed first by the dramatist and then by the Colonel as executors for Ralph Congreve (No. 94). The signatures are much alike for "Congreve" but very different for "W." The dramatist makes a sharp point for the first of the three upper prongs of the "W" and brings the middle prong approximately to the height of the other two. The Colonel rounds the first prong and brings the middle prong to about two-thirds the height of the other two. The Colonel regularly signs "Will" and lets the ll's fall together or slightly overlap at the top. When the dramatist signs "Will" or "William," the ll's are distinctly separate at the top.

[10] For the Congreve genealogy see Hodges, pp. 128, 129.

Government Service

No phase of Congreve's career is so well authenticated as his thirty-five years of government service. Of the many pertinent letters and documents, preserved chiefly at the Public Record Office, ten are here reproduced as Numbers 64, 77, 79, 81, 82, 83, 85, 86, 88, and 89; and many others are cited in footnotes.

Congreve began his service on 25 March 1695 as one of the five commissioners "for regulating and Licensing Hackney and Stage Coaches" at a yearly salary of one hundred pounds, and he held the post till Christmas, 1705.[11] The fact that three preceding commissioners had resigned because the salary was reduced from two hundred to one hundred pounds [12] indicates that the post was not merely a sinecure. The "Declared Accounts," or annual reports, of the commissioners showed that they rented an office in Surrey Street, very convenient to Congreve's lodgings in nearby Arundel Street, and employed a secretary and five other assistants.

While Congreve was on the commission for hackney coaches, he had two other shorter appointments. First he was one of eleven managers of the Malt Lottery, serving by virtue of a royal warrant issued on 23 April 1697. This lottery, like the Million Lottery that preceded it, was a government scheme for raising money. But it was less successful, and the Lords of the Treasury at first voted to allow only half the two hundred pounds provided for each manager of the Million Lottery. Thereupon Congreve joined five of his fellow managers in memorializing the Lords, comparing themselves to the

[11] See Congreve's original patent dated 12 July 1695 (P.R.O. Patent Roll 3378, 7 William III, Part I, No. 1) and the renewal dated 22 July 1702 (P.R.O., Declared Accounts for the Commissioners, 1702-1703) and also the annual Declared Accounts covering the period 1695-1705.

[12] See *The Post Boy* for 4-6 June 1695: "The Sallery of the Commissioners for Licensing of Hackney and Stagecoaches being reduced to 100 *l. per annum*, Mr. *Ashurst*, Mr. *Overbury* and Mr. *Isham* resigned their places, and are to be succeeded by Mr. *Herne*, Mr. *Clark* and Mr. *Congreve*." The Declared Accounts for 1694-1695 show that the salary had been two hundred pounds.

laborers in a poor mine, "the Pooreness of the Mine affording noe pretence against the payment of the Labourers" (No. 64). The second short appointment was the sinecure post as customs collector at Poole from 3 July 1700 to the end of 1703, with an annual salary of forty-eight pounds and the right to certain fees. This post, after payment of a deputy and other expenses, probably netted Congreve somewhat more than one hundred pounds yearly.[13]

At the end of 1705, Congreve gave up his commission for hackney coaches to begin a nine-year period as one of five commissioners for licensing wines.[14] This post carried a yearly salary of two hundred pounds, twice that of the one he had relinquished, but it was still properly described as a "little office" by Lord Halifax in 1712 when he exerted his influence with the Tory prime minister in Congreve's behalf (No. 79). Only the repeated efforts of Lord Halifax (No. 81) and Swift (Nos. 77, 89) enabled Congreve, a staunch Whig, to hold his government employment throughout the period of Tory power, 1710-1714. The office for wine licensing was at the foot of

[13] See the warrant for Congreve's original patent dated 3 July 1700 (P.R.O., T. 11/14, p. 86), the enrollment dated 1 August 1700 (P.R.O. Patent Roll 3416, 12 William III, Part III, No. 6), and the renewal of the patent dated 22 June 1702 (P.R.O. Patent Roll 3425, 1 Anne, Part II, No. 38). For the salary paid to Congreve, see P.R.O. Quarterly Treasury Accounts, General, T. 31/1, p. 73, etc. A manuscript "Account of the Several Patent Officers in the Revenue of Customs" preserved at the Library of Customs and Excise, London, shows that the customer at Poole had for the years 1779, 1780, 1781 an average salary of £48 and a total yearly net income of nearly £187.

[14] The Declared Accounts (P.R.O.) for the two years ending at Christmas, 1707, list Congreve as one of five "Commissioners and Agents for granting Licenses for Selling and Offering by Retail, all and every or any kind of Wine or Wines whatsoever in any City, Town, or place within the Kingdom of England, Dominion of Wales and Town of Berwick upon Tweed, being appointed to the said Office by Letters Patents under the Great Seale of England bearing date the XXVIth day of December in the fourth year [1705] of the Reigne of Her Majestie Queen Anne with full power and Authority to them or any two or more of them from time to time during her Majestiys pleasure. . . . And . . . to Each of them a yearly Salary of Two hundred pounds to Comence from the date of the said Letters Patents . . . paid quarterly . . . together with the usuall Fees and Profits belonging to the said Office." The Declared Accounts for the two years ending at Christmas, 1715, show that Congreve served as Commissioner till 21 December 1714.

Arundel Street conveniently near his lodgings. No doubt the work
of the office was done largely by the comptroller and his nine assistants,[15] but that the commissioners themselves sometimes func-
tioned at the office is shown by an extant wine license signed by Congreve. The commissioners also made reports to the lord treasurer,
as when Swift "saw Will. Congreve attending at the treasury, by
order, with his brethren, the commissioners of the wine licenses"
(No. 77).

Soon after the death of Queen Anne and the consequent return
of the Whigs to power, Congreve received, in place of his one "little
office," two appointments, at least one of which was lucrative; and
he held these for the remainder of his life. One of these was Undersearcher of Customs for the Port of London, for which a patent
was authorized on 3 November 1714; [16] the other was a commission

---

[15] The office assistants for the commissioners are shown by the Declared Accounts
and also by the Treasury Registers, P.R.O., T. 47/1, p. 1.

[16] For the warrant, see P.R.O., T. 11/16, p. 167; and for the original patent,
dated 4 November 1714, the Library of Customs and Excise, London. The original grant was only "during pleasure" of George I, but on 28 September 1727,
it was ordered continued under George II (see P.R.O., T. 11/19, p. 132). On
23 November 1714, Congreve and his proposed deputy, Joshua White (remembered in Congreve's will; see No. 148), were authorized to take the appropri-
ate oaths of office (P.R.O., T. 11/16, p. 171). The salaries are stated very precisely in a special report (P.R.O., T. 42/2) made by the Commissioners of the
Customs entitled "A List of all the Officers Employed in the Customs with the
Salaries and Allowances they Respectively receive, distinguishing therein such
as are paid out of Incidents from those that are placed upon the Establishment
or paid by Dormant Warrant as they stood at Michaelmas 1717." On p. 17 of
the report, Congreve is listed as one of the undersearchers with a yearly salary
of £12 paid by dormant warrant, *with no annual allowance by incidents*.
Each of the undersearchers was allowed a deputy at £60 annually. This difference in salary in favor of the deputy may be explained as a necessary living wage
for the man giving his full time to the work, whereas the position as undersearcher was only a sinecure. The great difference, however, is remarkable; and
it seems probable that the undersearchers had an income not indicated. In a
letter dated 1 September 1717, Lady Mary Wortley Montagu speaks of Congreve as "enjoying leisure with dignity in two lucrative employments" (Sherburn, Vol. I, p. 423). One of these was evidently the secretaryship of Jamaica,
and his only other employment was the post in the customs. Thomas Southerne
referred to Congreve's "Patent place in the Customs of 600 Pounds per annum"

as Secretary of Jamaica dated 14 December 1714 (No. 82). The duties of each office were carried out by a deputy, who under normal conditions left very little to the care of Congreve.

But conditions were anything but normal in Jamaica when Congreve became its secretary. Upon coming into office, Congreve named as his deputy Samuel Page, with Peter Beckford as substitute. When these nominations came before the Governor, Archibald Hamilton, they were protested on the ground that Beckford had often opposed the Governor in the Jamaica Assembly and Page was "only a Toole" of Beckford.[17] These objections, however, were overruled by the Board of Trade,[18] and Page was installed in office. After a few months, the Council of Jamaica, evidently dominated by the Governor, removed Page from the office of clerk of the council on the charge of incapacity. Almost immediately, the Assembly, in a committee report made by Beckford, commended Page for his "great exactness" and general efficiency.[19] The growing hostility between Governor and Assembly culminated the following month with Page's secret departure for London as a representative of the Assembly to lay before the Board of Trade charges that Hamilton was conspiring with the Spaniards.[18] Hamilton was arrested and brought to England. After months of delay, on 26 September 1717, he sent to the Board a long memorial in which he cited the bad character of Page and requested his dismissal from his post as deputy to the Secretary of Jamaica. A week later, the Board "ordered that a letter be writ to Mr. Congreve, Secretary of Jamaica, acquainting him with their lordships desire to speak with him on Wednesday next, upon several complaints that have been made to them against Mr. Page, his

(see No. 102). This amount would agree well enough with the "Account" for the years 1779, 1780, and 1781 (see note 13 above), when the average annual net value for the post of undersearcher was about £586.

[17] Governor Archibald Hamilton to the Board of Trade, 26 April 1715, P.R.O., C.O. 137/10, No. 79.

[18] Memorial of Governor Archibald Hamilton to the Board of Trade, 26 September 1717, P.R.O., C.O. 137/46, fols. 128-140.

[19] *Journals of the Assembly of Jamaica* (Jamaica, 1795), Vol. II, p. 195. The report was made on 9 February 1715/6.

deputy." [20] Congreve's reply is dated just two days later (No. 83). The Board of Trade found that Page had allowed his zeal to transport him "beyond the Rules of common Justice," [21] and on recommendation of the Board, the Privy Council, on 29 January 1717/8, ordered Congreve to remove Samuel Page as his deputy (No. 85).

While Page was on his way to London in March, 1716, he wrote to Governor Hamilton, naming Avery Wagstaffe or Peter Beckford to serve as deputy in his absence. [22] The Governor very naturally disregarded the wishes of his archenemy, and appointed his secretary, William Cockburn, to fill the vacancy. Five months later, after Hamilton had been replaced by a new governor, Cockburn was dismissed, and Beckford, acting as Congreve's lawyer, demanded a full accounting of the profits of the office. According to Cockburn's reckoning, the total income amounted to £595:3:10, half of which he was willing to relinquish as the share of the secretary; but Beckford demanded the whole of the proceeds in the name of the rightful deputy and won his suit against Cockburn for £641:5:8 (evidently the lawyer's estimate of the total income) as well as £31:7:6 to cover the cost of the suit. [23] When Cockburn appealed to the Board of Trade to be relieved of the judgment against him, Congreve made a counter appeal in support of the rights of "Samuel Page his late Deputy" (No. 86). After this appeal, the outcome of which we do not know, Samuel Page enters no more into the career of William Congreve. Page had been succeeded by some other person long before the Duke of Newcastle wrote in November, 1719,

[20] *Journal of the Commissioners for Trade and Plantations from March 1714/15 to October 1718* (London, 1924), p. 276.

[21] Report of the Board of Trade on the Memorial of Governor Archibald Hamilton, 24 October 1717, P.R.O., C.O. 138/14, p. 506.

[22] Samuel Page to Governor Archibald Hamilton, 6 March 1715/6, P.R.O., C.O. 137/12, No. 67.

[23] For the suit against Cockburn and the amounts here mentioned, see "The Humble Petition of William Cockburn Esqr.," which was before the Board of Trade about November, 1717. P.R.O., C.O. 138/16, pp. 21-25. Since the profits from the secretaryship were approximately £600 for five months, or £1,440 for twelve months, Congreve's share must have been about the £700 reported by Southerne (see No. 102).

to inquire about the death of Congreve's deputy in Jamaica (see No. 88).

The Law

Whether Congreve became a student of the law at the Middle Temple (see No. 55, dated 17 March 1690/1) to please himself or merely to satisfy his father, we do not know. Perhaps Steele had Congreve in mind when he described a bachelor of the Temple who "was placed there to study the Laws of the Land, and is the most learned of any of the House in those of the Stage." [24] As early as 1699, Charles Gildon wrote that Congreve first applied himself to the law but "was of too delicate a Taste, had a Wit of too fine a turn, to be long pleas'd with that crabbed, unpalatable Study." [25]

Congreve's three or four years at the Middle Temple may account for his effective use of legal terms and proceedings in his plays. In *The Way of the World*, V, xiii, for example, the complications of the plot are resolved when Mirabell shows that Mrs. Fainall, on "the wholesome Advice of Friends and Sages learn'd in the Laws of this Land," had made *"A Deed of Conveyance of the whole Estate real of* Arabella Languish, *Widow, in Trust* to Edward Mirabell." We have already seen how Congreve's legal training enabled him to help Dryden with his contracts for translating *Virgil* and the *Fables* and with his advertisement of second subscriptions of the *Virgil*. Congreve also participated in an indenture [26] with Richard Temple, Lord Cobham, and very naturally so, since the two men were close friends and often together in London or at Lord Cobham's country seat at Stowe in Buckinghamshire.

But it is not so readily evident how Congreve became involved in 1726 in the long-drawn-out chancery proceedings between the

[24] *The Spectator*, No. 2, Friday, 2 March 1710/11.

[25] "The Lives and Characters of the English Dramatick Poets," London, [1699], p. 21.

[26] Cobham et Stanyan, P.R.O., C. 54/5123, No. 18.

Duchess of Hamilton and the heirs of Lord Mohun. Certain it is that Lady Mohun named Congreve (No. 92) one of the trustees for her estate—apparently to protect herself against the Duchess— and that Congreve in turn declared (No. 95) he had been named without his knowledge or consent. The famous chancery suit in which Congreve thus became involved had been started as early as 1698 and had caused the famous duel between the Duke of Hamilton and Lord Mohun in 1712 in which each had killed the other.

55   CONGREVE'S ADMISSION TO THE MIDDLE TEMPLE

Martii 17mo.1690 [*1691*].

Congreve W.   Mr: Wilmus Congreve filius et heres
   ad. h.   apparens Wilmi Congreve de Stretton
                in Com Straffordiae Ar: admissus est   05-00-00
                in Societatem Medii Templi specialiter
                et obligatur una cum et dat pro fine

MANUSCRIPT: *Admissions to House & Chambers, 1658-1695,* Library of the Middle Temple. EDITIONS: Edmund Gosse, *Life of William Congreve,* London, 1888, p. 22; Hodges, p. 34.

56   DRYDEN TO EDWARD, LORD RADCLIFFE [1]

[*July 24, 1693*] [2]

MY LORD,

. . . Notwithstanding my haste, I cannot forbear to tell your Lordship, that there are two fragments of *Homer* Translated in this *Miscellany;* one by Mr. *Congreve,* (whom I cannot mention without the Honour which is due to his Excellent Parts, and that entire Affection which I bear him;) and the other by my self. Both the

Subjects are pathetical; and I am sure my Friend has added to the Tenderness which he found in the Original; and, without Flattery, surpass'd his Author. Yet I must needs say this in reference to *Homer,* that he is much more capable of exciting the Manly Passions, than those of Grief and Pity. . . . I wish Mr. *Congreve* had the leisure to Translate him, and the World the good Nature and Justice, to Encourage him in that Noble Design, of which he is more capable than any Man I know. . . .

I am My Lord,
Your Lordship's most Obedient Servant,
John Dryden.

EDITIONS: Dedication of *Examen Poeticum: being The Third Part of Miscellany Poems,* London, 1693; W. P. Ker, *Essays of John Dryden,* 2 vols., Oxford, 1900, Vol. II, pp. 1-14; *The Poetical Works of Dryden,* ed. by George R. Noyes, Cambridge, Massachusetts, 1950, pp. 382-386.

¹ Edward Radcliffe (1655-1705) succeeded his father as second Earl of Derwentwater in 1696. He was styled Viscount Radcliffe from 1688 (when his father was created first Earl of Derwentwater) until his succession to the earldom in 1696. He was a Tory and no doubt, like Dryden, sympathized with the exiled James II.

² Advertised to be published "on Monday next" in *The London Gazette* for Monday, 17 July, to Thursday, 20 July 1693.

57   CONGREVE TO JACOB TONSON

[Tunbridge] Satturday, Aug: 12 ('93).

DEAR MR TONSON

I received yours of Thursday by the post, by which I understand that you have delivered the things I wrote about to the Coachman; I expected them yesterday and to day but they are not come which makes me apprehend their loss thro' the negligence of the fellow. I am concerned about the letterrs because I expected some of buisinesse: pray enquire if they may be recovered. I am sorry for the trouble this must needs give you; and can onely wish my selfe twice as much to do you service. If you see Mr Wycherley [1] pray tell him with my service that I wrote to him to Shrewsbery. I don't know whether he received it or no. I suppose you received a letter from me by a private hand wherein I desired you if you had not provided [2] the things to omitt them, but since you have I think it is better, especially if I can [3] get them at all. I sent also by the same hand a letter for you to send to the post office for my father.[4] I hope you received them. I am dear Mr. Tonson,

> *Your most affectionate*
> *Friend and servant*
> *W: Congreve*

MANUSCRIPT: Formerly in the hands of Messrs. Sotheran, in London. EDITIONS: Summers, Vol. I, p. 105; Dobrée, p. 532.

[1] William Wycherley (1640?-1716), the celebrated author of *The Country Wife* and *The Plain Dealer*, was born at Clive (or Cleve) Hall near Shrewsbury. Congreve's letter to him has not been found. Wycherley is mentioned also in Nos. 109 and 114.

[2] In editing No. 57 from the manuscript, Dobrée read "provided" and Summers read "printed." The manuscript has not been located by the present editor.

[3] Read "can't" by Dobrée and Summers, but "can" is evidently what Congreve intended. Congreve did get "the things," as he wrote Tonson three days later (see No. 58).

[4] Congreve's father, Colonel William Congreve (1637-1708?), was then living at Lismore Castle in Ireland. See Nos. 18 and 105.

58   CONGREVE TO JACOB TONSON

[Tunbridge] Tuesday, [August 15, 1693] [1]

DEAR MR: TONSON.

I write this onely to acquaint you that yesterday I receivd the things which you sent, and for which I thank you; the reason of their delay was that they have layn a week at Senock.[2] If this comes time enough

I would have it prevent your sending me anything else. For I'm afraid my health will call me from the satisfaction of this place to the more noisy pleasures (or rather conveniencys) of Epsom.³ I have a continual heat in the palms of my hands, which I believe those waters are better for than Tunbridge; ³ I shall leave this place with great regrett, having never in my life been better pleased for the time. If I am necessitated to come away it will be either the latter end of this week or beginning of the next. You need not take notice of it for I would go to Epsom without being much seen in town. I should be glad if your occasions would give you leave to go thither for a day or two. I am dear Mr: Tonson your affectionate Friend

and servant W: Congreve

I thank you for giving my service to Dr:
Hobbs.⁴ Pray repeat it. And to whom else
you think it may be acceptable.

Address: *To Mr: Tonson att the Judges head*
           in Chancery Lane   London

Postmark: *AV/17*

MANUSCRIPT: The New York Public Library. EDITIONS: Gentleman's Magazine, June, 1835, p. 609; Dobrée, p. 533.

¹ This letter, dated merely "Tuesday," refers to "the things" about which Congreve had made inquiry in letter No. 57, dated "Satturday, Aug: 12 ('93)." The "Tuesday" of No. 58 was evidently Tuesday, August 15, since the postmark on the manuscript is "AV/17."

² "Senock," misread "Lenock" by Dobrée, is a common abbreviation for "Seven Oaks," a junction between London and Tunbridge. For this information the editor is indebted to the late Percy Dobell, Esq., of Tunbridge Wells.

³ Epsom is about fifteen miles southwest of the center of London; Tunbridge is about thirty miles southeast.

⁴ Thomas Hobbs was licensed by the Royal College of Physicians of London in 1684. See W. Munk, *The Roll of the Royal College of Physicians*, London, 2nd ed., 1878, Vol. II, p. 433. Dr. Hobbs gave Congreve a copy of Isbrandus de Diemerbroeck's *Anatome Corporis Humani*, Ultrajecti, 1672. This copy, with

the inscription "Willm. Congreve ex dono Dr. Hobbs," was sold in 1930 (see *Library*, No. 184). Among the Tonson Papers, Folio 41, in the Folger Shakespeare Library, in the handwriting of Jacob Tonson, are "Hints for use on Dr. Hobbs":

> I have often heard him say that, when in his youth, he . . . found his inclination to be a surgeon . . . because he woud bee usefull to his Country. . . . Nevour any Surgeon had soe much business, and was soe punctual in his word to every patient, nevour failing the hour he appointed. If we have now better Surgery than before it may be reasonably thought his example and great Succes was the occasion of that industry. The tenderness of his nature, his mild way of not onely handling but speaking to his patients, neither flattring them, nor surlily giving his opinion of their bad state. I have known him give money to poor patients and collect in some companys for patients that wanted bread as well as physick. He was Surgeon to the Person of King Charles and King James and particularly valewed by King Charles, whom he attended in his last illness. . . . He was soe punctually honest as nevour to be known to fail of his word, and as willingly and carefully took care of a patient recomended in meer charity, as of the best. . . .

59 DRYDEN TO JACOB TONSON (FROM FIVE LETTERS)

August 30th. [*1693*]

MR TONSON

. . . I am Mr Congreve's true Lover and desire you to tell him, how kindly I take his often Remembrances of me: I wish him all prosperity; and hope I shall never lose his Affection. . . .

Wednesday the 13th. of September [*1693*]

This is onely to acquaint you, that I have taken my place on the Oundle Coach for Tuesday next; and hope to be at London on Wednesday night. I had not confidence enough to hope Mr Southern and Mr Congreve woud have given me the favour of their company for the last foure miles; but since they will be so kind to a friend of theirs, who so truely loves both them and you, I will please my self with expecting it if the weather be not so bad, as to hinder them. . . .

Saturday June the 8th [*1695*]

Tis now high time for me to think of my second Subscriptions [for the translation of Virgil] [1]: for the more time I have for collecting them, the larger they are like to be. . . . Be pleasd to send me word what day will be most convenient to you; and be ready with the price of paper, and of the Books. No matter for any Dinner; for that is a charge to you, and I care not for it. Mr Congreve may be with us, as a Common friend; for as you know him for yours, I make not the least doubt, but he is much more mine. . . .

October the 29th [*1695*]

. . . You always intended I shoud get nothing by the Second Subscriptions, as I found from first to last. And your promise to Mr Congreve, that you had found a way for my benefit, which was an Encouragement to my paines, came at last, for me to desire Sir Godfrey Kneller and Mr Closterman [2] to gather for me. I then told Mr Congreve that I knew you too well to believe you meant me any kindness: and he promised me to believe accordingly of you, if you did not. But this is past, and you shall have your bargain if I live, and have my health: . . .

Friday Night, [*November or December 1695*]

Meeting Sir Ro: Howard [3] at the play-house this morning, and asking him how he likd my Seaventh Eneid, He told me you had not brought it: He goes out of town tomorrow, being Saturday, after dinner. I desire you not to fail of carrying my manuscript for him to read in the Country. . . . When you have leysure, I shou'd be glad to see how Mr Congreve and you have worded my propositions [4] for Virgil: When my Soons play [5] is acted I intend to translate again, if my health continue. Some time next week let me heare from you, concerning the Propositions.

Yours
J Dryden.

MANUSCRIPTS and EDITIONS: The excerpts follow *The Letters of John Dryden*, ed. by Charles E. Ward, Durham, Duke University Press, 1942, pp. 59, 60, 76,

77, 78, 79 from the original letters in the Pierpont Morgan Library and the William Andrews Clark Memorial Library. An earlier edition is provided by Malone, Vol. II, pp. 30, 40-46.

[1] According to Dryden's agreement with Tonson for the translation of Virgil, witnessed by Congreve on 15 June 1694, the first subscriptions at five guineas, with the coat of arms of each subscriber, were to be followed by second subscriptions after completion of the sixth *Aeneid*. See No. 61.

[2] Since both Kneller and Closterman had painted Dryden's portrait, and since Dryden had just written at their request the *Parallel of Painting and Poetry*, he knew them well enough to ask a favor of them: the collecting of second subscriptions for the *Virgil*. John Closterman (1656-1713) was born in Hanover and came to England in 1681. He was, of course, less well known than Sir Godfrey Kneller (1646-1723), who had come from Germany to England as early as 1676 and had immediately won fame as a portrait painter.

[3] Sir Robert Howard (1626-1698), whose sister Lady Elizabeth was Dryden's wife, was one of Dryden's early patrons. Dryden had assisted him in writing the *Indian Queen*, 1664. See *DNB*.

[4] Perhaps Dryden felt that Congreve's three or four years' study of the law at the Middle Temple especially fitted him to assist in the wording of the "propositions," or advertisement, for the second subscriptions. This advertisement is No. 63 below.

[5] *The Husband His Own Cuckold*, by John Dryden, Jr., was dedicated to his uncle, Sir Robert Howard.

60   DRYDEN TO WILLIAM WALSH [1]

December 12th [1693]

DEARE MR WALSH

. . . I have remembered you to all your friends; and in particular to Congreve; who sends you his play,[2] as a present from him selfe, by this conveyance; and much desires the honour of being better known to you. His Double Dealer is much censurd by the greater part of the Town: and is defended onely by the best Judges, who, you know, are commonly the fewest. Yet it gets ground daily, and has already been acted Eight times. The women thinke he has exposd their Bitchery too much; and the Gentlemen, are offended with him;

for the discovery of their follyes: and the way of their Intrigues, under the notion of Friendship to their Ladyes Husbands. My verses,[3] which you will find before it, were written before the play was acted. But I neither alterd them nor do I alter my opinion of the play. . . .

> *I am Dear Sir,*
> *Your most faithfull Servant. John Dryden.*

MANUSCRIPT: Pierpont Morgan Library, New York. EDITIONS: Robert Bell, *Poetical Works of John Dryden*, 1854, Introduction; Ward, pp. 61-64.

[1] William Walsh (1663-1708), the poet and critic, joined Congreve and Vanbrugh in translating, or adapting, Molière's *Monsieur de Pourceaugnac* for the stage. The English version was acted in 1704 with the title *Squire Trelooby*. See Hodges, pp. 73-74. Walsh was, like Congreve and Vanbrugh, a Whig and a member of the Kit-Cat Club.

[2] *The Double-Dealer*, the publication of which was announced by the *London Gazette* for 4-7 December 1693, though the first edition bears the date 1694.

[3] Prefixed to the first edition of *The Double-Dealer*.

61   DRYDEN-TONSON CONTRACT FOR THE *Virgil*

15th June 1694

John Dryden to translate Ecl. Georg. and Eneids of Virgil.

to do nothing in the mean time, except the Translation of Fresnoy,[1] or any Poem or Book in Prose, not above 1s price, when printed.

for the sole Benefit of Ja. Tonson.

Mr Tonson to pay to Mr Dryden £200. viz. 50 in part when the Ecl. and Georg. are don: 50£ when the first 4 Æn. are finishd. 50£ at the end of the 8th book: and 50£ when the whole is completed.

Tonson to provide 100 Plates, us'd formerly with Ogelbys Virgil: and to mend such as want it.

must endeavour to procure 100 Subscribers, at 5 Guninees each. viz. 3 of them down, and 2 upon the delivery of a Book. which

Books, and the Graving the Title and Arms of the Subscribers to be at Tonsons charge.

Mr Dryden to have whatever Shall be subscrib'd by anybody more than 5 Guineas.

Tonson (if requir'd) to make Oath how much he shall have received.

Shall also deliver to Mr Dryden as many Books as he Shall demand, paying him what the Charge of the large Paper comes to more than the Common paper.

If any difference upon this Article; to be determined by 3 Referees.

No more of the large Paper to be printed, than for the Subscribers: And, till they are dispos'd of; no Second Edition.

When 6th Eneid finish'd, Mr Dryden may give notice, that none but Subscribers can have the large Paper &c.

If the Number of the five Guinea Subscribers Shall not amount to 100 by that time the Ecl. Georg. and 6th Eneid are finish'd, Mr Dryden to be at Liberty to make a new Bargain &c.

Signed Sealed and delivered
in the presence of
T Wester (?)
Will: Congreve

MANUSCRIPTS: British Museum Add. MS. 36933 (signed by Jacob Tonson for Dryden, with a marginal summary which is here printed instead of the detailed contract); Add. Charter 8429 (signed by Dryden for Tonson). EDITIONS: Summarized and partly quoted by C. E. Ward, *Review of English Studies,* Vol. XIII (1937), pp. 301-303, and *Publications of Modern Language Association,* Vol. LIII (1938), pp. 809-810.

¹ *Parallel of Painting and Poetry.* See No. 59, note 2.

62   CONGREVE TO JACOB TONSON

August 20 (*95*)

DEAR MR: TONSON

I thank you for your letter and the kind offers in it, but my Mother [1]
dos not intend to come to town till I write her word, that I am
leaving this place. I am very glad you have had so much satisfaction in the country and that Dr: Hobbs [2] has improved his health.
Mr: Jekel [3] and I drank your Healths; and were [4] in hopes it was
so because you stayd so long. I think I have already found benefit
from these waters, but the present prospect of wett weather disheart-
ens me. I am glad you approve so much of my picture. If you should
see Sir Godfrey [5] again before you goe out of town pray give him
my service, and if he has not finish'd the picture give him a Hint:
for I should be glad it were don before my return. I thank you for
the agreeable news [6] you sent me. I hope to hear more of the same
kind every post. I am Dear Mr Tonson your

faithfull friend and
servant Will: Congreve

Address: *To Mr: Tonson*
att the Judges head near the inner-
Temple gate in Fleet-street.
London

MANUSCRIPT: The New York Public Library. EDITIONS: *Gentleman's Magazine*,
June, 1835, p. 609; Dobrée, pp. 533-534.

[1] This is the only Congreve letter that mentions his mother. She is mentioned
frequently, however, in letters written to Congreve's father by the Earl of
Burlington and others while the father and mother were living in Ireland,
about 1690-1702, at Youghal and at Lismore Castle. One of these letters, from
the Marquis of Carmarthen, commander of an English Fleet based at Cork, apparently explains how the mother had gone to England during the summer of
1695. In that letter, dated 18 July 1695, the Marquis invited Mrs. Congreve
and Lady Mary Boyle to take passage in his own ship to Plymouth. See the Lismore Papers: Early Correspondence, National Library of Ireland. For other
information about the mother, see Hodges, pp. 2, 3, 55, 56.

[2] See No. 58, note 4.

[3] Probably Joseph Jekyll (1663-1738), who preceded Congreve at the Middle Temple and sat for many years in Parliament. He and Congreve were both staunch Whigs, friends of Lord Halifax. Jekyll was knighted in 1700. See *DNB*.

[4] Misread "now" by Dobrée.

[5] Sir Godfrey Kneller painted at least three pictures of Congreve: the one mentioned here; the one bought by the National Portrait Gallery in 1859; and the Kit-Cat picture painted in 1709 and now with the Kit-Cat portraits in the National Portrait Gallery, London. In his will, Sir Godfrey left a ring to Congreve.

[6] Possibly the agreeable news was about the popular demand for the quarto edition of *Love for Love*, which had been published first in the preceding May and reissued several times since.

63   ADVERTISEMENT OF SECOND SUBSCRIPTIONS
      TO DRYDEN's *Virgil*

[ca. *November or December, 1695*]

I have intrusted my much Honourd Friend Mr. Atterbury,[1] to receive the Money subscribed to me for the Translation of Virgil; and to give receipts to the Subscribers for the same.

The Price of the Book is two Guinneys: one of which is to be payd to Mr. Atterbury at the time of Subscription: the other to my Stationer Mr. Tonson, at the receipt of the Book.

The Paper, print and figures of the Book, to be the best: and equall in all respects to those Books, for which Five Guinneys are subscribd: onely the Coats of Armes are not inserted to these Second Subscribers.

The Names and Titles of these Second Subscribers, shall be printed in a List before the Book.

By agreement betwixt me and my Stationer, no more Books are to be printed on the finest paper, than onely those, which are bespoken by the Subscribers.[2]

All the Eclogues, all the Georgigs, and the first six Eneids, are already Translated: and I judg the Whole Work will be finished by Lady Day [3] next.

John Dryden.

MANUSCRIPT: Cambridge University Library, Add. MS. 4429(11), a Dryden holograph. EDITIONS: *Review of English Studies*, Vol. XIII (1937), pp. 304-305; *The Letters of John Dryden*, ed. by Charles E. Ward, Durham, Duke University Press, 1942, p. 172.

[1] Francis Atterbury (1662-1732), later Bishop of Rochester, was chaplain to William and Mary.

[2] See the Dryden-Tonson Contract for the *Virgil*, No. 61.

[3] 25 March 1696.

64   CONGREVE et al. TO THE LORDS OF THE TREASURY

[*London, 1698*] [1]

MAY IT PLEASE YOUR LORDSHIPS

The Managers of the Malt Lottery, understanding by Mr Humes that your Lordships for that their Service; have ordered them but half the reward given them for Management of the Million Lottery, humbly crave leave to lay before your Lordships the difference of their Service therein.

In the Million Lottery there were 100,000 Tickets of 10 li. each, and of these 3 Collumns in every Booke soe that 100,000 × 3 = 300,000 Tickets to be Examined.

In the Malt Lottery there were 130,000 Tickets of 10 li. each and of these 4 Collumns in each Booke soe that 130000 × 4 = 520000 Tickets to be Examined.

Soe that the Figureing and examining of the Million Lottery is to that of the Malt : : 30 : 52:

2dly. That the Managers of the Malt Lottery denyed themselves Coatch hyre att 5s per diem, dinners etc. allowed in that of the Million, and therefore have reason to hope that their Good Management will not be drawne into a precedent to prejudice their Allowance.

3dly. The proveing and Tallying the Malt Tickets has bin soe Managed as to be contained in 13 Bookes, which by breakeing the Tenn Pound Tickets into 20s. Tickets of the Million Lottery made a Vast Number of Bookes, which amounted to about 5000 li.

4thly. The payment 1,200,000 li. in Malt Tickets into the Exchequer was an affaire very Nice and Troublesome, like to which they had nothing in the Million Lottery.

Lastly, even the unsuccesfullness of the Affaire ought to be noe argument against theire Services. The Pooreness of the Mine affording noe pretence against the payment of the Labourers.

All which is Humbly Submitted, etc.

> *Chr: Montagu*
> *Pet: Hume*
> *Jno Isham*
> *Will: Congreve*
> *Dally Thomas*
> *Jno Thrale*

Endorsement: *Adhere to the former resolucon.*

MANUSCRIPT: P.R.O., Treasury Papers, T. 1, Vol. 50, No. 43.

[1] This document was not dated, but it was evidently written during the first months of 1698. The six persons who signed the document and five others were appointed by royal warrant on 23 April 1697 "to be Managers of the Lottery [to prepare books, deliver tickets, and oversee the drawing of lots] as provided in the Act for the Duties on malt &c." See William A. Shaw, *Calendar of Treasury Books . . . preserved in the Public Record Office*, London, 1933, Vol. XII, p. 126. It was hoped, so the Act stated, that this project would provide greatly needed funds "as well towards carrying on the Warr against France as for the necessary Occasions of His Majesties Household" (8-9 William III. C. 22). The Managers were to be paid for their services "in such Proportions as shall be thought fitt and reasonable." When the Malt Lottery proved less successful than the earlier Million Lottery had been, the Lords of the Treasury ordered on 2 February 1697/8 that "the Commissioners of the Malt Lottery have 100 l. each" (Shaw, Vol. XIII, p. 60). Apparently about this time Congreve and his five colleagues made their appeal to the Lords of the Treasury. Although the first decision was to "Adhere to the former resolucon," the Lords

evidently changed their minds later, for on 9 August 1698 they ordered "100 guineas each to the Commissioners who executed the Act for the Malt Lottery Tickets" (Shaw, Vol. XIII, p. 107).

65   DRYDEN TO MRS. ELIZABETH STEWARD [1]
   (FROM TWO LETTERS)

March the 4th 1698 [*1699*]

MADAM

. . . This Day was playd a reviv'd Comedy of Mr Congreve's calld the Double Dealer, which was never very takeing; in the play bill was printed,—Written by Mr Congreve; with Severall Expressions omitted: What kind of Expressions those were you may easily ghess; if you have seen the Monday's Gazette, wherein is the Kings Order,[2] for the reformation of the Stage: but the printing an Authours name, in a Play bill, is a new manner of proceeding, at least in England. . . .

Tuesday March the 12th 1699[*1700*]

. . . Congreves New Play [3] has had but moderate success; though it deserves much better. . . .

Your most Obligd, Obedient Servant,
John Dryden.

MANUSCRIPTS and EDITIONS: *The Letters of John Dryden,* ed. by Charles E. Ward, Durham, Duke University Press, 1942, pp. 112, 113, 134 from the originals in the Pierpont Morgan Library and the Roberts Collection, Haverford College. For an earlier edition, see Malone, Vol. II, pp. 80-81, 128.

[1] Daughter of Elizabeth Creed, Dryden's cousin, who had married John Creed, one of the early members of the Royal Society, Secretary for the Commissioners for Tangiers, closely associated with Pepys.

[2] From the *London Gazette,* No. 3474, Monday, 27 February 1698/9:

> His Majesty being informed, That notwithstanding an Order made the 4th of *June, 1697,* by the Earl of *Sunderland,* then Lord Chamberlain of His Majesty's Houshold, to prevent the Prophaneness and Immorality of the Stage; several Plays have lately been Acted, containing Expressions contrary to Religion, and good Manners: And whereas the Master of the

Revels has represented, That, in Contempt of the said Order, the Actors
do often neglect to leave out such Prophane and Indecent Expressions,
as he has thought proper to be omitted. These are therefore to signify
His Majesty's Pleasure, That you do not hereafter presume to Act any
thing in any Play, contrary to Religion or good Manners, as you shall
answer it at your utmost Peril. —*Given under my Hand this 18 of* February *1698, in the Eleventh Year of His Majesty's Reign.*

Pere. Bertie.

An Order has been likewise sent by His Majesty's Command, to the Master
of the Revels, Not to Licence any Plays containing Expressions contrary
to Religion and good Manners, and to give Notice to the Lord Chamberlain of His Majesty's Houshold, or in his Absence, to the Vice-Chamber-
lain, if the Players presume to Act any thing which he has struck out.

[3] *The Way of the World.*

66   DRYDEN–TONSON CONTRACT FOR THE *Fables* [1]

March 20th: 1698/9

I Doe hereby Promise to Pay John Dryden Esqr: or Order on the
25th: of March 1699 the Sume of Two hundred and fifty Guineas in
Consideration of Tenn thousand Verses which the said John Dryden
Esqr: is to Deliver to me Jacob Tonson when finished whereof Seaven
thousand five hundred Verses more or lesse are allready in the said
Jacob Tonson's possession and I Doe hereby promise and Engage my
selfe to make up the said Sume of two hundred and fifty Guineas
[to] three hundred pounds to the said John Dryden Esqr: his heires
Executors Administrator's or assignes att the beginning of the Second
Impression of the said Ten thousand Verses.[2] In Wittnesse whereof
I have hereunto Sett my hand and Seale this 20th: day of March
1698/9.

Sealed and Delivered being
first Stampt pursuant to the Acts
of parliament for that purpose in   *Jacob Tonson.*
the presence of
      Ben: Portlock
      Will: Congreve

MANUSCRIPTS: The William Andrews Clark Library, Los Angeles, two copies, both signed by Jacob Tonson and witnessed by Ben: Portlock and Will: Congreve, and almost identical in wording. Probably one copy was for Tonson and the other for Dryden. EDITIONS: Malone, Vol. I, p. 560; William Roberts, *The Earlier History of English Bookselling*, London, 1889, pp. 167-168. Both Malone and Roberts follow the copy (perhaps Tonson's) that adds "sterling" after "three hundred pounds." The present edition follows the other copy (perhaps Dryden's) that omits "sterling" but adds "heires" before "Executors."

[1] Since Dryden says that Congreve and Tonson jointly "worded" the propositions for *Virgil* (see No. 59), Congreve may well have had a hand in drawing up the agreement for Dryden's last work, the *Fables*. Congreve's several years' study of the law should have fitted him to assist his good friend.

[2] Actually, Dryden composed nearly eleven thousand lines for Tonson, who made good his contract by paying thirty-one pounds five shillings to Dryden's heirs. See *The Poetical Works of Dryden*, ed. by George R. Noyes, Boston, 1950, p. lxii.

67   CONGREVE TO JOHN DRUMMOND

London January 15th: 1700[*1701*]

SIR

Upon my arrival in England my affairs obliged me to a long Journey into the West. Just at my return to London I met with your Kind Obliging letter; I beg you to believe, that tho' that has prevented my writing first; yet nothing could have made me longer deferr returning you my thanks for all the great civillitys and obligations I received from you at Amsterdam.[1] I shall receive a great deal of pleasure if I can by any means contribute to your entertainment by recommending or writing anything worthy of your leisure hours: and I will not fail with the first opportunity to enjoyn Mr: Tonson to take care answerable to your directions.[2] My impatience of writing to you at this time is the occasion that I send you nothing worth your consideration, for I am so lately come to town that I am a perfect stranger to the news of it. I have observed in the country and by the lists of the members for the new Parliament,[3] that there will be but little alteration in it from the last. How the present Juncture of affairs may vary the pro-

ceedings of the same Persons, onely time can shew. The reception of
the Emperors minister [4] you may be sure is as well as possible; and
I doubt not will have a good issue. All Persons of sence and integrity in the love of their country, are convinced of the necessity
of enabling the King to make a war if he shall Judge it fitt. And I
hope the Parliament will see our condition in a true light when they
shall meet.[5] I will send you a Pamphlet newly publishd which I
think very well and Justly explains the state of Europe in Generall
as well as of England and Holland in particular at this time. The
Author of it is not certainly Known; but his good understanding is
very evident in the treatise he has set forth entituld the Duke of
Anjous succession Considerd as to its Legality and Consequences.[6]
Mr: Abell tho' he has receivd 300 li. of the money belonging to
the new Play-house [7] has not yet sung and is full of nothing but
lies and shifting tricks. His character I suppose is not new to you.
Mr: Mein [8] is heartily your servant and I can answer for the rest of
my fellow travellers tho' I have not seen them since my last coming
to town. Pray Sir on any occasion wherein you think me capable of
serving you lay your commands on me and be assured you cannot
oblidge me more than by giving me opportunitys of shewing how
sensible I am of your Kindnesse and that I am with great truth Sir

Your very affectionate
humble servant

When you favour me with   *Will: Congreve*
a letter, pray direct for me
next door below the blew ball [9]
in Arundell Street in the Strand.

Address: *To Mr: John Drummond*
       Mercht: in Amsterdam

MANUSCRIPT: Additional Abercairney MSS., Scottish Record Office, H.M.
General Register House, Edinburgh.

[1] This statement is our only evidence that Congreve got as far as Amsterdam on
his visit to the Continent during the late summer and autumn of 1700. Perhaps
Congreve returned by the middle of October, as he intended when writing from
Rotterdam on September 27 (see No. 5). He was certainly back in London by

December 10 (No. 6), when he wrote Keally about his Continental trip. Congreve was naturally embarrassed because he had allowed more than a month to pass before thanking John Drummond, the prosperous Scottish merchant who had befriended him in Amsterdam. The "long Journey into the West" was probably to Poole, the southwestern seaport for which Congreve had been appointed collector of customs during the preceding summer.

² Evidently the bookseller Jacob Tonson had been asked to send certain books to Drummond in Amsterdam. See also No. 68.

³ Luttrell shows that Parliament had been dissolved in December and elections held during the first part of January. On February 4 and 6 he reported about 150 new members among nearly four hundred who had come up to London.

⁴ Luttrell reported that Count Wratislaw, envoy of the Emperor, arrived in England on December 28 and was received "with great respect" by King William at Hampton Court on December 30.

⁵ Parliament passed a resolution on 14 February 1700 [1701] "That they will stand by and support his majestie and his government" in the controversy with France. See Luttrell for 15 February 1700 [1701].

⁶ The Library of Congress has the second and third editions of this pamphlet, both published in 1701.

⁷ Lincoln's Inn Fields Theatre had been called "the new Play-house" since its opening with the first production of Congreve's *Love for Love* on 30 April 1695. Since Congreve had a share with Thomas Betterton in this theatre, he was naturally concerned that Abell was failing to live up to his agreement. For Congreve's high opinion of Abell as a singer, see No. 6.

⁸ Charles Mein. See Nos. 3, 4, 6, etc.

⁹ The Blue Ball is mentioned also in No. 12.

68   CONGREVE TO JOHN DRUMMOND

London April: 10th: 1701

SIR

Nothing but an indisposition, of which I am yet hardly recoverd,¹ could have hinderd my answering your letter, both in respect of the great desire I have to continue the pleasure of your acquaintance and in regard of giving you the best account I am able of the state of our

affairs, in such manner as might be either serviceable or entertaining
to you. But as to the latter, we are in so much uncertainty that I
think no body can pretend to do more than guess what we shall do,
and even that with more presumption than probability. We observe
our parliament to make such slow steps that tho' we conclude the
necessity of affairs will draw us into a warr; yet we cannot foresee
any time when we may venture to expect a commencement of it. Our
Parliamant are still proceeding to a further inspection into Treatys.[2]
What issue it will have further than the ratification of that of 77,[3]
I cannot guesse. I fancy we shall wait your motions in Holland and
avoid as far as possible to make our selves principalls; at least this
appears to be the sense of this present session. How much more
vigourous their sentiments will be the next, time will shew. But
sure nothing can prevent a war sooner or later,[4] before we can think
our selves in any prospect of safety. I have not seen Mr: Tonson of
some time but he promised me faithfully to take care of supplying
you from time to time with such books as might be acceptable to you,
and accordingly took a memorandum of directions. I hear of ill suc-
cesse in Mr Foules affairs. I hope you are no sufferer by it. If Mr:
Vander Heyden is married I wish him Joy. And all success to you
in every undertaking. I am very sorry I can write you no letter at
this time more to the purpose which I would answer, being very
willing to appear to my power very much

Your humble servant
Will: Congreve

Address: *To Mr: John Drummond*
         Mercht: in Amsterdam

MANUSCRIPT: Additional Abercairney MSS., Scottish Record Office, H.M. General Register House, Edinburgh.

[1] Congreve mentioned his having been "something uneasy and unwell" in writing Keally on 26 March 1701. (No. 8)

[2] On 15 February 1700 [1701], according to Luttrell, the Commons asked
King William "to lay before the house all treaties and alliances made with any
prince or state since the war," and four days later the Lords asked the King for
the same information.

[3] On 20 February 1701, the Commons gave the King "assurance of support and assistance in performance of the treaty made with the states general, 3 March 1677, . . . which was, in case of an attack, to assist them with 10,000 land men and 20 men of war." See Luttrell for 20 February 1700 [1701] and 3 April 1701.

[4] The War of the Spanish Succession did break out during 1701.

69   CONGREVE TO JACOB TONSON

London July 1st: 1703

DEAR MR: TONSON.

My having been at the Bathe prevented my receiving your letter so soone as I should have don, had I been in town. And I was in hopes you would have been here before, but by your staying so much longer I hope you will doe your buisinesse effectually. I shewd your letter to my Lord Halifax[1] and desired him to do you right to Sir Harry Furnes.[2] I hope the weather will continue fair for your return[3] since it is changed so much for the better. I thank you for the care and trouble you have taken about my linnen. I could wish for halfe a dozen a degree Courser if your time and leisure permits you. Your Nephew[4] told me of Copies that were dispersed of the Pastoral[5] and likely to be printed so we have thought fit to prevent them and print it our selves. I believe barn-elms[6] wants you and I long to see it but dont care to satisfie my curiosity before you come. My humble service to Mr: Addison.[7] I am

> *Yours most faithfull*
> *and affectionately Willm: Congreve.*

Address: *The address has been torn away except for the final word,* "*Amsterdam.*"

MANUSCRIPT: Historical Society of Pennsylvania, Philadelphia. EDITIONS: *Gentleman's Magazine*, June, 1835, pp. 609-610; Hodges, p. 97.

[1] See No. 6, note 7.

13

London July 1st 1703

Dear Mr Tonson.

My having been at the Bathe prevented my receiving your letter so soone as I should have Don had I been in town, & I was in hopes you wou'd have been here before, but by your staying so much longer I hope you will doe your businesse effectualy. I send your letter to my Lord Halifax & desire him to do you right to Sr Harry Furnese. I hope the weather will continue fair for yr returne since it is changed so much for the better. I thank you for the care & trouble you have taken about my linnen I cou'd wish for halfe a dozen a degree Courser if yr time & leisure permits you. Your Nephew tell me of Copies that were dispersed of the Pastoral & likely to be printed so we have thought fit to prevent 'em & print it our selves. I believe Barn-elms wants you & I long to see it but dont care to satisfie my curiosity before you come. my humble service to Mr Addison I am

yr most faithfull
& affectionatly   Will: Congreve.

Congreve to Jacob Tonson

[2] Luttrell mentioned Sir Henry Furnese as sheriff of London (4 July 1700) and director of the Bank of England (21 November 1700). John Macky (*A Journey Through England*, London, 1722, Vol. I, p. 88) mentioned Sir Henry as one "who remitted the Money to the Armies abroad" and built a fine seat near Dover. He died in 1712 at the age of fifty-four.

[3] The address shows that Tonson was then in Amsterdam.

[4] Jacob Tonson II, son of Tonson's brother Richard, who had a printing shop at Gray's-Inn-Gate before his death in 1691. The widow continued the business until 1698, when Tonson moved there from his old shop at the Judges' Head in Chancery Lane and took the widow's son, his nephew, as partner. See also Nos. 98-101, 153.

[5] *The Tears of Amaryllis for Amintas; a pastoral on the death of the Marquis of Blandford*, London, 1703.

[6] See p. 79.

[7] See Nos. 28 and 120. Addison was still on his extended tour of the Continent.

70   LICENSE TO VANBRUGH AND CONGREVE AS MANAGERS OF THE HAYMARKET THEATRE

December 14, 1704

ANNE R. License for a New Company of Comedians.
WHEREAS We have thought fitt for the better reforming the Abuses, and Immoralty of the Stage [1] That a New Company of Comedians should be Establish'd for our Service, under stricter Government and Regulations than have been formerly

We therefore reposing especiall trust, and confidence in Our Trusty and Welbeloved John Vanbrugh and Willm. Congreve Esqrs. for the due Execution, and performance of this our Will and Pleasure, do Give and Grant unto them the said John Vanbrugh, and Willm. Congreve full power and Authority to form, constitute, and Establish for Us, a Company of Comedians with full and free License to Act and Represent in any Convenient Place, during Our Pleasure all Comedies, Tragedys Plays, Interludes Operas, and to perform all other Theatricall and Musicall Entertainments whatsoever and to settle such Rules and Orders for the good Government of the said Company, as the Chamberlain of our Household shall from time to time direct and approve of GIVEN at our Court at St. James this 14th. day of December in the third Year of Our Reign.

By her Majestys Command

Kent [2]

MANUSCRIPT: P.R.O., L.C. 5/154, p. 35. EDITIONS: *London Gazette*, 21-25 December 1704; Nicoll, Vol. II, p. 275.

[1] The reason here stated for the establishment of the new dramatic company might seem to be a recognition of Jeremy Collier's *Short View of the Immorality and Profaneness of the English Stage*, 1698; but it should be noted that Vanbrugh and Congreve, the managers chosen for the new company, had been the dramatists most vigorously attacked by Collier.

[2] Henry Grey, Duke of Kent. See No. 26, note 5.

71   COMPLAINT OF CHRISTOPHER RICH AGAINST VANBRUGH AND
      CONGREVE

9th December 1705

Mr. Rich [1] Complains to the Lord Chamberlain of her Majesties Household.

That Mr. Vanbrugh and Mr. Congreve (in Violation of the standing Orders and Rules of the Lord Chamberlains Office concerning the Playhouses and contrary to the Lawes of the Land) have seduced away and Entertain'd Mrs. Mary Hooke alias Harcourt to Act in the Playhouse in the Haymarkett, altho they were acquainted and well knew That in October 1702 she Entred into Articles with Mr. Rich for five Years, with Security for Performance. That she lately Return'd from Dublyn on Purpose to Serve out her Articles with Mr. Rich. But Mr. Vanbrugh and Mr. Congreve bidding her a *much* higher Salary than she *Expected* or (as Mr. Rich beleives) they intend to Pay her, she hath Deserted Mr. Rich his Service.

He now humbly Prays his Lordship That she may be restrayn'd from Acting in the Company in the Hay Markett until she hath Served out her Articles with him.

Persons belonging to Mr. Rich which since Christmas last have been Entertain'd by Mr. Vanbrugh and Mr. Congreve in the Haymarket. Mr. Powell,[2] Mr. Bowen,[3] Mr. Doggett,[4] Mr. Mins, Mr. Husbands, Mrs. Bignall, Mrs. Baker.

6 Nov 1703   Upon a false surmise of Mr Congreves at 3 in the afternoon our Reviv'd Play [5] stopt so that the best part of the Audience was lost.

1705   Mr Swynys Play [6] stopt that day it was first to be acted altho it was for the benefitt of Mr Johnson who was then in prison and no Just reason for Stopping it but kindness to Mr Vanbrugh.

MANUSCRIPT: P.R.O., L.C. 7/3. EDITION: Nicoll, Vol. II, p. 289 (summary with some quotations).

[1] Christopher Rich (d. 1714), "an old snarling Lawyer" turned theatrical manager at Drury Lane, "as sly a Tyrant as ever was at the Head of a Theatre." See Cibber, Vol. I, pp. 233, 252.

[2] George Powell (1658?-1714), one of the chief actors at Drury Lane, is discussed at length by Cibber (Vol. I, pp. 237-243, 251-256, etc.).

[3] Perhaps the singer James Bowen mentioned by Anthony Aston (Vol. II, p. 312).

[4] Thomas Doggett (d. 1721), won great fame as the creator of Fondlewife in Congreve's *Old Bachelor* and of Sailor Ben in his *Love for Love*. Colley Cibber said of Doggett: "*Congreve* was a great Admirer of him, and found his Account in the Characters he expresly wrote for him" (Vol. II, p. 159). Anthony Aston called Doggett "the most faithful, pleasant Actor that ever was" (Vol. II, p. 310).

[5] *Love and Danger or Mistaken Jealousy* (Nicoll, Vol. II, p. 290).

[6] *The Quacks, or Love's the Physician* . . . As it was Acted (after being twice forbid) at the Theatre Royal in Drury-Lane, 1705. The Preface explains that the play "was to be stiffled, because the other House were to Act one upon the same Subject." See Nicoll, Vol. II, pp. 22, 290, 342, 343.

72   THE LORD CHAMBERLAIN ON THE COMPLAINT OF THE
BARONESS

February 24, 1705/6 [1]

I received your letter about the Buisness of Mr Vanbrook with the Barroness, and think it will be very difficult for me to make them agree who are so wide in their proposals to each other, therefore will lett alone a little longer ('till I come to town) in hopes they may patch up of themselves, rather then give my self the trouble (if I can avoid it) to make an Agreement which very likely will please neither; But as for the former Bargain which Mr Vanbrook does not deny, I shall alwais think him obliged to perform and pay her the 50[li]: And she shall sing the 5 times for it, or six if he insists upon it, though the time is Elapsed in which she was to performe it.

MANUSCRIPT: P.R.O., L.C. 7/3. EDITION: Nicoll, Vol. II, p. 289.

[1] Although this letter is dated five days earlier than No. 73, it refers to the bargain discussed in that letter.

73   COMPLAINT OF THE BARONESS AGAINST
VANBRUGH AND CONGREVE

March 1, 1705 [*1706*]

Sigre. Nicola Haym made a verbal bargaine for his Scholler [the Baroness] [1] with Mr Vanbrugh and Mr Congreve, some small time before the first opening of the Theatre in the Haymarket,[2] by which they were to give her one hundred Guineas for to sing ten times, but those ten times were to be performd before the end of November 1705, but his saide Scholler has onely sung five times. She insists on the liberty to sing where she pleases, the time agreed on being expir'd, and demands also the rest of the money due to her on the saide bargaine.

To shew that they did make this bargaine besides the Testimony of Sigre. Nicola Haym who declares that it was made at the time abovementioned at the Sign of the Cock in Bow Street one afternoon where was present also Mr. Ecles,[3] but he cannot witnes it, what was spoken having been in a language he understands not.

That this treaty did end in November last, there are these proofes. The saide Sigre. Nicola declar'd his Scholler would not come on the Stage under one hundred Guinneas, and on this it was concluded she should sing ten times either in the Pastoral [4] with which the house was to be open'd, or in other playes between the Acts, and as the winter was almost spent, the Theatre being first opend in the Ester holly dayes twas yeilded to these Gentlemen that the time for her to sing in, should not expire till the last of November as is saide above, and to this they declar'd them selves satisfyed and content.

That Sigre. Nicola's Scholler not having sung but five times dose not proceede from her, for he sent to these Gentlemen, two letters before the opening of their Playhouse this winter, to acquaint them that she was ready to sing any time they should apoint, but they never gave an answer to ether of them. Upon this my Scholler went her self to know when they would have her sing and also advertisd them that the time agreed for was neare expiring. Mr Vanbrugh's answer was that he could not tell when she should sing, but after this they made her sing two different nights, and it is not any want on her side that she has not sung the remaining times.

As to the money, and the bargaine these Gentlemen have often ownd both this winter, to Sigre Nicola and his Scholler, and they have it also in a letter under Mr Vanbrugh's own hand to her nor can these Gentlemen complaine (in this bargaine) of any one but them selves, for when Mr Congreve after the Acting of the Pastoral [4] saide to Sigre. Nicola that he would give his Scholler 50 Guineas for what had been done and that they should both be at liberty and the bargaine end, this Sigre. Nicola and his Scholler declard they would agree to, but Mr Congreve withdrew his proposition. This makes it plaine that they were satisfyed with their bargaine, but if they were not why did they not when they were aplyd to both by letter and personally that they should make their Advantage of her singing within the time mentioned above, why did they not then say that they would not let her sing any more, for she might then if she had lost what is due from them, the Season not being spent, have searcht her profit elswhere.

MANUSCRIPT: P.R.O., L.C. 7/3. EDITION: Nicoll, Vol. II, pp. 288-289 (summary with some quotations).

[1] Nicolino, or Nicola, Haym seems to have been music teacher and manager for the Baroness, here called his "Scholler." Between 1705 and 1727, Nicolino Haym adapted the librettos or the music for more than a dozen operas produced in London. See Nicoll, Vol. II, pp. 226, 228, 274, 275, 390-400. The Baroness was apparently the "scholar, Joanna Maria" named in Haym's agreement with Christopher Rich. See Nicoll, Vol. II, p. 275.

[2] Opened 9 April 1705. See Cibber, Vol. I, p. 319; Nicoll, Vol. II, p. 271.

[3] Probably John Eccles, the composer, mentioned in Nos. 3 and 8.

[4] *The Loves of Ergasto, or The Triumphs of Love.* See Nicoll, Vol. II, p. 400; Cibber, Vol. I, p. 325.

74   CONGREVE'S ACCOUNT WITH HOARE'S BANK

March 30, 1706–July 23, 1723

1706

Mr William Congreve Dr.	Cr.
Ap 23 To my note the 30 March 10/15/—	Mar 30—By mony reced p 2 notes 20G and 10G 32/5/—
June 1 To my note the 30 March 21/10/—	

1707

July 31 To part of 30 the 28 May .... 10/—/—	May 28. By mony reced p. note ..... 30/—/—
Augt. 19 To cleare ditto 20/—/—	

1712

Mar. 23. To my note 25 Feb 24 /15/—	Feb. 25. By mony reced p note ...24/15/—

1714

May 11. To part 100 the 8   May   8 (By note) .. 100/—/—
      May 32/5/—   14 By notes

   14 To cleare ditto
        67/15/—

   20 To my note 14 May   20 and 15/10
        20/—/—   35/10/—

June 2   To my note 14 May   [Including 24/15/—   160:5—
        15/10/—   from 1712]

1723

July 23   To note 20 July   July 20 By note ...... 30/—/—
       30/—/—

MANUSCRIPT: Hoare's Bank in Fleet Street, London, Ledgers 7/169, 170; 9/17, 18; 16/128, 129; 25/248, 249. EDITION: Hodges, p. 100.

75   CONGREVE TO JACOB TONSON

June 27. 1709

Received then of Jacob Tonson Sen. one hundred Fifty Seven Pounds Seven Shillings which Sume is in full of all emounts depending between us to this day. I say received by me

Witness   *Wm Congreve*
   Jacob Tonson Jun [1]

MANUSCRIPT: Folger Shakespeare Library, Washington, D.C.

[1] See No. 69, note 4.

76 JACOB TONSON TO CONGREVE

June the 18th. 1710

I promise to pay to Mr Congreve or his order the Sum of twenty guyneas when ever his vollume of poems [1] which I am now printing shall come to be reprinted and at any time he shall demand give him an account what part of this Impression are disposed of.

Witness my hand
Jacob Tonson Sen

MANUSCRIPT: British Museum 28,275, f. 12. EDITION: D. Crane Taylor, *William Congreve*, p. 206.

[1] *The Third Volume of the Works of Mr. William Congreve; Containing Poems upon Several Occasions*, London: Printed for *Jacob Tonson*, at *Shakespear's Head* over-against *Catherine Street* in the *Strand*. MDCCX.

77 SWIFT TO STELLA

Chelsea, June 22, 1711

I went late to-day to town, and dined with my friend Lewis.[1] I saw Will. Congreve attending at the treasury, by order, with his brethren, the commissioners of the wine licenses. I had often mentioned him with kindness to lord treasurer; [2] and Congreve told me, that after they had answered to what they were sent for, my lord called him privately, and spoke to him with great kindness, promising his protection, &c. The poor man said, he had been used so ill of late years, that he was quite astonished at my lord's goodness, &c. and desired me to tell my lord so; which I did this evening, and recommended him heartily. My lord assured me he esteemed him very much, and would be always kind to him; that what he said was to make Congreve easy, because he knew people talked as if his lordship designed to turn every body out, and particularly Congreve; which indeed was true, for the poor man told me he apprehended it. As I left my lord treasurer, I called on Congreve (knowing where he dined) and told him what had passed between my lord and me: so I have a worthy man easy, and that is a good day's work.

EDITIONS: See No. 41.

[1] See No. 41, note 4.

[2] Robert Harley, Earl of Oxford. See No. 45, note 5.

78   CONGREVE'S ACCOUNT IN BANK OF ENGLAND STOCK

William Congreve Esq of St. Clement Danes.   [credit]
Bank Stock   [April 24, 1712–May 22, 1717]

28 Apr 1713 To John Calfe of the Strand Colour Seller	£300	*New Account*
		24 Apr 1712 By Thomas Carbonnel £500
		6 June 1712 By Solomon de Paz Morenu 300
Closed		
22 May 1717 to Col Ralph Congreve to Stretton Stafford-shire	£900	25 Nov 1712 By Charles Jenner 200
		27 Nov 1712 By John Warner 100
		31 Aug 1715 by Thomas Snow 100
	£1200	£1200

MANUSCRIPT: Bank of England Stock, Folio 1/4478.

79   CHARLES MONTAGU, EARL OF HALIFAX,[1] TO ROBERT HARLEY,
     EARL OF OXFORD [2]

25. April 1712

MY LORD

I can not omit returning Your Lordship my particular thanks for
continuing Mr Congreve in his little Office,[3] for though Mr Congreve deserves so much Your favour, I flatter my selfe that my
solicitation had some weight with Your Lordship, and shall allways
be acknowledged with the utmost gratitude. . . . In the great Un-
certaintys We are in of News from abroad I will not importune
Your Lordship for an Audience, but when some matters are a little
better known, I hope You will allow me to presse into Your Presence, for I think I could serve You. I am with great Respect, My
Lord

Your Lordships Most
Humble and Obliged Servant
Halifax

MANUSCRIPT: Harley Papers XXIX (January-September 1712), British Museum
Loan 29/199, formerly among the Portland MSS. at Welbeck Abbey. EDITION
(not complete): *Historical Manuscripts Commission Report*, 1899, Vol. V, p.
166.

[1] See No. 6, note 7.

[2] See No. 45, note 5.

[3] Congreve was continued in his "little Office" as commissioner for licensing
wines, but three of the five commissioners were changed. See the Declared Accounts at the P.R.O. for the two years ending at Christmas, 1713.

80   RALPH CONGREVE TO CONGREVE

15th. day of March 1713/4 OS:

Know all Men by these presents that I Ralph Congreve Esq [1] Lieutenant Governor of Gibraltar for diversse good considerations me thereunto moveing have nominated constituted and appointed and by these presents do Nominate Constitute and appoint William Congreve Esqr of London My true and Lawfull attourney for me and in my name and to my use either to Buy in the South Sea Stock,[2] or to sell or dispose of any sum or sums which I now have or may have in the said Stock as my said Attourney shall see convenient, Acquittances or other discharges for me and in my name to Make, Seal and Deliver, Attourneys one or more to make and att pleasure to revoke, and to do all other Acts and things whatsoever concerning the premises as fully and in every respect as I my self might or cou'd do were I personally present, and I hereby Ratify and Confirm whatsoever my said Attourney shall Lawfully do or cause to be don by virtue of these presents. In Wittness Whereof I have hereunto set my hand and seal this 15th. day of March 1713/4 OS: att Gibraltar

Signed, seal'd and Delivered　　　　　　*R: Congreve*
　　in the Presents off
　　　Lud: Petrie
　　　John Beaver

MANUSCRIPT: Edinburgh University Library, Laing MSS. II, 640/24.

[1] Ralph Congreve was the seventh child and third surviving son of John Congreve (of Stretton Hall, Staffordshire), the older brother of the dramatist's father. Ralph was born on 3 February 1668/9 and died 18 November 1725. He was an ensign in the army as early as 1690, a captain in the Battle of Blenheim, 1704, a colonel in the Battle of Almansa, 1707, and Lieutenant-governor of Gibraltar from 1713 till 1716. See *Erdswick Book* and Charles Dalton, *English Army Lists and Commission Registers*, 1661-1714, London, 1892-1896, Vol. III, p. 50, Vol. V, pp. 43, 61, Vol. VI, p. 371. See No. 93 for his will, in which he named his cousin William Congreve the dramatist as one of three executors. See also No. 148.

² Formed in 1711, the South Sea Company continued in business throughout the eighteenth century. In 1720, it was the center of feverish speculation, beginning the year at less than 130, rising to 1,000 by July, and falling to 135 by November. Congreve's ownership of South Sea stock from 1716 to 1723 is shown by manuscript notes preserved at the following libraries: the Bodleian, Christ Church, Oxford, Harvard, Huntington, and Wellesley. At his death in 1729, Congreve owned £3,000 in Old South Sea Annuities (see No. 90).

81   CHARLES MONTAGU, EARL OF HALIFAX, TO ROBERT HARLEY, EARL OF OXFORD

Thursday [*May 13, 1714*]

MY LORD

Poor Congreve is again alarmd by Reports He has had, that their Commission [of wine licenses] is renewing. He does not doubt the continuance of Your Lordships favour to Him, depending on the assurances Your Lordship has given Him, as well as Me, of Your Care and Protection of Him. But I beg Your Lordship will enable Me, to ease Him, entirely of His fears. What was the Meaning of some People Yesterday? I am with great Respect

My Lord
Your Lordships most
Humble and most Obliged Servant
Halifax

Endorsed by Lord Oxford: *Lord Halifax*
May: 13: 1714
Mr Congreve
answered that night

MANUSCRIPT: Harley Papers XXXII (January-June 1714), British Museum Loan 29/203, formerly among the Portland MSS. at Welbeck Abbey. EDITION (not complete): *Historical Manuscripts Commission Report*, 1899, Vol. V, p. 438.

82   CONGREVE'S COMMISSION AS SECRETARY OF JAMAICA

December 14, 1714

George by the Grace of God of Great Britain, France and Ireland, King defender of the Faith &c [revokes the patent as Secretary of Jamaica granted by Queen Anne to John Baber, Esq., on August 12, 1702]. And further Know ye, that We reposing especial trust and Confidence in the faithfulness, Experience and Ability of Our Trusty and Wellbelov'd William Congreve Esqr. of Our Special Grace certain knowledge and mere motion. Have Given and Granted, and by these presents do give and grant unto the said Wm Congreve the Offices and Places of Secretary of Our Island of Jamaica in America, and Commissary or Steward General of all such Provisions and Stores as are or shall be from time to time provided and sent for Our Forces in Our said Island of Jamaica, And of Clerk of the Enrollments for the Enrolling and Registering all Deeds and Conveyances made and passed in that Our Island, and also of all Bills of Sale and Letters Patents or other Acts or matters usually Enrolled or which by the Laws of that Our Island shall be directed to be Enrolled. And him the said Wm Congreve Secretary of Our said Island and Commissary or Steward General of all such Provisions and Stores as are or shall be from time to time provided and sent for Our Forces in Our said Island and Clerk of the Enrollments for the Enrolling and Registring all Deeds and Conveyances made and passed in that Our Island, and also of all Bills of Sale and Letters Patents or other Acts or matters usually Enrolled or which by the Laws of that Our Island shall be directed to be enrolled, We do make Ordain and Constitute by these presents. To have, hold, Exercise and Enjoy the said Offices and Places to him the said William Congreve by himself or such his Sufficient Deputy or Deputies as shall from time to time be first Approved of and Sworn by Our Governor or Lieutenant Governor of Our said Island or some of Our Council there for the time being in that behalf Authorized for and during our pleasure together with all Fees, Profits, Privileges, Perquisites and Advantages whatsoever to the said Offices and Places

or any of them Jointly or Severally in any wise belonging or which
are or shall be Established or Allowed for or in respect of the Exercise or Execution of the said Offices and places respectively in as full
and ample manner to all intents and purposes as the said John Baber
or any other person or persons have held or of right to have held
and enjoy'd the same. And Our further Will and Pleasure is and
We do hereby Charge and Command the said Wm Congreve to
perform and Execute the several Offices and Places aforesaid with
care and Diligence, and to give a good Account thereof to Us and
to Our Governor and Council Upon Our said Island for the time
being. Provided always, and We do hereby direct and Command him
the said Wm Congreve to Transport himself to the said Island by
the first Opportunity,[1] and from his said Arrival there to reside upon
Our said Island, and not to be Absent from thence without Our
Royal License and Leave under Our Signet and Sign Manuel first
had and Obtained in that behalf. In witness whereof We have
Caused these Our Letters to be made Patents. Witness Our self at
Westminster the 14th of December in the first Year of Our Reign.

By Writ of Privy Seal
Cocks

MANUSCRIPT: P.R.O., C.O. 137/12, Part II, No. 69.

[1] A few months after Congreve was made Secretary to Jamaica, he was granted
permission to remain in England and conduct the office through a deputy.

83   CONGREVE TO THE SECRETARY OF THE BOARD OF TRADE

Ashley[1] *October the 5th.* *1717*

SIR

After a Fitt of Illness of two Month's continuance, I am but just
gott into the Country for the recovery of my health, and am altogether unable to waite upon the Lords Commissioners[2] as you
signify to me they desire I shou'd doe.

I beg the favour of you to acquaint them of this from me with all due respects to their Lordships.

And if you please you may also intimate to their Lordships that I have already given Satisfaction to both the Principal Secretarys of State [3] in what relates to me concerning Mr. Page.[4] I am,

Sir

Your most humble servant

Wm Congreve

MANUSCRIPT: P.R.O., C.O. 137/12, No. 72. EDITION: Hodges, p. 102.

[1] The country estate of Lord Shannon. See No. 54, note 1.

[2] Lords Commissioners of Trade and Plantations, or Board of Trade. These titles were used interchangeably.

[3] One of these was Congreve's good friend Joseph Addison.

[4] Samuel Page, Congreve's deputy as Secretary of Jamaica. See also Nos. 85, 86.

84   CONGREVE TO THOMAS PELHAM-HOLLES,[1] DUKE OF NEW-CASTLE

[*London January 27, 1717/18*]

MY LORD,

It is the Fortune of this Edition of the Dramatick Works of the late Mr. *Dryden*, to come into the World at a Time, when Your Grace has just given Order for Erecting, at Your own Expence, a Noble Monument to his Memory.[2]

This is an Act of Generosity, which has something in it so very Uncommon, that the most unconcern'd and indifferent Persons must be moved with it: How much more, must all such be affected by it, who had any due Regard for the personal Merits of the Deceas'd; or are capable of any Taste and Distinction, for the Remains and elegant Labours of one of the greatest Men that our Nation has produced.

That, which distinguisheth Actions of pure and elevated Generosity, from those of a mix'd and inferiour Nature, is nothing else but the absolutely disinterested Views of the Agent.

My Lord, this being granted, in how fair a Light does Your Munificence stand? a Munificence to the Memory, to the Ashes of a Man whom You never saw; whom You never can see: And who, consequently, never could by any personal Obligation, induce You to do this Deed of Bounty; nor can he ever make You any Acknowledgement for it when it shall be done.

It is evident Your Grace can have acted thus from no other Motive but Your pure Regard to Merit, from your intire Love for Learning, and from that accurate Taste and Discernment, which by Your Studies you have so early attained to in the Politer Arts.

And these are the Qualities, my Lord, by which You are more distinguish'd, than by all those other uncommon Advantages with which You are attended. Your great Disposition, Your great Ability to be beneficent to Mankind, could by no means answer that End, if You were not possess'd of a Judgment to direct You in the right Application, and just Distribution of Your good Offices.

You are now in a Station,[3] by which You necessarily preside over the liberal Arts, and all the Practicers and Professors of them. Poetry is more particularly within Your Province: And with very good Reason may we hope to see it revive and flourish, under Your Influence and Protection.

What Hopes of Reward may not the living Deserver entertain, when even the Dead are sought out for; and their very Urns and Ashes made Partakers of Your Liberality?

As I have the Honour to be known to You, my Lord, and to have been distinguish'd by You, by many Expressions and Instances of Your Good-will towards me; I take a singular Pleasure to congratulate You upon an Action so intirely Worthy of You. And as I had the Happiness to be very Conversant, and as intimately acquainted, with Mr. *Dryden*, as the great Disproportion in our Years could allow me to be; I hope it will not be thought too assuming in me, if in Love to his Memory, and in Gratitude for the many friendly Offices, and favourable Instructions, which in my early Youth I received from him, I take upon me to make this publick Acknowledgment to Your Grace, for so publick a Testimony as You are pleas'd to give the World of that high Esteem in which You hold the Performances of that eminent Man.

I can in some Degree justify my self for so doing, by a Citation of a kind of Right to it, bequeath'd to me by him. And it is indeed, upon that Pretension that I presume even to make a Dedication of these his Works to You.

In some very Elegant, tho' very partial Verses which he did me the Honour to write to me, he recommended it to me to *be kind to his Remains*. I was then, and have been ever since most sensibly touched with that Expression: and the more so, because I could not find in my self the Means of satisfying the Passion which I felt in me, to do something answerable to an Injunction laid upon me in so Pathetick and so Amicable a Manner.

You, my Lord, have furnish'd me with ample Means of acquitting my self, both of my Duty and Obligation to my *departed Friend*. What kinder Office lyes in me, to do to these, his most valuable and unperishable Remains, than to commit them to the Protection, and lodge them under the Roof of a Patron, whose Hospitality has extended it self even to his Dust?

If I would permit my self to run on in the way which so fairly opens it self before me, I should tire Your Grace with reiterated Praises and Acknowledgments, and I might possibly (notwithstanding my pretended Right so to do) give some handle to such who are inclinable to Censure, to tax me of Affectation and Officiousness; in thanking You, more than comes to my Share, for doing a Thing, which is, in truth, of a Publick Consideration, as it is doing an Honour to your Country. For so unquestionably it is, to do Honour to him, who was an Honour to it.

I have but one thing to say either to obviate, or to answer such an Objection, if it shall be made to me, which is, that I loved Mr. *Dryden.*

I have not touch'd upon any other publick Honour, or Bounty done by You to Your Country: I have industriously declined entring upon a Theme of so extensive a Nature; and of all Your numerous and continual Largesses to the Publick, I have only singled out this, as what most particularly affected me. I confess freely to Your Grace, I very much admire all those other Donations, but I much more love this; and I cannot help it, if I am naturally more delighted with any thing that is Amiable, than with any thing that is Wonderful.

Whoever shall Censure me, I dare be confident, You, my Lord, will Excuse me, for any thing that I shall say with due Regard to a Gentleman, for whose Person I had as just an Affection as I have an Admiration of his Writings. And indeed Mr. *Dryden* had Personal Qualities to challenge both Love and Esteem from All who were truly acquainted with him.

He was of a Nature exceedingly Humane and Compassionate; easily forgiving Injuries, and capable of a prompt and sincere Reconciliation with them who had offended him.

Such a Temperament is the only solid Foundation of all moral Virtues, and sociable Endowments. His Friendship, where he profess'd it, went much beyond his Professions; and I have been told of strong and generous Instances of it, by the Persons themselves who received them: Tho' his Hereditary Income was little more than a bare Competency.

As his Reading had been very extensive, so was he very happy in a Memory tenacious of every thing that he had read. He was not more possess'd of Knowledge than he was Communicative of it. But then his Communication of it was by no means pedantick, or impos'd upon the Conversation; but just such, and went so far as by the natural Turns of the Discourse in which he was engag'd it was necessarily promoted or required. He was extream ready and gentle in his Correction of the Errors of any Writer, who thought fit to consult him; and full as ready and patient to admit of the Reprehension of others in respect of his own Oversight or Mistakes. He was of very easy, I may say of very pleasing Access: But something slow, and as it were diffident in his Advances to others. He had something in his Nature that abhorr'd Intrusion into any Society whatsoever. Indeed it is to be regretted, that he was rather blameable in the other Extream: For by that means, he was Personally less known, and consequently his Character might become liable both to Misapprehensions and Misrepresentations.

To the best of my Knowledge and Observation, he was, of all the Men that ever I knew, one of the most Modest, and the most Easily to be discountenanced, in his Approaches, either to his Superiors, or his Equals.

I have given Your Grace this slight Sketch of his personal Character, as well to vindicate his Memory, as to justify my self for the Love which I bore to his Person; and I have the rather done it, because I hope it may be acceptable to You to know that he was worthy of the Distinction You have shewn him, as a Man, as well as an Author.

As to his Writings, I shall not take upon me to speak of them; for, to say little of them, would not be to do them right: And to say all that I ought to say, would be, to be very Voluminous. But, I may venture to say in general Terms, that no Man hath written in our Language so much, and so various Matter, and in so various Manners, so well. Another thing I may say very peculiar to him; which is, that his Parts did not decline with his Years: But that he was an improving Writer to his last, even to near seventy Years of Age; improving even in Fire and Imagination, as well as in Judgement: Witness his Ode on St. *Cecelia*'s Day, and his Fables, his latest Performances.

He was equally excellent in Verse, and in Prose. His Prose had all the Clearness imaginable, together with all the Nobleness of Expression; all the Graces and Ornaments proper and peculiar to it, without deviating into the Language or Diction of Poetry. I make this Observation, only to distinguish his Stile from that of many Poetical Writers, who meaning to write harmoniously in Prose, do in truth often write meer Blank Verse.

I have heard him frequently own with Pleasure, that if he had any Talent for *English* Prose, it was owing to his having often read the Writings of the great Archbishop *Tillotson*.[4]

His Versification and his Numbers he could learn of no Body: For he first possess'd those Talents in Perfection in our Tongue. And they who have best succeeded in them since his Time, have been indebted to his Example; and the more they have been able to imitate him, the better they have succeeded.

As his Stile in Prose is always specifically different from his Stile in Poetry; so, on the other hand, in his Poems, his Diction is, where-ever his Subject requires it, so Sublimely, and so truly Poetical, that its Essence, like that of pure Gold, cannot be destroy'd. Take his Verses, and divest them of their Rhimes, disjoint them in their Numbers, transpose their Expressions, make what Arrangement and Disposition you please of his Words, yet shall there Eternally be Poetry, and something which will be found incapable of being re-solv'd into absolute Prose: An incontestable Characteristick of a truly poetical Genius.

I will say but one Word more in general of his Writings, which is, that what he has done in any one Species, or distinct Kind, would have been sufficient to have acquir'd him a great Name. If he had written nothing but his Prefaces, or nothing but his Songs, or his Prologues, each of them would have intituled him to the Preference and Distinction of excelling in his Kind.

But I have forgot my self; for nothing can be more unnecessary than an Attempt to say any thing to Your Grace in Commendation of the Writings of this great Poet; since it is only to Your Knowl-edge, Taste and Approbation of them, that the Monument which You are now about to raise to him is owing. I will therefore, my Lord, detain You no longer by this Epistle; and only intreat You to believe, that it is address'd to Your Grace, from no other Motive, than a sincere Regard to the Memory of Mr. *Dryden*, and a very sensible Pleasure which I take in applauding an Action by which You are so justly, and so singularly entitled to a Dedication of his Labours, tho' many Years after his Death; and even tho' most of them were produced by him, many Years before You were born.

I am with the greatest Respect,
My LORD,
Your Grace's
most Obedient and
most Humble Servant,
William Congreve.

EDITIONS: *The Dramatick Works of John Dryden, Esq; in Six Volumes,* London: Printed for J. Tonson, 1717, I, Epistle Dedicatory; Summers, Vol. IV, pp. 181-185; Dobrée, pp. 478-484. Advertised as "just published" in *The Daily Courant* for 27 January 1717/18, No. 5076.

[1] Thomas Pelham-Holles, first Duke of Newcastle (1693-1768), was one of the youngest members of the Kit-Cat Club. For Congreve's other letters to the Duke of Newcastle, see Nos. 88 and 134.

[2] Notwithstanding the Duke of Newcastle's order for "a Noble Monument," if he actually gave such an order in 1717, no monument to the memory of John Dryden appeared in Westminster Abbey until years later, when one was erected at the expense of John Sheffield, Duke of Buckinghamshire. See Malone, Vol. I, pp. 385-389.

[3] The Duke of Newcastle was then Lord Chamberlain of His Majesty's Household and thus had supervision of theatrical productions. See also No. 134.

[4] John Tillotson (1630-1694), Archbishop of Canterbury.

85　CHARLES SPENCER, EARL OF SUNDERLAND,[1] TO CONGREVE

Whitehall January 29th. 1717/8

SIR

I send you the Copy of an Order of Council directing the Removal of Mr. Samuel Page from being your Deputy, as Secretary of Jamaica; and I am to signify to you His Majesty's Pleasure, that you forthwith comply with the said Order. I am

Sir

Your most humble Servant
Sunderland

MANUSCRIPT: P.R.O., C.O. 324/33, p. 130. This seems to be the minute book of the Privy Council, into which was copied the letter to Congreve. In the margin to the left at the beginning of the letter appears "Mr Congreve."

[1] Charles Spencer, third Earl of Sunderland (1674-1722), was a son-in-law of the Duke of Marlborough. See *DNB*.

86   CONGREVE'S PETITION BEFORE THE BOARD OF TRADE

February 9, 1717/18

Wm. Congreve Secretary of Jamaica against Allowing Mr. Cockburn an Apeale referred to the Committee.

Upon reading this day at the Board the humble Petition of Wm. Congreve Esqr. Secretary of the Island of Jamaica, on behalf of himself and Samuel Page his late Deputy, praying to be heard against the Granting of Mr. Cockburne liberty of Appealing from a Decree lately passed in Jamaica, in a Suit between him and the petitioners touching the Fees and profitts of the Secretarys Office received by the Said Cockburne, during the time he Officiated therein: It is Ordered in Councill, that the Said Petition (a copy whereof is hereunto annexed) [1] Be, and it is hereby referred to the Right Honourable the Lords of the Committee for hearing Appeales from the plantacons to hear the partys therein Concerned by their Councill Learned, And Report their Opinion thereupon to this Boarde.

MANUSCRIPT: P.R.O., P.C. 2/86, p. 104.

[1] The petition, apparently lost, is fortunately summarized in these minutes of the Board of Trade. Next month, the committee on Appeals found "the proceedings of the Said Cause not transmitted from Jamaica in an Authentick manner" and were "pleased to leave it undetermined, Whether Such Appeale ought to be Allowed or not, untill All the proceedings shall be brought over in due Form." See P.R.O., P.C. 2/86, p. 111. The final decision is not known.

87   ACCOUNTS OF CONGREVE AND HIS COUSIN IN 4% ANNUITIES (DEBENTURES), 1718-1739, AT THE BANK OF ENGLAND

May 14, 1719–October 15, 1720

William Congreve Esq of St. Clements Dane Middlesex Esq. [The dramatist]

4% Annuities (Debentures)   *New Account*
          1718-1739   14 May 1719. By
22 Dec 1719 to Major ⎤   Henry Metcalfe £1000
  Wm Congreve [1] as ⎟   26 June 1719. By
  contra (Error)   ⎬ 245:9:8   Debentures 3/359 £ 215:10
  Debrs. 4   ⎦   26 June 1719. By
21 June 1720 To Wil-   Debentures 1/575 £   29:19:8
  liam Nicoll of the   31 Dec 1719 By Sir
  Bank of England   1500.   George Caswall   £ 500
      Closed   ─────────
                    ─────────
                    £1745:9:8   £1745:9:8

Major William Congreve [1] of Highgate Middlesex [The cousin]
  4% Annuities (Debentures)   *New Account*
          1718-1739   22 Dec. 1719 By Wm
15 Oct 1720 To Subs. For.   Congreve Esq. (Er-
  940   £571:12:6   ror)
      Closed   Debrs. 3/359 ...£215:10:–
                                   By ditto (Error)
                                      Debr 1/575 ....   29:19:8
                                   22 Jan 1719 By Deb-
                                      entures 3/2097 .. 144:8:10
                                   Jan 1719 By ditto
                                      3/593 ....   69:19:4
                                   11 July 1720. By Wil-
                                      liam Nicoll 111:14:8
                                                       ─────────
                                                       £571:12:6

MANUSCRIPT: Bank of England £4% Annuities (Debentures) 1718-1739,
Folios 139 and 224.

[1] Colonel William Congreve of Highgate. See No. 93, note 4.

88 CONGREVE TO THOMAS PELHAM-HOLLES, DUKE OF NEW-CASTLE [1]

Wotton August 9. 1719

MY LORD

I have the honour of your Graces Letter of the 3d instant, but just now; it having missed me by a day in Worcestershire. I take it as a high Obligation that you would lay your commands on me in any thing in my power. But the gentleman who has applyd to your Grace in this particular, has been misinformd; for my Deputy is not the person dead; but one deputed by him,[2] upon his late return into England, himselfe now preparing, as by letter he informs me, to return spedily to Jamaica. Next to the happynesse it would have been to me to have been able to have Obeyd your Graces Commands; it is the greatest, to know you had the goodnesse to think of me, upon any occasion wherein I might possibly have shewne my respect to you, or to any one for whom you are concerned, for I am as with the Greatest Justice, so with the greatest inclination and respect

My Good Lord
　Your Graces most
　　Obedient and most humble
　　servant.
　　William Congreve.

MANUSCRIPT: British Museum Add. MS. 32685, ff. 47, 48. EDITIONS: Summers, Vol. I, p. 96; Dobrée, pp. 520-521.

[1] See No. 84, note I.

[2] This was probably the person referred to by Governor Nicholas Lawes of Jamaica in his letter to the Board of Trade dated 28 April 1719: "Some days agoe Mr. Daniel who acted as Secretary of this Island, died." See P.R.O., C.O. 138/16, p. 218.

89   SWIFT TO POPE

Dublin, January 10, 1721 [New Style].

. . . But, whatever opportunities a constant attendance of four years might have given me for endeavouring to do good offices to particular persons, I deserve at least to find tolerable quarter from those of the other Party; for many of which I was a constant advocate with the Earl of Oxford, and for this I appeal to his Lordship: He knows how often I press'd him in favour of Mr. Addison, Mr. Congreve,[1] Mr. Row, and Mr. Steel, although I freely confess that his Lordship's kindness to them was altogether owing to his generous notions, and the esteem he had for their wit and parts, of which I could only pretend to be a remembrancer. For I can never forget the answer he gave to the late Lord Hallifax,[2] who upon the first change of the Ministry interceded with him to spare Mr. Congreve: It was by repeating these two lines of Virgil,

> *Non obtusa adeo gestamus pectora Pœni,*
> *Nec tam aversus equos Tyria Sol jungit ab urbe.*[3]

Pursuant to which, he always treated Mr. Congreve with the greatest personal civilities, assured him of his constant favour and protection, adding that he would study to do something better for him.

I remember it was in those times a usual subject of raillery towards me among the Ministers, that I never came to them without a Whig in my sleeve; . . .

EDITIONS: For comment on the early editions of this letter, see Sherburn, Vol. II, p. 64. The excerpt printed here under No. 89 follows Sherburn, Vol. II, pp. 67-68.

[1] For Swift's appeal to Robert Harley, Earl of Oxford, in behalf of Congreve, see No. 77.

[2] For the appeals of Charles Montagu, Lord Halifax, for Congreve, see Nos. 79, 81.

[3] *Aeneid*, Vol. I, pp. 567-568.

90 CONGREVE'S ACCOUNT IN OLD SOUTH SEA ANNUITIES AT THE
   BANK OF ENGLAND

William Congreve Esq Surry   June 25, 1723–February 12,
                    Street   1728/9
                    later   The Honorable Francis Earle
            Surrey Street   of Godolphin Executor [1]

Old South Sea Annuities
New Acct.

Closed 12 Feb 1728. To Henrietta Duchess of Marlborough.[2] Wife of Francis Earl of Godolphin } £3000	25 June 1723 By Joint Stock S.S.A.	£1600
	7 July 1724 By Cuthbert Routh	200
	15 Dec 1724 By Thomas Snow	200
	9 Jan 1728 By Bridget Abell	1000
£3000		£3000

MANUSCRIPT: Bank of England Old South Sea Annuities, Folios 3/539, 18/421.

[1] Named executor in Congreve's will probated 3 February 1728/9. See No. 148.

[2] Although the Earl of Godolphin withdrew the £3,000 as executor, the Bank of England noted the account as closed to Henrietta, Duchess of Marlborough, since Congreve's will had named her as residuary legatee.

91 CONGREVE TO JACOB TONSON

August 8th: 1723

DEAR MR TONSON

My Kinsman Coll Congreve [1] desires by me that you would do him the favour to lend him my picture [2] to have a Copy taken of it. I am sure there will be great Care taken of it. I am sorry I am not in

town now you are to have the pleasure of seeing you. I hope you
are well. I am with unalterable esteem and friendship Dear Jacob

Ever Yours

Wm Congreve.

MANUSCRIPT: Folger Shakespeare Library, Washington, D.C. EDITIONS: *Gentleman's Magazine*, June 1835, p. 610; Hodges, p. 98.

[1] Colonel William Congreve (1671-1746) of Highgate, cousin of the dramatist.
See No. 93, note 4.

[2] This was painted by Sir Godfrey Kneller in 1709 and was one of the famous
Kit-Cat collection handed down through many generations until it was acquired
in 1945 by the National Portrait Gallery, London. The copy made in 1723
came down in the family of Colonel William Congreve to Lady Petheran,
daughter of the second baronet, and was left by her husband, Sir Comer Petheran, to General Sir Walter Norris Congreve (1862-1927). It is now owned
by the general's son, Major Christopher Congreve. The copy is clearly shown
in a painting of "Lady Congreve and Children" by Philip Reinagle, Kt., which
is now in the National Portrait Gallery of Ireland in Dublin. The dramatist's
portrait appears in the painting hanging in a prominent position over the fire-
place.

92   ELIZABETH, DUCHESS OF HAMILTON *vs.* CONGREVE
   AND OTHERS

August 14, 1725

TO THE RIGHT HONOURABLE PETER LORD KING [1] BARON OF OCKAM
   LORD HIGH CHANCELLOR OF GREAT BRITAIN

Complaining Sheweth unto your Lordship Your Oratrix the most
Noble Elizabeth Dutchess Dowager of Hamilton and Brandon
Relict of the most Noble James late Duke of Hamilton and Brandon deceased That heretofore that is to say in or about Michaelmas
Terme which was in the Year of our Lord One Thousand Six Hundred and Ninety Eight the said Duke in right of your Oratrix then
his Wife and Your Oratrix did Exhibit their Bill of Complaint
into this Honourable Court against the Right Honourable the Lady
Gerrard Relict and Administratrix of Digby Lord Gerrard Your

Oratrix's Father deceased . . . for a discovery of the Personall
Estate of the said Digby Lord Gerrard so as the said Duke and
Your Oratrix might have an Account and their Share thereof and
also for an Account of the Rents and profitts of the real Estate of
the said Digby Lord Gerrard which descended and came to Your
Oratrix upon his Death in October which was in the Year of our
Lord One Thousand Six Hundred and Eighty four as his Daughter
and Heir for Satisfaction to be made to Your Oratrix for the same.
. . . [The complaint of the Duchess of Hamilton tells how the
suit to recover what she considered due her from her father's estate
had been continued from 1698 till 1726 while the estate was passed
along by Lady Gerrard to her brother Charles, Earl of Maccles-
field; by him to Charles, Lord Mohun; by Lord Mohun to his
wife Elizabeth, Lady Mohun; and finally by Lady Mohun, on her
death in 1725, to several trustees. The complaint mentions the
deaths of Lord Mohun and the Duke of Hamilton in 1712 but not
the fact that each had killed the other in a duel growing out of
the suit.] But the said Elizabeth Lady Mohun having as Your
Oratrix is informed in her life time made and Executed some Deed
of limitation and Appointment or Some other Instrument of Conveyance of all her reall and Personall Estate and thereof appointed
the most Noble John Duke of Argyle and the Right Honourable
Archibald Earl of Ilay William Congreve of the Parish of St.
Clements Danes in the County of Middlesex Esqr. Moses Beranger
of London Esqr. and Charles Mordaunt of the Parish of St. Anns
Westminster in the said County of Middlesex Esqr. or some of them
Trustees thereof they the said John Duke of Argyle Archibald Earl
of Ilay William Congreve Moses Beranger and Charles Mordaunt
or some or One of them or some other Person or Persons for their
some or One of their Use or Uses privily Consent means or pro-
curement by Vertue of such Deed of Limitation or Appointment
or other Instrument of Conveyance or under Colour thereof having
not only entred upon all such real Estate whereof the said Elizabeth Lady Mohun dyed seized or Interested in but also possessed
themselves of all the Personall Estate of the said Elizabeth Lady
Mohun as well what was her owne as what came to her from her

said Husband the said Charles Lord Mohun and also all the Jewells Pictures Furniture and Household Stuffe and other Goods and Chattells. . . . To the end therefore that the said Bill Answer Suite and proceedings may stand and be revived for the Benefitt of Your Oratrix against the said John Duke of Argyle Archibald Earl of Ilay William Congreve Moses Beranger and Charles Mordaunt and may be in the same plight and Condition as they were in at the Death of the said Elizabeth Lady Mohun and that the said John Duke of Argyle Archibald Earl of Ilay William Congreve Moses Beranger and Charles Mordaunt may either admitt Assetts of the said Elizabeth Lady Mohun's Estate to answer and Satisfy what shall be coming to Your Oratrix by vertue of the said Decree or that they may discover the said Elizabeth Lady Mohun's Personall Estate which they or any of them know or believe She or any other in trust for her or to her Use or benefitt was or were possessed of Interested in or any way entituled unto and the particulars wherein the same consisted and where or in whose Hands or possession the same was and set forth the particulars and full Value of the same and every part thereof to the utmost of the knowledge or beleife of them or any of them May it please your Lordship to grant unto Your Oratrix Your Lordships Letters directed to the said John Duke of Argyle and Archibald Earl of Ilay requiring them to appear and Answer the premises And in Default of their so doing his Majesties most gracious Writt or Writts of Subpena ad revivendum et respondendum to be directed to the said John Duke of Argyle and Archibald Earl of Ilay and also his Majesties most gracious writt or writts of Subpena to them the said William Congreve Moses Beranger and Charles Mordaunt to be directed thereby Commanding them at a certain day and under a Certain Pain therein to be limitted personally to be and appear before Your Lordship in this High and Honourable Court of Chancery and true Answer make to all and Singular the Matters above alledged and set forth and also to stand to and abide such Order direction and Decree therein as to Your Lorship shall seem meet &tc.

Nicholls   *Tho Betts*

MANUSCRIPTS: P.R.O. C 11/2172/19, dated 14 August 1725; C 11/2221/53, dated 2 May 1726. The second manuscript, dated 2 May 1726, follows the earlier manuscript in so far as Congreve is concerned, each manuscript naming Congreve five times. Congreve's answer (No. 95), dated 14 May 1726, could refer to the complaint dated 14 August 1725 or to that dated 2 May 1726, for the answer applies equally well to either. No. 92 follows the reading of the earlier, and clearer, manuscript.

[1] Peter King (1669-1734), created first Baron King of Ockham in Surrey in 1725, was Lord Chancellor from 1725 till 1733. See *DNB*.

93   WILL OF RALPH CONGREVE

November 6, 1725

In the Name of God Amen. I Ralph Congreve[1] of Clarges Street[2] Esqr, do make this my last Will and Testament. Imprimis I give to my Dear Wife[3] and Children for their use during their lives my house in Clarges Street with all the Furniture. I Confirm to my dear Wife two hundred and Sixty pounds a year dureing her life to be paid to her by way of Dower out of the profitts or Dividends arising from Bank or South Sea Stock or out of the Rents of such an Estate as shall be purchased for Six Thousand pounds according to the Marriage Settlement which six Thousand pounds or Estate so purchased I confirme to my Eldest Son after his Mothers Decease and in default of such Issue to the second or other sons and in default of Heirs Male to my Eldest Daughter and in default of such Issue to my Second or other Daughters or to the Survivor of them with all the rest of my real and personall Estate goods and Chattells whatsoever. Item I give to all my Younger Children one thousand pounds to each of them as soon as they shall attain to their age of one and twenty years. All the rest of my real and personall Estate I also give to be Divided amongst them with all my Jewells and plate at such time and proportion to each of them as my Dear Wife shall think proper and I do appoint my said Dear Wife to be Guardian of all my Dear Children so long as she shall remain unmarried and upon her Marrying or Decease I do appoint my Executors hereafter named to be Guardians of all my Dear Children reserving to my self a power to make a Codicil to this Will. And of this my last will and Testament I do make my Cozen William Congreve Esqr, my Brothers Colo. Willm Congreve [4] and my Wives Brother Colo. Hanmer [5] my lawfull Executors and I give to each of them the sum of Fifty pounds to buy mourning. If it please God that all my Children should dye before they marry or attaine to the age of one and twenty years I give to my Brother Charles [6] and to my Sister Mary [7] twenty pounds a year to each of them for their lives. All the rest of the Interest or profits of all my real or personall Estate I give to my Dear Wife during her life and after her Decease I give to my Brother Colonel William Congreve my house in Clarges Street and one thousand pounds to be equally Divided amongst his Children then living or to the Survivor of them. I also give a thousand pounds in like manner to my Brother John Congreves Esqr.[8] Children. I also give to my brother Charles Congreves Children then living to each of them one hundred pounds and two hundred pounds to my Neice Powel.[9] Lastly I give and Devise all the rest and Residue of my real and personall Estate to my Dear wife Ann Congreve and to her disposal and I do hereby revoke all former Wills by me made. In Witness whereof I have hereunto set my hand and seal this 6th day of November in the year of our Lord one thousand seven hundred and twenty five. Ra: Congreve signed sealed published and Declared by the said Ralph Congreve to be his last Will in the presence of us who have in his presence and by his Desire Subscribed our names as Witnesses thereunto Wm. Pickering George Lodge Edward Page.

Probated: *London, December 3, 1725.*

MANUSCRIPT: Somerset House, London, P.C.C. Romney 247.

[1] See No. 80.

[2] Clarges Street, called "Clergy" Street on the "New Map of the City of London" printed by Thomas Taylor in 1723, was about a mile and a half west of Congreve's lodgings in Surrey Street. Clarges Street runs north from Piccadilly.

[3] Ralph Congreve married Anne, sister of Colonel William Hanmer (see No. 94, note 2) in October, 1717. See *Erdswick Book*. The oldest son was Ralph Congreve (later of Aldermaston, Berkshire), who was buried on 15 December 1775. The oldest daughter, Anne (remembered by the dramatist in his will), died unmarried at Aldermaston.

[4] Colonel William Congreve of Highgate (1671-1746) was a lieutenant as early as 1690 under Captain William Congreve (probably the dramatist's father), a captain by 1696, a major by 1706, and a lieutenant-colonel by 1712. He served throughout the Marlborough campaigns and was retired in 1736 on sixteen shillings six pence per day, "being incapable from age and long service." He was the ancestor of Sir William Congreve, Bart. (1772-1828), inventor of the Congreve rocket. See *Erdswick Book* and Dalton, *English Army Lists*, Vol. II, p. 271, Vol. IV, pp. 25, 129, Vol. V, p. 167, Vol. VI, p. 198. Colonel William Congreve of Highgate was mentioned as chief mourner at the dramatist's funeral on 26 January 1728/29. See No. 149, note 1.

[5] See No. 94, note 2.

[6] Born 2 December 1667. See *Erdswick Book*.

[7] Born 9 August 1661. See *Erdswick Book*.

[8] Born 25 December 1666. See *Erdswick Book*.

[9] Daughter of Ralph's sister Martha (born 2 June 1674), who married Henry Powel on 31 March 1706. See *Erdswick Book*.

94   CONGREVE, COLONEL WILLIAM CONGREVE, AND WILLIAM
     HANMER TO CHARLES LOCKYER

26th. February 1725 [1726]

Wee William Congreve of Surrey Street Esq; William Congreve of Highgate Esq; [1] And William Hanmer of Golden Square Esq; [2] Executors of the Last Will and Testament of Ralph Congreve late of Clarges Street Esquire Deceased. Do hereby desire And Authorize you to pay to Anne Congreve the Widdow of the said Ralph Congreve All Dividend's That shall hereafter become Due upon Three thousand two hundred pound's Capitall South Sea Stock Late belonging to the said Ralph Congreve And in the Booke's of the Said Company in his Name And for your so Doing this Shall be your

WEE William Congreve of Surrey Street Esqr William Congreve of Highgate Esqr And William Hanmer of Golden Square Esqr Exors of the Last Will and Testament of Ralph Congreve Late of Clarges Street Esquire decd Do hereby desire And Authorize you to pay to Anne Congreve Widow of ye said Ralph Congreve All dividends that shall hereafter become Due upon Three thousand two hundred pounds Capitall South Sea Stock Late belonging to the said Ralph Congreve And in the Books of the said Company in his Name And for your So Doing this shall be your Sufficient Warrant Wittness our hands this 26th day of Feby in the Year of Our Lord 1725

Wm Congreve
Will Congreve
Will. Hanmer.

To Charles Lockyer Esqr
Accompt to the South Sea
Company

sufficient Warrant. Wittness our hand's this 26th. day of February in the Year of Our Lord 1725 [1726].

To Charle's Lockyer Esqr   *Wm Congreve*
Accomptant to the South Sea   *Will Congreve*
Company ————————   *Will: Hanmer.*

MANUSCRIPT: Harvard Theatre Collection.

[1] See No. 93, note 4.

[2] Brother of Anne, widow of Ralph Congreve. Ralph had named William Hanmer one of three executors for his will. See the will, No. 93. Golden Square is north of Piccadilly, not far from Clarges Street. William Hanmer, a descendant of the well-known Wiltshire family, made a career in the English army. He was appointed lieutenant of Grenadiers on 13 May 1709, lieutenant-colonel in the Coldstream Guards on 20 December 1717, and colonel of a Regiment of Marines on 25 December 1740. He died in September, 1741. See Charles Dalton, *George the First's Army, 1714-1727*, 2 vols., London, 1910-12, Vol. I, pp. 128, 212, 291, 292.

95 CONGREVE'S ANSWER TO ELIZABETH, DUCHESS OF HAMILTON

May 14, 1726

The severall Answer of William Congreeve Esquire one of the Defendants to the Bill of Complaint of the most noble Elizabeth Dutchess of Hamilton and Brandon Relict of the most noble James late Duke of Hamilton and Brandon deceased Complainant.

  This Defendant saveing and reserving to himselfe now and at all times hereafter all manner of benefitt and advantage by way of Exception or otherwise to the Errors in the Complainant's said Bill of Complaint contained For answer thereunto or unto so much thereoff as this Defendant is advised is materiall for him to answer unto This Defendant answereth and sayth That it may be true that such severall proceedings were had in this Honourable Court in such manner as the Complainant hath particularly sett forth the same But this Defendant is an absolute stranger thereto save by

the said Bill of Complaint and this Defendant says that if such
deed of Limitation or appointment or any other Instrument of
Conveyance Deed or writing was or were made and executed by
Elizabeth Lady Mohun to the effect in the Complainant's Bill for
that purpose mentioned And this Defendant nominated a Trustee
therein sure Deed was made and executed without this Defendant's
knowledge or Privity or being acquainted with save as by the Complainant's Bill in manner aforesaid. This Defendant says he never
acted as Trustee for or on the behalf of the said Lady Mohun or
ever entered upon or possessed himselfe of any part of her Reale
or Personall estate. And this Defendant further says that if it shall
appeare to this Honourable Court he is a Trustee as in the said
Bill is Charged this Defendant is willing and desirous to relinquish
or Assigne the same and act and doe therein as this Honourable
Court shall direct being Indempnifyed, Without that that any other
matter Cause or thing in the Complainant's said Bill of Complaint
contained materiall or effectuall in the Law for this Defendant to
make answer unto and not herein and hereby well and sufficiently
answered unto Confessed or avoided Traversed or denyed is true
to the knowledge and beleife of this Defendant all which matters
and things this Defendant is ready and willing to justifye maintaine
and prove as this Honourable Court shall direct and humbly prays
to be hence dismissed with his reasonable Costs and Charges in this
behalfe most wrongfully sustained.

Knight   *Thos: Kilpin*

MANUSCRIPT: P.R.O., C 11/2221/53.

96   CONGREVE TO HUMPHRY MORICE [1]

Surry street November 22. 1726

SIR

I had the favour of your letter yesterday and have no Objection to Mr Maxwells renewall of his authority, besides that your recommendation is of great weight with me. I suppose Mr Maxwell would be single in the office. I would not do a hard thing by Mr Wood tho I never see nor hear anything of him. But as he makes no application, I believe he dos not think of it. However, as you were also his security I frankly leave the determination of it to you, and shall in this or any thing in my little power be glad to shew you how much I am with great respect Sir

> *Your most*
> *humble and Obedient*
> *servant*
> *Wm Congreve.*

MANUSCRIPT: Bank of England. EDITION: Hodges, p. 100.

[1] Humphry Morice (1671?-1731) was deputy-governor, 1725-1726, and governor, 1727-1728, of the Bank of England. During that period Congreve wrote Humphry Morice the two letters (Nos. 96, 97) still preserved at the Bank.

97   CONGREVE TO HUMPHRY MORICE

Surry street february 7th 1726/7

SIR

I had the favour of yours and sent to Mr Walter who has all along drawn up the writings in this affair, but he is out of town on the Dorsetshire Election. He is expected to return by the beginning of next week and then I will not fail to let you know what day the writing may be executed. I heartily wish you your health and am Sir with particular respect

> *Your most Obedient*
> *humble servant*
> *Wm Congreve*

MANUSCRIPT: Bank of England. EDITION: Hodges, p. 101.

98   JACOB TONSON TO JACOB TONSON II [1]

> *March the 11th 1727* [*1728*]

SIR

. . . I am mightily pleased with your writing mr Congreve is much better in health and that he intends for the Bath. That alone would have made me resolve on going there if I had not wanted it for my own health. Pray give my most humble service to him and let him know the pleasure I promise my self in having again (as I hope) his company. Pray let me know if any one, or who, goes with him. . . .

> *April the 22d 1728*

. . . After the return of the waggon (which wil bee handsomly loaden with Golden Pippin and Red streak I am Sure the best in the Country and more of the last vintage) I design for the bath, and promise my Self a very great pleasure in meeting my most worthy freind mr Congreve there. . . .

> *Your affectionate Servant*
> *Ja: Tonson*

MANUSCRIPTS: Bodleian Library MS. Eng. Letters C. 129 (first passage); The University of Texas Library (second passage). EDITIONS: Lawrence Edwards, "The Letters of Jacob Tonson," unpublished dissertation, University of Tennessee, Knoxville, 1956, pp. 35-36, 42; Sarah Lewis Carol Clapp, *Jacob Tonson in Ten Letters by and About Him*, The University of Texas Press, 1948, p. 10 (second passage only).

[1] See No. 69, note 4.

99   JACOB TONSON TO JACOB TONSON II

January the 27th 1728 [*1729*]

SIR

. . . The Death of my old acquaintance and freind mr Congreve [1]
does really much concern me, tho his long indisposition makes it
the less Surprizing. I flatterd my self with my Seeing him at the
Bath this Spring woud have been a sufficient reason for my going
there, but my decay of strenth, a consequence of a decay of appetite, makes it necessary and after Easter week I propose the journy.
You shall have a long notice before I goe—pray let me know how
Mr Congreves Circumstances were at his Death. I beleive they must
be considerable, and to whom left and his executors. His collection
of Books were very genteel and wel chosen. I wish you coud think
them worth your buying; [2] I think there were in [his] books several notes of his own or corrections and every thing from him wil
be very valuable. —I hope the Dutchess of Marlborough wil order
a monument [3] for him. But I think if these monuments are not soon
finished they wil lye undertaken longer than any Aldermans. I think
Dr Radclifs [4] is not yet up. I hope you have all your healths. I am
indifferent; noe reason to complain when I think how old I am.

> *Your Affectionate Servant*
> *Ja: Tonson.*

MANUSCRIPT: Bodleian Library MS. Eng. Letters C. 129. EDITION: Lawrence
Edwards, "The Letters of Jacob Tonson," unpublished dissertation, University
of Tennessee, Knoxville, 1956, pp. 89-90.

[1] Congreve died at five o'clock on the morning of Sunday, 19 January 1728/9,
eight days before the date of Tonson's letter to his nephew.

[2] Since Congreve's will (No. 148) had left his personal things, including his
books, to Henrietta, Duchess of Marlborough, they could not have been bought.
His books were indeed "very genteel and wel chosen," as shown by the manuscript list of titles which Congreve had made about 1726-1728. See *Library*.

[3] The Duchess of Marlborough did order a monument for Congreve. See No.
152.

[4] Dr. John Radcliffe (1650-1714), a wealthy London physician who had be-
queathed funds to Bartholomew's Hospital. See *DNB*.

100   JACOB TONSON TO JACOB TONSON II

February 3de 1728[9]

SIR

I have Received all yours and am mightily pleased with your advertisement about Rymer.[1] It is a noble undertaking and as wel performed. Congreves works in quarto [2] wil most certainly doe but the Sooner the better. Let a mans worth be nevour so great after Death it gets strangely out of the minds of his Surviving acquaintance. If mr Addisons works were now to bee published there woud not, I beleive, be the same number of Subscribers [3] — What the Prints say of mr Congreves agee must needs bee a mistake. They say 57, wanting 12 days.[4] Now I wel know that Juvenal in folio was printed and published 1693, and the Satyr [5] he translated was done a Yearee before and he coud not bee [have been] less than 20 or rather more. Pray let me know how it stands. . . . Let me know who you design to Supervise mr Congreves works; He took a great deal of care himself in the 8° edition I printed.[6] I beleive that wil be the best coppy for you to follow. Sure Waller [7] wil at last come out. I hope to See you this Summer or this Spring — I fancy mr Lintot [8] woud come with you if asked; but with him or any else you wil be most heartily welcome.

Your Affectionate Servant,
Ja: Tonson.

MANUSCRIPT: University of Texas Library. EDITIONS: Sarah Lewis Carol Clapp, *Jacob Tonson in Ten Letters by and About Him*, The University of Texas Press, 1948, pp. 16-18; Lawrence Edwards, "The Letters of Jacob Tonson," unpublished dissertation, University of Tennessee, Knoxville, 1956, pp. 90-92.

[1] For advertisements about the subscription to Rymer's *Foedera*, see *The London Gazette*, No. 6747, 25-28 January 1728/29, and No. 6748, January 28-February 1. The Tonson edition of the *Foedera* in seventeen folio volumes was indeed a "noble undertaking."

[2] The edition that actually appeared in 1730 was in duodecimo, not in quarto: *The Works of Mr. William Congreve: In Three Volumes. Consisting of His Plays and Poems. The Fifth Edition. London:* Printed for J. Tonson in the *Strand.* MDCCXXX.

³ Addison's *Works*, in four volumes, 1721, was one of Tonson's very successful publications by subscription. Congreve's name does not appear in the long list of subscribers, nor is the title found in Congreve's manuscript list of books in his library.

⁴ Congreve was nearly fifty-nine (not fifty-seven) when he died on 19 January 1728/29. If "the Prints" were correct in saying that he lacked only twelve days of reaching his next birthday, he must have been born on January 31 instead of January 24, the date painted into a portrait of Congreve at the age of twelve and apparently indicating the date of his birth. See Hodges, p. 6.

⁵ The eleventh satire of Juvenal, with notes, was Congreve's contribution to *The Satires of Juvenal and Persius*, London, Jacob Tonson, 1693, pp. 217-238.

⁶ *The First-Third Volume of the Works of Mr. William Congreve:* Printed for *Jacob Tonson*, at *Shakespear*'s Head over-against *Catherine Street* in the *Strand*. MDCCX.

⁷ *The Works of Edmund Waller* was published in 1729.

⁸ Barnaby Bernard Lintot (1675-1736) was Tonson's chief competitor and also, as this letter shows, a personal friend. Congreve's receipt, dated 1 June 1715, to "Mr. Lintott" for the first volume of Pope's Homer is preserved at the Huntington Library.

IOI   JACOB TONSON TO JACOB TONSON II

[*Ledbury, Herefordshire*, ca. *March, 1729*]
. . . I have Received yours and hope your letter to Mrs Beale ¹ will effectually bring her to reason. For the old Batchelour ² it was printed for Peter Buck, and I beleive the entering of it in the Hall Book ³ wil shew the time of printing it which was immediately upon its being Acted. Buck before that printed a little novel in 12,⁴ written by Mr Congreve and which has been Since reprinted by Wellington.⁵ Buck, alsoe about thee same time printed a 12º of miscellany Poems ⁶ in which were Several poems of Mr Congreves, which Poems hee revised and then put them into my 3d. part of M. Poems ⁷ and that was published in 1693—I think the head should bee done by Virtue,⁸ from the Kitcat Picture. Smith ⁹ did the messo-

tinto print from that, but I think there is a stifness about thee mouth which is not in the painting. . . .

　　Pray let me heare from you about the Grant [10] as soon as may be. If the Book mentioned in the Prints to be written by K. James [11] is good for any thing I woud have it.

Your Affectionate Servant
Ja: Tonson

MANUSCRIPT: Bodleian Library MS. Eng. Letters C. 129. EDITION: Lawrence Edwards, "The Letters of Jacob Tonson," unpublished dissertation, University of Tennessee, Knoxville, 1956, pp. 134-135.

[1] A widow with whom Tonson and his nephew negotiated the purchase of a tract of land from June, 1728, until the agreement was finally signed on 22 May 1729. The nephew's letter to Mrs. Beale evidently proposed the "Terms" referred to in Tonson's letter of 31 March 1729, thus suggesting March as the month in which the undated letter No. 101 was written. It was evidently written before the final agreement on 22 May 1729 and after Tonson had seen the advertisement (see the end of No. 101) of *Memoirs of the English Affairs, Chiefly Naval, from . . . 1660 to 1673*, by King James II, advertised as published "This Day" in *The London Evening-Post* for 11-13 February 1729.

[2] See No. 105.

[3] The Hall Book of the Company of Stationers recorded the daily business transactions.

[4] *Incognita: or, Love and Duty Reconcil'd.* A Novel. Licens'd Decemb. 22, 1691. London, Printed for *Peter Buck*, at the Sign of the *Temple*, near *Temple Bar* in *Fleet-street*, 1692.

[5] *Incognita: or, Love and Duty Reconcil'd.* A Novel. By Mr. Congreve. London, Printed for *R. Wellington* at the *Dolphin* and *Crown* in St. *Paul's* Churchyard, 1713.

[6] *Miscellany Poems upon Several Occasions* . . . London, for Peter Buck, 1692. But the old publisher's remarkable memory failed him here: the size was octavo, not duodecimo. See *Library*, No. 411.

[7] *Examen Poeticum*, 1693.

[8] George Vertue (1684-1756), distinguished engraver and antiquarian. See *DNB*.

[9] John Smith (1652-1742), a mezzotint engraver. See Nos. 43 and 45.

[10] A grant from the Crown relating to Tonson's Herefordshire estate, "The Hazels."

[11] See note 1 above.

102   THOMAS SOUTHERNE ON CONGREVE

January 12, 1735/6[1]

Mr Will: Congrave was the Son of a younger brother of a good old family in Staffordshire, who was employd in the Stewardship of part of the great estate of the Earl of Burlington in Ireland, where he resided many years. His only Son the Poet was born in that Country,[2] went to the free school at Kilkenny, and from thence to Trinity College in Dublin, where he had the advantage of being educated under a polite schollar, and ingenious Gentleman Dr St George Ash,[3] who was after Provost of that College, then Bishop of Cloghar, and then Bishop of Derry. This Bishop had the great good fortune of haveing the two famousest Witts his pupills the most extraordinary Dr Swift, Dean of St Patricks, and Mr Will: Congreve, tho not at the same time.[4] Mr Congreve was of the Middle Temple. His first performance was an ~~ingenious~~ Novel, calld incognita. Then he began his Play the old Batchelor haveing little Acquaintance withe the traders in that way, his Cozens recommended him to a friend [5] of theirs, who was very usefull to him in the whole course of his play. He engagd Mr Dryden in its favour, who upon reading it sayd he never saw such a first play in his life, but the Author not being acquainted with the stage or the town, it woud be pity to have it miscarry for want of a little Assistance: the stuff was rich indeed, it wanted only the fashionable cutt of the town. To help that Mr Dryden, Mr Arthur Manwayring,[6] and Mr Southerne red it with great care, and Mr Dryden putt it in the order it was playd. Mr Southerne obtaind of Mr Tho: Davenant who then governed the Playhouse, that Mr Congreve shoud have the privilege of the Playhouse half a year before his play was playd, which I never knew allowd any one before. It was playd with great success. That play made him many friends. Mr Montacue,[7] after Lord Hallyfax, was his Patron, putt him into the Commission for hackney coaches, and then into the Pipe [8] [Wine] Office, and then gave him a Patent place in the Customs of 600 Pounds per annum and Secretary to Jamaica, that payd him 700 Pounds a year by deputy on the Exchange at London.

Endorsed: *Memoirs relating to Mr. Congreve*
written by Mr. Thomas Southerne and communicated
to me from him by the Hands of
Dr Thomas Pellet, January 12th 1735/6

MANUSCRIPT: British Museum Add. MSS. 4221, f. 341. EDITIONS: Edmund Gosse, *Life of William Congreve*, London, 1888, pp. 187-188; revised ed., New York, 1924, pp. 175-176.

[1] This document was written by Thomas Southerne, as the endorsement states, for Thomas Birch (1705-1766), who used the information in a life of Congreve contributed to the *General Dictionary, Historical and Critical*, Vol. IV, 1736. Thomas Southerne (1660-1746), ten years older than Congreve, preceded him both at Trinity College, Dublin, and at the Middle Temple. Since he had already produced a half-dozen plays on the London stage, he was in a position to help Congreve with his first play. Many years later, Congreve was able to return the favor by recommending that the Lord Chamberlain approve the acting of one of Southerne's plays. See No. 134.

[2] Perhaps Southerne wanted to believe that Congreve was born in Ireland, just as he himself and Swift had been. But Congreve's statement that he was born in England is supported both by the baptismal record at the Church of All Saints in Bardsey, Yorkshire, and also by the certified contemporary bishop's transcript still preserved at the Borthwick Institute of Historical Research in the city of York, England.

[3] St. George Ashe (1658?-1718) became Provost of Trinity College, Dublin, in 1692, three years after Congreve left for England. He was made Bishop of Cloyne in 1695, of Clogher in 1697, and of Derry in 1717. See *DNB*.

[4] Southerne's memory at the age of seventy-five was much less dependable than that of Jacob Tonson, who at the same age was giving his nephew remarkably accurate details of events that had occurred nearly forty years before. Swift and Congreve were together at Trinity College, Dublin, for nearly two years.

[5] Edmund Gosse, in editing this document, says that the "friend" was probably Southerne himself. Perhaps the "Cozens" were Ralph and William Congreve (see No. 93, notes 3 and 4), who might have known Southerne as a fellow army officer.

[6] Arthur Maynwaring, or Mainwaring (1668-1712), was an able political writer, a Whig, and a member of the Kit-Cat Club. See *DNB*.

[7] Charles Montagu. See No. 6, note 7.

[8] The Public Record Office gives detailed information about Congreve's other offices, but nothing yet has been found there about a place in the "Pipe Office." The Wine Office, not the Pipe Office, followed the hackney coaches. Southerne was right about the £700 yearly from the secretaryship, but he was possibly wrong about the £600 yearly from the place in the customs. See Hodges, pp. 98-99, and note 16 on pp. 85-86 above.

III $\mathcal{D}$ENNIS, ADDISON, POPE, & OTHERS:

CHIEFLY LITERARY CRITICISM

When Congreve speaks of his art, so Virginia Woolf advises,[1] we should listen with all our ears. Congreve does comment on his art in many of the letters and documents brought together in this section, and his comment is largely on that comparatively rare subject of dramatic criticism: comedy.

Congreve printed a dedicatory letter with each of his plays. For his two very popular comedies—*The Old Bachelor* and *Love for Love*—written to satisfy the audience, he supplied very little critical comment (Nos. 105, 107). For the less popular *Double-Dealer* and *The Way of the World*, written to satisfy his own standards and not "prepar'd for that general Taste which seems now to be predominant in the Pallats of our Audience," he provided more—and significant—criticism (Nos. 106, 122). When he saw that he could not be true to his own developing critical taste and still satisfy his audience, he stopped writing for the popular stage.

[1] See "Congreve's Comedies," *The Moment and Other Essays*, New York, 1948, p. 31.

During the summer of 1695, while Congreve was at the height of his popularity as a writer of comedy, the critic John Dennis drew Congreve and Walter Moyle, two of his fellow wits at Will's Coffeehouse, into a correspondence (Nos. 108-115) that led to Congreve's most important critical utterance. This was his essay *Concerning Humour in Comedy*, in the form of a letter to Dennis dated 10 July 1695 (No. 110). The next five letters, largely personal, serve to round out the correspondence and express some telling critical views. In No. 114, for example, Walter Moyle shows incidentally the wits' sour verdict on Dr. Blackmore's poetry. It is characteristic of Congreve that, in his reply to Moyle, he avoided any slur against the doctor-poet. Perhaps, like Dr. Johnson later, Congreve did not find Blackmore's poetry altogether contemptible [2] but did not care "to contradict a multitude" any more than he did later when he failed to share the general enthusiasm for Swift's *Tale of a Tub* (No. 18).

One of Congreve's most important documents was *A Discourse on the Pindarique Ode* (No. 125), published in 1706 after a careful study of the form actually used by Pindar. Congreve explained the metrical principles rigidly used by the Greek poet and did much to correct the widespread abuse of the Pindaric form. The *Discourse*, with its footnotes much in the modern manner, exhibits Congreve the scholar as well as Congreve the critic. Most of the books he cites were in his own extensive and scholarly library.

Addison's three letters to Congreve from France and Switzerland were possibly a means of expressing appreciation. Congreve had won fame and patrons while Addison was still at Oxford. To one of these patrons, the powerful Lord Treasurer Charles Montagu, Congreve introduced Addison, and Montagu provided a governmental stipend which enabled Addison to make a three-year study tour on the Continent in preparation for diplomatic service.

When Pope came to publish his correspondence a few years after Congreve's death, he could find only five letters from Congreve (Nos. 131, 133, 135, 137, 144) and none that he had written to him. Pope had apparently not asked Congreve, as he had some

---

[2] See *Library*, Nos. 46, 47, 48, 422, for the titles of four long poems by Blackmore in Congreve's library.

of his other friends, to return his letters. In fact, Congreve was already dead before Pope began actively to collect and edit his correspondence, and from the papers that Congreve may have left at his death not a single manuscript letter written to him has come to light. Thus Pope found himself, when he came to publish his correspondence in 1735, without any of the letters that he knew he had written to Congreve. Apparently Pope proceeded to fill the gap by fabricating letters to Congreve from those he had written to other friends. If these manufactured letters are poor substitutes for those Pope actually had written to Congreve, at least they have the value of showing what Pope in 1735 thought—or wished—he had written his friend fifteen or twenty years earlier.

The half-dozen persons who dedicated literary works to Congreve could not have expected any financial reward. They turned to him rather as one who had given assistance or had encouraged them by his own example. Charles Hopkins came with his tragedy (No. 119), Steele with his *Poetical Miscellanies* (No. 126), Charles Beckingham with his poems in memory of Nicholas Rowe (No. 130), and Peter Davall with his translation of the *Memoirs of the Cardinal de Retz* (No. 142). Most famous of all, Alexander Pope came with his completed Homer as "a memorial of my friendship, with one of the most valuable men as well as finest writers, of my age and country . . . and to have the honour and the satisfaction of placing together, in this manner, the names of Mr. Congreve, and of A. Pope" (No. 136).

Two of Congreve's letters are in kindly response to assistance asked of him: one to Catharine Trotter, who needed help with her tragedy (No. 124); the other to Giles Jacob, who was seeking for his *Poetical Register* information about Congreve and his many literary acquaintances (No. 132). Two of the letters written to him were from old friends who were turning to Congreve as a recognized arbitrator in a literary dispute. John Dennis addressed to him his defense of the reputation of Wycherley (No. 138), and Steele his defense of Addison (No. 139).

During his last years, Congreve was visited by distinguished for-eigners who had come to do him homage: young Voltaire, who sought out Congreve about 1726 (No. 143) and later called him the English Molière; [3] and the Italian actor and dramatist Louis Riccoboni, who conversed "more than once" with Congreve, the Englishman "most esteemed for Comedy" (No. 145).

103   CONGREVE TO MRS. KATHARINE LEVESON [1]

[*December 22, 1691*] [2]

MADAM,

A Clear Wit, sound Judgment and a Merciful Disposition, are things so rarely united, that it is almost inexcusable to entertain them with any thing less excellent in its kind. My knowledge of you were a sufficient Caution to me, to avoid your Censure of this Trifle,[3] had I not as intire a knowledge of your Goodness. Since I have drawn my Pen for a Rencounter, I think it better to engage where, though there be Skill enough to Disarm me, there is too much Generosity to Wound; for so shall I have the saving Reputation of an unsuccess-ful Courage, if I cannot make it a drawn Battle. But methinks the Comparison intimates something of a Defiance, and savours of Arro-gance; wherefore since I am Conscious to my self of a Fear which I cannot put off, let me use the Policy of Cowards and lay this Novel unarm'd, naked and shivering at your Feet, so that if it should want Merit to challange Protection, yet, as an Object of Charity, it may move Compassion. It has been some Diversion to me to Write it, I wish it may prove such to you when you have an hour to throw away in Reading of it: but this Satisfaction I have at least before-hand, that in its greatest failings it may fly for Pardon to that In-dulgence which you owe to the weakness of your Friend; a Title

[3] *Letters Concerning the English Nation*, by Mr. de Voltaire, London, 1733, p. 236.

which I am proud you have thought me worthy of, and which I think can alone be superior to that

Your most Humble and
Obliged Servant
CLEOPHIL.

EDITIONS: *Incognita*, London, 1692; *Incognita*, ed. by H. F. B. Brett-Smith, New York and Boston, 1922, pp. 3-4; Summers, Vol. I, p. 109; Dobrée, p. 3.

¹ Daughter of Robert Leveson, of an old Staffordshire family. See Hodges, p. 30.

² Date of licensing as recorded on the title page of *Incognita*. Publication of the novel was announced in *The London Gazette* for 18-22 February 1691/2.

³ Notwithstanding this modest reference to *Incognita* as a "Trifle," Congreve shows by his careful "Preface to the Reader" (No. 104) that he has not taken his literary work lightly. The reference to his works as "Trifles" appears again in the dedicatory letter to *Love for Love*, 1695 (No. 107), in the letter to Giles Jacob, 1719 (No. 132), and in the famous conversation with Voltaire, about 1726 (No. 143).

104   CONGREVE TO THE READER OF *Incognita*

[December 22, 1691] ¹

READER,

Some Authors are so fond of a Preface, that they will write one tho' there be nothing more in it than an Apology for its self. But to show thee that I am not one of those, I will make no Apology for this, but do tell thee that I think it necessary to be prefix'd to this Trifle, to prevent thy overlooking some little pains which I have taken in the Composition of the following Story. Romances are generally composed of the Constant Loves and invincible Courages of Hero's, Heroins, Kings and Queens, Mortals of the first Rank, and so forth; where lofty Language, miraculous Contingencies and impossible Performances, elevate and surprize ² the Reader into a giddy Delight, which leaves him flat upon the Ground whenever he gives of, and vexes him to think how he has suffer'd himself to be pleased and transported, concern'd and afflicted at the several Passages which he has Read, *viz.* these Knights Success to their Damosels Misfortunes, and such like, when he is forced to be very well convinced that 'tis all a lye. Novels are of a more familiar nature; Come near us, and represent to us Intrigues in practice, delight us with Accidents and odd Events, but not such as are wholly unusual or unpresidented, such which not being so distant from our Belief bring also the pleasure nearer us. Romances give more of Wonder, Novels more Delight. And with reverence be it spoken, and the parallel kept at due distance, there is something of equality in the Proportion which they bear in reference to one another, with that betwen Comedy and Tragedy; but the *Drama* is the long extracted from Romance and History: 'tis the Midwife to Industry, and brings forth alive the Conceptions of the Brain. *Minerva* walks upon the Stage before us, and we are more assured of the real presence of Wit when it is delivered *viva voce*—

> *Segnius irritant animos demissa per aurem,*
> *Quam quæ sunt oculis subjecta fidelibus, & quæ*
> *Ipse sibi tradit spectator.*—— [3]
>
> Horace.

Since all Traditions must indisputably give place to the *Drama*, and since there is no possibility of giving that life to the Writing or Repetition of a Story which it has in the Action, I resolved in another beauty to imitate *Dramatick* Writing, namely, in the Design, Contexture and Result of the Plot. I have not observed it before in a Novel. Some I have seen begin with an unexpected accident, which has been the only surprizing part of the Story, cause enough to make the Sequel look flat, tedious and insipid; for 'tis but reasonable the Reader should expect it not to rise, at least to keep upon a level in the entertainment; for so he may be kept on in hopes that at some time or other it may mend; but the 'tother is such a balk to a Man, 'tis carrying him up stairs to show him the Dining-Room, and after forcing him to make a Meal in the Kitchin. This I have not only endeavoured to avoid, but also have used a method for the contrary purpose. The design of the Novel is obvious, after the first meeting of *Aurelian*[4] and *Hippolito* with *Incognita* and *Leonora,* and the difficulty is in bringing it to pass, maugre all apparent obstacles, within the compass of two days. How many probable Casualties intervene in opposition to the main Design, *viz.* of marrying two Couple so oddly engaged in an intricate Amour, I leave the Reader at his leisure to consider: As also whether every Obstacle does not in the progress of the Story act as subservient to that purpose, which at first it seems to oppose. In a Comedy this would be called the Unity of Action; here it may pretend to no more than an Unity of Contrivance. The Scene is continued in *Florence* from the commencement of the Amour; and the time from first to last is but three days. If there be any thing more in particular resembling the Copy[5] which I imitate (as the Curious Reader will soon perceive) I leave it to show it self, being very well satisfy'd how much more proper it had been for him to have found out this himself, than for me to prepossess him with an Opinion of something extraordinary in an Essay began and finished in the idler hours of a fortnight's time: for I can only esteem it a laborious idleness, which is Parent to so inconsiderable a Birth. I have gratified the Bookseller in pretending an occasion for a Preface; the other two Persons concern'd are the Reader and my self, and if he be but pleased with what was produced for that end, my satisfaction follows of course, since it will be proportion'd to his Approbation or Dislike.

EDITIONS: *Incognita,* London, 1692; *Incognita,* ed. by H. F. B. Brett-Smith, New York and Boston, 1922, pp. 5-7; Summers, Vol. I, pp. 111-112; Dobrée, pp. 5-7.

[1] Date of licensing as recorded on the title page of *Incognita.*

[2] The expression "to elevate and surprise," used in *The Rehearsal* to satirize the unnaturalness of heroic plays, here suggests Congreve's dislike for romances. See *Incognita,* ed. by Brett-Smith, p. 71, and Summers, Vol. I, p. 244. Congreve had a copy of *The Rehearsal,* the fifth edition, 1687. See *Library,* No. 406.

[3] Horace, *Ars Poetica,* lines 180-182, translated by Francis Howes:

> *Those [facts] which a tale shall through the ear impart*
> *With fainter characters impress the heart*

Than those which, subject to the eye's broad gaze,
The pleased spectator to himself conveys.

[4] Aurelian, Hippolito, and other names used in *Incognita*, are apparently derived from Dryden's comedy, *The Assignation; or, Love in a Nunnery*. See Summers, Vol. I, p. 244.

[5] That is, "*Dramatick* Writing," mentioned by Congreve in the first sentence of the paragraph. This Preface shows unmistakably that Congreve's first interest is the drama.

105   CONGREVE TO CHARLES BOYLE,[1] LORD CLIFFORD
       OF LANESBOROUGH

[March, 1693] [2]

MY LORD,

It is with a great deal of Pleasure, that I lay hold on this first Occasion, which the Accidents of my Life have given me of Writing to your Lordship: For since at the same time, I write to all the World, it will be a means of publishing (what I would have every Body know) the Respect and Duty which I owe and pay to you. I have so much Inclination to be yours, that I need no other Engagement: But the particular Ties, by which I am bound to your Lordship and Family,[3] have put it out of my Power to make you any Compliment; since all Offers of my self, will amount to no more than an honest Acknowledgment, and only shew a Willingness in me to be grateful.

I am very near wishing, That it were not so much my Interest to be your Lordship's Servant, that it might be more my Merit; not that I would avoid being obliged to you, but I would have my own Choice to run me into the Debt; that I might have it to boast, I had distinguish'd a Man, to whom I would be glad to be obliged, even without the Hopes of having it in my Power, ever to make him a Return.

It is impossible for me to come near your Lordship, in any kind, and not to receive some Favour; and while in appearance I am only making an Acknowledgment (with the usual under-hand dealing of the World) I am at the same time, insinuating my own Interest. I cannot give your Lordship your due, without tacking a Bill of my own Privileges. 'Tis true, if a Man never committed a Folly, he would never stand in need of a Protection: But then Power would have nothing to do, and good Nature no Occasion to shew it self; and where those Qualities are, 'tis pity they should want Objects to shine upon. I must confess this is no reason, why a Man should do an idle thing, nor indeed any good Excuse for it, when done; yet it reconciles the Uses of such Authority and Goodness, to the Necessities of our Follies; and is a sort of Poetical Logick, which at this Time I would make use of, to argue your Lordship into a Protection of this Play. It is the first Offence I have committed in this kind, or indeed, in any kind of Poetry, tho' not the first made Publick; [4] and, therefore, I hope will the more easily be pardoned: But had it been Acted, when it was first written, more might have been said in its behalf; Ignorance of the Town and Stage, would then have been Excuses in a young Writer, which now, almost four Years [5] Experience, will scarce allow of. Yet I must declare my self sensible of the good Nature of the Town, in receiving this Play so kindly, with all its Faults, which I must own were, for the most part, very industriously cover'd by the Care of the Players; for, I think, scarce a Character but receiv'd all the Advantage it would admit of, from the Justness of the Action.

As for the Criticks, my Lord, I have nothing to say, to, or against, any of them of any kind; from those who make just Exceptions, to those who find fault in the wrong place. I will only make this general Answer in behalf of my Play (an Answer, which *Epictetus* advises every Man to make for himself, to his Censurers) *viz. That if they who find some Faults in it, were as intimate with it as I am, they would find a great many more.* This is a Confession, which I needed not to have made; but however, I can draw this use from it, to my own Advantage, that I think there are no Faults in it but what I do know; which, as I take it, is the first step to an Amendment.

Thus I may live in hopes (some time or other) of making the
Town amends; but you, my Lord, I never can, tho' I am ever
Your LORDSHIP's
most Obedient, and
most Humble Servant,
Will. Congreve.

EDITIONS: Dedication to the first edition of *The Old Batchelour*, 1693; *Works*
(1710), Vol. I; *Works* (1719), Vol. I; Summers, Vol. I, pp. 161-162; Dobrée,
Comedies, pp. 15-17. The text for No. 105 follows the *Works* (1719), which
improves the 1710 edition by omitting four needless commas.

[1] Charles Boyle (1639-1694), to whom Congreve dedicated his *Old Bachelor*,
was the grandson of the first Earl of Cork, who built up the extensive Irish
estates that were later managed by Congreve's father. Charles Boyle became
Baron Clifford of Lanesborough on the death, in 1691, of his mother, who was
Baroness Clifford in her own right. Charles Boyle died four years before his
father, Richard Boyle, second Earl of Cork and first Earl of Burlington. See
GEC *Peerage*, Vol. II (1912), pp. 430-433.

[2] The date is inferred from a reference in the Epilogue implying that Lent
(which started that year on the last day of February) had already begun and the
fact that the third printing of the play was announced in *The London Gazette*
for March 23-27. Evidently the great popularity of the play called for three
printings within a few weeks. Tonson said (No. 101) that the play was printed
"immediately upon its being acted."

[3] The "particular Ties" between the Boyle family and the Congreves probably
date back to 1674, when the four-year-old William went with his parents to
live at the Irish seaport of Youghal, then one of the chief residences of the
Boyles. It was to Youghal, and to Lismore Castle about twenty miles away,
that Congreve's father returned in 1690 to look after the vast Cork-Burlington
estates in Ireland. These he found in a sad state after the recent Protestant-
Catholic conflict. Referring to the ruin reported at Lismore Castle, Lord Clifford
wrote from London to Congreve's father on 25 January 1690/91: "I hope my
Father [the Earl of Burlington] will repaire it again, but if he should not, and
I should live to have it, I will make it much better than ever it was sence I
knew it, for I think it the finest seat in your Country. I begge the favour of you
to present my service to your Wife and to all my Friends at Youghall and
assure your selfe that I shall be ready upon all occasions, to serve you, and in-
courage you to continue in the employment you are in, for no body has a
greater opinion of your integrity, and honesty than your assured Frende, and
Servant, Clifforde." See Lismore Papers: Early Correspondence, National Library of Ireland. The Earl did repair Lismore Castle, and Congreve's father

and mother were in residence there until the father retired about 1702. See also Nos. 18, 31, 57; Hodges, pp. 10, 55, 56.

[4] Congreve is here saying that *The Old Bachelor* was written before his translation of the Eleventh Satire for Dryden's *Juvenal* (published in October, 1692) or his short poems published during the same year. He is said to have written *Incognita* before *The Old Bachelor*, but Congreve may be leaving the little novel out of consideration on the ground that it had been published under an assumed name and thus not "made publick." Or possibly he considered the novel unworthy of classification as "Poetry"—that is, literature. It is noteworthy that he did not list *Incognita* among the books in his library. See *Library*, p. 14.

[5] Congreve apparently came up to London about the middle of 1689, "almost four years" before March, 1693. Perhaps he penned a first draft of *The Old Bachelor*, as tradition says, under an old oak at Stretton, his grandfather's seat, where he would naturally have visited during 1689 on his way from Dublin to London.

106   CONGREVE TO CHARLES MONTAGU (LATER EARL OF HALIFAX)[1]

[ca. *December 7, 1693*]

SIR,

I Heartily wish this Play were as perfect as I intended it, that it might be more worthy your acceptance; and that my Dedication of it to you, might be more becoming that Honour and Esteem which I, with every Body, who are [2] so fortunate as to know you, have for you. It had your Countenance when yet unknown; and now it is made publick, it wants your Protection.

And give me leave, without any Flattery to you, or Vanity in my self, to tell my Illiterate Criticks, as an answer to their Impotent Objections, that they have found fault with that, which has been pleasing to you. This Play in relation to my concern for its Reputation, succeeded before it was Acted, for thro' your early Patronage it had an audience of several Persons of the first Rank both in Wit and Quality; and their allowance of it, was a Consequence of your approbation. Therefore if I really wish it might have had a more popular reception; it is not at all in consideration of my self; but because I wish well, and would gladly contribute to the benefit of the Stage, and diversion of the Town. They were (not long since) so kind to a very imperfect Comedy of mine, that I thought my self justly indebted to them all my endeavours for an entertainment that might merit some little of that Applause, which they were so lavish of, when I thought I had no Title to it. But I find they are to be treated cheaply, and I have been at an unnecessary expence.[3]

I would not have any Body imagine, that I think this Play without its Faults, for I am Conscious of several, and ready to own them; but it shall be to those who are able to find them out.[4] I confess I design'd (whatever Vanity or Ambition occasion'd that design) to have written a true and regular Comedy, but I found it an undertaking which put me in mind of—*Sudet multum, frustraque laboret ausus idem.*[5] And now to make amends for the vanity of such a design, I do confess both the attempt, and the imperfect performance. Yet I must take the boldness to say, I have not miscarried in the whole; for the Mechanical part of it is perfect.[6] That, I may say with as little vanity, as a Builder may say he has built a House according to the Model laid down before him; or a Gardiner that he has set his Flowers in a knot of such or such a Figure. I design'd the Moral first, and to that Moral I invented the Fable, and do not know that I have borrow'd one hint of it any where. I made the Plot as strong as I could, because it was single, and I made it single, because I would avoid confusion, and was resolved to preserve the three Unities of the Drama, which I have visibly done to the utmost severity. This is what I ought not to observe upon my self; but the Ignorance and Malice of the greater part of the Audience is such, that they would make a Man turn Herauld to his own Play, and Blazon every Character. However,[7] Sir, this Discourse is very impertinent to you, whose Judgment, much better can discern the Faults, than I can excuse them; and whose good Nature, like that of a Lover, will find out those hidden Beauties (if there are any such) which it would be great immodesty in [8] me to discover. I think I don't speak improperly when I call you a *Lover* of Poetry; for it is very well known she has been a kind [9] Mistress to you; she has not deny'd you the last Favour; you have injoy'd her,[10] and she has been fruitful [11] in a most Beautiful Issue—If I break off abruptly here, I hope every Body will understand that it is to avoid a Commendation, which, as it is your due, would be most easie for me to pay, and too troublesome for you to receive.

I have since the Acting of this Play hearkned after the Objections which have been made to it; for I was Conscious where a true Critick might have put me upon my defence. I was prepared for their [12] Attack; and am pretty confident I could have vindicated some parts, and excused others; and where there were any plain Miscarriages, I would most ingenuously have confess'd them. But I have not heard any thing said sufficient to provoke an Answer. Some little snarling and barking there has been, but I don't know one well-mouth'd Curr that has opened at all.[13] That, which looks most like an Objection, does not relate in particular to this Play, but to all or most that ever have been written; and that is Soliloquy. Therefore I will answer it, not only for my own sake, but to save others the trouble, to whom it may hereafter be Objected.

I grant, that for a Man to Talk to himself, appears absurd and unnatural; and indeed it is so in most Cases; but the circumstances which may attend the occasion, make great alteration. It oftentimes happens to a Man, to have designs which require him to himself, and in their Nature, cannot admit of a Confidant. Such, for certain, is all Villany; and other less mischievous intentions may be very improper to be Communicated to a second Person. In such a case therefore the Audience must observe, whether the Person upon the Stage takes any notice of them at all, or no. For if he supposes any one to be by, when he talks to himself, it is monstrous and ridiculous to the last degree. Nay, not only in this case, but in any part of a Play, if there is expressed any knowledge of an Audience, it is insufferable. But otherwise when a Man in Soliloquy reasons with himself, and *Pro's* and *Con's*, and weighs all his Designs: We ought not to imaging that this Man either talks to us, or to himself; he is only thinking, and thinking such Matter, as were inexcusable Folly in him to speak. But because we are conceal'd Spectators of the Plot in agitation, and the Poet finds it necessary to let us know the whole Mystery of his Contrivance; he is willing to inform us of this Persons Thoughts, and to that end is forced to make use of the expedient of Speech, no other better way being yet invented for the Communication of Thought.

Another very wrong Objection has been made by some who have not taken leisure to distinguish the Characters. The Hero of the Play as they are pleas'd to call him, (meaning *Mellefont*) is a Gull, and made a Fool, and cheated. Is every Man a Gull and a Fool that is deceived? At that rate I'm afraid the two Classes of Men, will be reduc'd to one, and the Knaves themselves be at a loss to justifie their Title: But if an Open-hearted Honest Man, who has an entire Confidence in one whom he takes to be his Friend, and whom he has obliged to be so; and who (to confirm him in his Opinion) in all appearance, and upon several tryals has been so: If this Man be deceived by the Treachery of the other; must he of necessity commence Fool immediately, only because the other has proved a Villain? Ay, but there was Caution given to *Mellefont* in the first Act by his Friend *Careless*. Of what Nature was that Caution? Only to give the Audience some light into the Character of *Maskwell*, before his appearance; and not to convince *Mellefont* of his Treachery; for that was more than *Careless* was then able to do: He never knew *Maskwell* guilty of any Villany; he was only a sort of Man which he did not like. As for his suspecting his Familiarity with my Lady *Touchwood:* Let them examine the Answer that *Mellefont* makes him, and compare it with the Conduct of *Maskwell*'s Character through the Play.

I would have them again look [14] into the Character of *Maskwell*, before they accuse any Body [15] of weakness for being deceiv'd by him. For upon summing up the enquiry into this Objection, find they have only mistaken [16] Cunning in one Character, for Folly in another.

But there is one thing, at which I am more concerned than all the false Criticisms that are made upon me; and that is, some of the Ladies are offended: I am heartily sorry for it, for I declare I would rather disoblige all the Criticks in the World, than one of the Fair Sex. They are concerned that I have represented some Women Vi-

cious and Affected: How can I help it? It is the Business of a Comick
Poet to paint the Vices and Follies of Humane kind; and there are
but two Sexes that I know, *viz. Men,* and *Women,*[17] which have a
Title to Humanity: And if I leave one half of them out, the Work
will be imperfect. I should be very glad of an opportunity to make
my Complement [18] to those Ladies who are offended: But they can
no more expect it in a Comedy, than to be Tickled by a Surgeon,
when he's letting them Blood. They who are Virtuous or Discreet,
I'm sure cannot [19] be offended, for such Characters as these distinguish them,[20] and make their Beauties more shining and observ'd:
And they who are of the other kind, may nevertheless pass for such,
by seeming not to be displeased, or touched with the Satyr of this
Comedy. Thus have they also wrongfully accused me of doing them
a prejudice, when I have in reality done them a Service.

I have heard some whispering, as if they intended to accuse this
Play of Smuttiness and Bawdy: But I declare I took a particular care
to avoid it, and if they find any in it, it is of their own making, for
I did not design it to be so understood. But to avoid my saying any
thing upon a Subject, which has been so admirably handled before,
and for their better instruction, I earnestly recommend to their
perusal, the Epistle Dedicatory before the *Plain-Dealer.*[21]

You will pardon me, Sir, for the freedom I take of making
Answers to other People, in an Epistle which ought wholly to be
sacred to you: But since I intend the Play to be so too, I hope I may
take the more liberty of Justifying it, where it is in the right. I hear
a great many of the Fools are angry at me, and I am glad of it; for
I Writ at them, not to them. This is a bold confession, and yet I
don't think I shall disoblige one Person by it; for no Body can take
it to himself, without owning the *Character.*[22]

I must now, Sir, declare to the World, how kind you have been
to my Endeavours; for in regard of what was well meant, you have
excused what was ill perform'd, I beg you would continue the same
Method in your acceptance of this Dedication. I know no other way
of making a return to that *Charity* [23] you shew'd, in protecting an
Infant, but by Enrolling it in your Service, now that it is of Age and
come into the World. Therefore be pleased to accept of this as an

Acknowledgment of the Favour you have shewn me, and an earnest
of the real Service and Gratitude of,

SIR,

Your Most Obliged
Humble Servant
William Congreve.

EDITIONS: Dedication to the first edition of *The Double-Dealer*, 1694 (but advertised in *The London Gazette* on 7 December 1693); the edition of 1706; *Works* (1710), Vol. I, pp. 139-148; *Works* (1719), Vol. I, pp. 117-122; Summers, Vol. II, pp. 9-12; Dobrée, *Comedies*, pp. 113-117. Of all Congreve's letters and documents, No. 106 has had the most extensive changes—chiefly by way of deletions—in the later editions. Congreve had been puzzled, and extremely irritated, by the harsh criticism of *The Double-Dealer*, his second comedy, produced just nine months after *The Old Bachelor*. He was a good enough critic of his own work to recognize serious defects in his first play, as he said in the Dedication to *The Old Bachelor* (see No. 105), and to know that he had produced for his audience a much more commendable play in the second. And, besides, Dryden—the best critic of the age—had already penned in the warmest terms his approval of *The Double-Dealer*. When the audience almost hissed this better comedy off the stage, the twenty-three-year-old Congreve quite lost his temper and, in the Dedication to the first editions of the play, spoke of his critics as "Fools" and characterized them as "Illiterate," "snarling and barking" "their Impotent Objections," swayed by "Ignorance and Malice" and showing that "they are to be treated cheaply" and that he had wasted his time in doing his best work for them. All this and much more Congreve omitted or changed in later editions, beginning first with the edition of 1706 and going still further in the collected *Works*, 1710. No. 106 reprints the Dedication of the first edition and indicates omissions and changes applicable to the 1706 and 1710 editions.

[1] See No. 6, note 7.

[2] The reading "are," 1694 and 1706, becomes "is" in 1710 and 1719.

[3] This whole paragraph was omitted in 1706 and later editions.

[4] The eighteen words from "and" to "out" were omitted in 1706 and later editions.

[5] Horace, *Ars Poetica*, line 241.

[6] "perfect," 1694, 1706; "regular," 1710, 1719.

[7] The passage, from "which I have visibly" through "However" was omitted first in 1710.

[8] "in," 1694; "for," 1706 and later.

[9] "kind," 1694; "very kind," 1706 and later.

[10] The words "you have injoy'd her" were omitted 1710, 1719.

[11] "fruitful," 1694, 1706; "fruitful to you," 1710, 1719.

[12] "their," 1694, 1706; "the," 1710, 1719.

[13] This sentence was omitted 1706 and later.

[14] "have them again look," 1694; "beg them again to look," 1706 and later.

[15] "any Body," 1694; later, "Mellefont."

[16] "find they have only mistaken," 1694; later, "it may be found they have mistaken."

[17] "Humane kind; and there are but two Sexes that I know, *viz. Men*, and *Women*," 1694; later, "Human-kind; and there are but two Sexes, Male, and Female, *Men*, and *Women*."

[18] "Complement," 1694; later, "Compliment."

[19] "I'm sure cannot," 1694; "can hardly," 1706; "should not," 1710, 1719.

[20] In 1706 and later, "them" is italicized.

[21] This paragraph was revised for the 1706 edition and omitted entirely in 1710, 1719.

[22] The last two sentences were omitted 1706 and later.

[23] "*Charity*," 1694; later, "Humanity," not in italics.

107   CONGREVE TO CHARLES SACKVILLE, EARL OF DORSET [1]

[ca. *May, 1695*]

MY LORD,

A Young Poet, is liable to the same Vanity and Indiscretion with a Young Lover; and the Great Man who [2] smiles upon one, and the Fine Woman who [2] looks kindly upon t'other, are both [3] of them in Danger of having the Favour publish'd with the first Opportunity.

But there may be a different Motive, which will a little distinguish the Offenders. For tho' one shou'd have a Vanity in ruining another's Reputation, yet the other may only have an Ambition to advance his own. And I beg Leave, my Lord, that I may plead the latter, both as the Cause and Excuse of this Dedication.

Whoever is King, is also the Father of his Country; and as no body can dispute Your Lordship's *Monarchy* in *Poetry;* so all that are concern'd ought to acknowledge Your Universal Patronage: And it is only presuming on the Privilege of a Loyal Subject, that I have ventur'd to make this my Address of Thanks, to Your Lordship; which at the same Time, Includes a Prayer for Your Protection.

I am not Ignorant of the Common Form of Poetical Dedications, which are generally made up of Panegyricks, where the Authors endeavour to distinguish their Patrons, by the shining Characters they give them, above other Men. But that, my Lord, is not my Business at this time, nor is Your Lordship *now* to be distinguish'd. I am contented with the Honour I do my self in this Epistle; without the Vanity of attempting to add to, or explain Your Lordship's Character.

I confess it is not without some strugling, that I behave my self in this Case, as I ought: For it is very hard to be pleased with a Subject, and yet forbear it. But I chuse rather to follow *Pliny*'s Precept, than his Example, when in his Panegyrick to the Emperor *Trajan,* he says,

> *Nec minus considerabo quid aures ejus pati possint,*
> *Quam quid virtutibus debeatur.*[4]

I hope I may be excus'd the Pedantry of a Quotation, when it is so justly apply'd. Here are some Lines in the Print, (and which your Lordship read before this Play was Acted) that were omitted on the Stage; and particularly one whole Scene in the Third Act, which not only helps the Design forward with less Precipitation, but also heightens the ridiculous Character of *Foresight,* which indeed seems to be maim'd without it. But I found my self in great Danger of a long Play, and was glad to help it where I could. Tho' not withstanding my Care, and the kind Reception it had from the Town;

I could heartily wish it yet shorter: But the Number of Different Characters represented in it, would have been too much crowded in less room.

This Reflection on Prolixity, (a Fault, for which scarce any one Beauty will attone) warns me not to be tedious now, and detain Your Lordship any longer with the Trifles of,

MY LORD,

Your Lordship's Most

Obedient and Most

Humble Servant,

William Congreve.

EDITIONS: Dedication to the first edition of *Love for Love*, 1695; *Works* (1710), Vol. I, pp. 303-306; *Works* (1719), Vol. I, pp. 247-249; Summers, Vol. II, pp. 89-90; Dobrée, *Comedies*, pp. 214-216. No. 107 follows the 1710 edition.

[1] Charles Sackville, sixth Earl of Dorset and first Earl of Middlesex (1638-1706), in his post as Lord Chamberlain had helped Thomas Betterton, Mrs. Barry, Mrs. Bracegirdle, and others revolt from the Drury Lane Theatre and set up their own playhouse in Lincoln's Inn Fields. Congreve very fittingly dedicated to the Lord Chamberlain his *Love for Love*, the first play to be performed at the new theatre on 30 April 1695.

[2] "who," 1710, 1719; "that," 1695.

[3] "both," 1710, 1719; "each," 1695.

[4] *Panegyricus*, caput III.

108   JOHN DENNIS [1] TO CONGREVE

[June, 1695?]

DEAR SIR,

I have now read over the Fox, in which thô I admire the strength of *Ben. Johnson*'s Judgment, yet I did not find it so accurate as I expected. For first the very thing upon which the whole Plot turns, and that is the Discovery which *Mosca* makes to *Bonario;* seems to me, to be very unreasonable. For I can see no Reason, why he should make that Discovery which introduces *Bonario* into his Masters House. For the Reason which the Poet makes *Mosca* give in the Ninth Scene of the third Act, appears to be a very Absurd one. Secondly, *Corbaccio* the Father of *Bonario* is expos'd for his Deafness, a Personal defect; which is contrary to the end of Comedy Instruction. For Personal Defects cannot be amended; and the exposing such, can never Divert any but half-witted Men. It cannot fail to bring a thinking Man to reflect upon the Misery of Human Nature; and into what he may fall himself without any fault of his own. Thirdly, the play has two Characters, which have nothing to do with the design of it, which are to be look'd upon as Excrescencies. Lastly, the Character of *Volpone* is Inconsistent with it self. *Volpone* is like *Catiline, alieni appetens, sui profusus;* but that is only a double in his Nature, and not an Inconsistence. The Inconsistence of the Character appears in this, that *Volpone* in the fifth Act behaves himself like a Giddy Coxcombe, in the Conduct of that very Affair which he manag'd so Craftily in the first four. In which the Poet offends first against that Fam'd rule which *Horace* gives for the Characters.

Servetur ad imum,
Qualis ab incepto processerit, et sibi constet.[2]

And Secondly, against Nature, upon which, all the rules are grounded. For so strange an Alteration, in so little a time, is not in Nature, unless it happens by the Accident of some violent passion; which is not the case here. *Volpone* on the sudden behaves himself without common Discretion, in the Conduct of that very Affair which he had manag'd with so much Dexterity, for the space of three Years together. For why does he disguise himself? or why does he repose the last Confidence in *Mosca?* Why does he cause it to be given out that he's Dead? Why, only to Plague his Bubbles. To Plague them, for what? Why only for having been his Bubbles. So that here is the greatest alteration in the World, in the space of twenty-four hours, without any apparent cause. The design of *Volpone* is to Cheat, he has carried on a Cheat for three years together, with Cunning and with Success. And yet he on a sudden in cold blood does a thing, which he cannot but know must Endanger the ruining all.

I am,

Dear Sir,

Your most Humble

Servant.

EDITIONS: Dennis, pp. 73-75; *Familiar Letters*, Vol. I, pp. 148-150; Hooker, Vol. II, pp. 384-385.

[1] John Dennis (1657-1734) must be credited with drawing out Congreve's significant discussion of humor in comedy (see No. 110). See Hooker, Vol. II, p. 521. Congreve recognized the soundness of Dennis as a critic and took great pains to set down his own ideas on the difficult subject of comedy.

[2] Horace, *Ars Poetica*, lines 126-127, translated by Francis Howes:

> *Let them one tenor to the last pursue,*
> *Consist throughout and to themselves be true.*

109   JOHN DENNIS TO CONGREVE

[June, 1695?]

DEAR SIR,

I will not augment to Trouble which I give you by making an Apology for not giving it you sooner. Thô I am heartily sorry that I kept such a trifle as the inclos'd,[1] and a trifle writ Extempore, long enough to make you expect a labour'd Letter. But because in the Inclos'd, I have spoken particularly of *Ben. Johnson*'s Fox, I desire to say three or four words of some of his Plays more generally. The Plots of the Fox, the silent Woman, the Alchimist, are all of them very Artful. But the Intrigues of the Fox, and the Alchimist, seem to me to be more dexterously perplexed, than to be happily disentangled. But the Gordian knot in the Silent Woman is untyed with so much Felicity, that that alone, may Suffice to show *Ben Johnson* no ordinary Heroe. But, then perhaps, the Silent Woman may want

the very Foundation of a good Comedy, which the other two cannot be said to want. For it seems to me, to be without a Moral. Upon
which Absurdity, *Ben Johnson* was driven by the Singularity of
Moroses Character, which is too extravagant for Instruction, and fit,
in my opinion, only for Farce. For this seems to me, to Constitute
the most Essential Difference, betwixt Farce and Comedy, that the
Follies which are expos'd in Farce are Singular; and those are particular, which are expos'd in Comedy. These last are those, with
which some part of an Audience may be suppos'd Infected, and to
which all may be suppos'd Obnoxious. But the first are so very odd,
that by Reason of their Monstrous Extravagance, they cannot be
thought to concern an Audience; and cannot be supposed to instruct
them. For the rest of the Characters in these Plays, they are for the
most part true, and Most of the Humorous Characters Master-pieces.
For *Ben Johnson*'s Fools, seem to shew his Wit a great deal more
than his Men of Sense. I Admire his Fops, and but barely Esteem
his Gentlemen. *Ben* seems to draw Deformity more to the Life than
Beauty. He is often so eager to pursue Folly, that he forgets to take
Wit along with him. For the Dialogue, it seems to want very often
that Spirit, that Grace, and that Noble Railery, which are to be found
in more Modern Plays, and which are Virtues that ought to be
Inseparable from a finish'd Comedy. But there seems to be one
thing more wanting than all the rest, and that is Passion, I mean
that fine and that delicate Passion, by which the Soul shows its
Politeness, ev'n in the midst of its trouble. Now to touch a Passion
is the surest way to Delight. For nothing agitates like it. Agitation
is the Health and Joy of the Soul, of which it is so entirely fond,
that even then, when we imagine we seek Repose, we only seek
Agitation. You know what a Famous Modern Critick[2] has said of
Comedy.

> *Il faut que ses acteurs badinent noblement,*
> *Que son Noeud bien formé se denoue aisement;*
> *Que l'action Marchant ou la raison la guide,*
> *Ne seperde Jamma dans une Scens vuide,*
> *Que son Stile humble et doux se releue a propos,*
> *Que ses discours par tout fertiles en bons mots,*

Soient pleins de passions finement maniéès,
Et les Scenes toujours l'une al'autre lieés,

I leave you to make the Application to *Johnson*—Whatever I have said my self of his Comedies, I submit to your better Judgment. For you who, after Mr. *Wicherly*, are incomparably the best Writer of it living; ought to be allowed to be the best Judge, too,

I am,

Yours, &c.

EDITIONS: Dennis, pp. 76-79; *Familiar Letters*, Vol. I, pp. 150-152; Hooker, Vol. II, pp. 385-386.

[1] A reference to the preceding letter, No. 108, which was apparently enclosed with No. 109.

[2] Boileau, *l'Art Poétique*, Vol. III, pp. 405-412, translated by Sir William Soame and Dryden (1683):

> *With well-bred conversation you must please,*
> *And your intrigue unravelled be with ease;*
> *Your action still should reason's rules obey,*
> *Nor in an empty scene may lose its way.*
> *Your humble style must sometimes gently rise,*
> *And your discourse sententious be and wise,*
> *The passions must to nature be confined,*
> *And scenes to scenes with artful weaving joined.*

110   CONGREVE TO JOHN DENNIS

July 10, 1695.

DEAR SIR,

You write to me, that you have Entertained your self two or three days, with reading several Comedies, of several Authors; and your Observation is, that there is more of *Humour* in our English Writers, than in any of the other Comick Poets, Ancient or Modern.[1] You desire to know my Opinion, and at the same time my Thought, of that which is generally call'd *Humour* in Comedy.

I agree with you, in an Impartial Preference of our English

Writers, in that Particular. But if I tell you my Thoughts of *Humour,* I must at the same time confess, that what I take for true *Humour,* has not been so often written even by them, as is generally believed: And some who have valued themselves, and have been esteem'd by others, for that kind of Writing, have seldom touch'd upon it. To make this appear to the World, would require a long and labour'd Discourse, and such as I neither am able nor willing to undertake. But such little Remarks, as may be contained [2] within the Compass of a Letter, and such unpremeditated Thoughts, as may be Communicated between Friend and Friend, without incurring the Censure of the World, or setting up for a *Dictator,* you shall have from me, since you have enjoyn'd it.

To Define *Humour,* perhaps, were as difficult, as to Define *Wit;* for like that, it is of infinite variety. To Enumerate the several *Humours* of Men, were a Work as endless, as to sum up their several Opinions. And in my mind the *Quot homines tot Sententiæ,* might have been more properly interpreted of *Humour;* since there are many Men, of the same Opinion in many things, who are yet quite different in Humours. But thô we cannot certainly tell what *Wit* is, or, what *Humour* is, yet we may go near to shew something, which is not *Wit* or not *Humour;* and yet often mistaken for both. And since I have mentioned *Wit* and *Humour* together, let me make the first Distinction between them, and observe to you that *Wit is often mistaken for Humour.*

I have observed, that when a few things have been Wittily and Pleasantly spoken by any Character in a Comedy; it has been very usual for those, who make their Remarks on a Play, while it is acting, to say, *Such a thing is very Humorously spoken: There is a great Deal of Humour in that Part.* Thus the Character of the Person speaking, may be, Surprizingly and Pleasantly, is mistaken for a Character of *Humour;* which indeed is a Character of *Wit.* But there is a great Difference between a Comedy, wherein there are many things *Humorously,* as they call it, which is *Pleasantly* spoken; and one, where there are several Characters of *Humour,* distinguish'd by the Particular and Different Humours, appropriated to the several Persons represented, and which naturally arise, from the different Constitutions, Complexions, and Dispositions of Men. The saying of Humorous Things, does not distinguish Characters; For every Person in a Comedy may be allow'd to speak them. From a Witty Man they are expected; and even a *Fool* may be permitted to stumble on them by chance. Thô I make a Difference betwixt *Wit* and *Humour;* yet I do not think that Humorous Characters exclude Wit: No, but the Manner of *Wit* should be adapted to the *Humour.* As for Instance, a Character of a Splenetick and Peevish *Humour,* should have a Satyrical Wit. A Jolly and Sanguine *Humour,* should have a Facetious Wit. The Former should speak Positively; the Latter, Carelessly: For the former Observes, and shews things as they are; the latter, rather overlooks Nature, and speaks things as he would have them; and his *Wit* and *Humour* have both of them a less Alloy of Judgment than the others.

As *Wit,* so, its opposite, *Folly, is sometimes mistaken for Humour.*

When a Poet brings a *Character* on the Stage, committing a thousand Absurdities, and talking Impertinencies, roaring Aloud, and Laughing immoderately, on every, or rather upon no occasion; this is a Character of Humour.

Is any thing more common, than to have a pretended Comedy, stuff'd with such Grotesques, Figures, and Farce Fools? Things, that either are not in Nature, or if they are, are Monsters, and Births of Mischance; and consequently as such, should be stifled, and huddled out of the way, like *Sooterkins;* that Mankind may not be shock'd with an appearing Possibility of the Degeneration of a God-like *Species.* For my part, I am as willing to Laugh, as any body, and as easily diverted with an Object truly ridiculous: but at the same time, I can never care for seeing things, that force me to entertain low thoughts of my Nature. I dont know how it is with others, but I confess freely to you, I could never look long upon a Monkey, without very Mortifying Reflections; thô I never heard any thing to the Contrary, why that Creature is not Originally of a Distinct *Species.* As I dont think *Humour* exclusive of *Wit,* neither do I think it inconsistent with *Folly;* but I think the Follies should be only such,

as Mens Humours may incline them to; and not Follies intirely
abstracted from both Humour and Nature.

Sometimes, *Personal Defects are misrepresented for Humours.*

I mean, sometimes Characters are barbarously exposed on the
Stage, ridiculing Natural Deformities, Casual Defects in the Senses,
and Infirmities of Age. Sure the Poet must both be very Ill-natur'd
himself, and think his Audience so, when he proposes by shewing a
Man Deform'd, or Deaf, or Blind, to give them an agreeable Entertainment; and hopes to raise their Mirth, by what is truly an
object of Compassion. But much need not be said upon this Head to
any body, especially to you, who in one of your Letters to me concerning Mr. *Johnson*'s *Fox*, have justly excepted against this Im-
moral part of *Ridicule* in *Corbaccio's* Character; and there I must
agree with you to blame him, whom otherwise I cannot enough admire, for his great Mastery of true Humour in Comedy.

External Habit of Body is often mistaken for Humour.

By *External Habit*, I do not mean the Ridiculous Dress or
Cloathing of a Character, thô that goes a good way in some received
Characters. (But undoubtedly a Man's Humour may incline him
to dress differently from other People) But I mean a Singularity of
Manners, Speech, and Behaviour, peculiar to all, or most of the same
Country, Trade, Profession, or Education. I cannot think, that a
Humour, which is only a Habit, or Disposition contracted by Use
or Custom; for by a Disuse, or Complyance with other Customs, it
may be worn off, or diversify'd.

Affectation is generally mistaken for Humour.

These are indeed so much alike, that at a Distance, they may
be mistaken one for the other. For what is *Humour* in one, may be
Affectation in another; and nothing is more common, than for some
to affect particular ways of saying, and doing things, peculiar to
others, whom they admire and would imitate. *Humour* is the Life,
Affectation the Picture. He that draws a Character of *Affectation*,
shews *Humour* at the Second Hand; he at best but publishes a Translation, and his Pictures are but Copies.

But as these two last distinctions are the Nicest, so it may be
most proper to Explain them, by Particular Instances from some

Author of Reputation. *Humour* I take, either to be born with us, and so of a Natural Growth; or else to be grafted into us, by some accidental change in the Constitution, or revolution of the Internal Habit of Body; by which it becomes, if I may so call it, Naturaliz'd.

Humour is from Nature, *Habit* from Custom; and *Affectation* from Industry.

Humour, shews us as we *are.*

Habit, shews us, as we appear, under a forcible Impression.

Affectation, shews what we would be, under a Voluntary Disguise.

Thô here I would observe by the way, that a continued Affectation, may in time become a Habit.

The Character of *Morose* in the *Silent Woman,* I take to be a Character of Humour. And I choose to Instance this Character to you, from many others of the same Author, because I know it has been Condemn'd by many as Unnatural and Farce: And you have your self hinted some dislike of it,[3] for the same Reason, in a Letter to me, concerning some of *Johnson*'s Plays.

Let us suppose *Morose* to be a Man Naturally Splenetick and Melancholly; is there any thing more offensive to one of such a Disposition, than Noise and Clamour? Let any Man that has the Spleen (and there are enough in *England*) be Judge. We see common Examples of this Humour in little every day. 'Tis ten to one, but three parts in four of the Company that you dine with, are Discompos'd and Startled at the Cutting of a Cork, or Scratching a Plate with a Knife: It is a Proportion of the same Humour, that makes such or any other Noise offensive to the Person that hears it; for there are others who will not be disturb'd at all by it. Well; But *Morose* you will say, is so Extravagant, he cannot bear any Discourse or Conversation, above a Whisper. Why, It is his excess of this Humour, that makes him become Ridiculous, and qualifies his Character for Comedy. If the Poet had given him, but a Moderate proportion of that Humour, 'tis odds but half the Audience, would have sided with the Character, and have Condemn'd the Author, for Exposing a Humour which was neither Remarkable nor Ridiculous. Besides, the distance of the Stage requires the Figure

represented, to be something larger than the Life; and sure a Pic-
ture may have Features larger in Proportion, and yet be very like
the Original. If this Exactness of Quantity, were to be observed in
Wit, as some would have it in Humour; what would become of
those Characters that are design'd for Men of Wit? I believe if a
Poet should steal a Dialogue of any length, from the *Extempore*
Discourse of the two Wittiest Men upon Earth, he would find the
Scene but coldly receiv'd by the Town. But to the purpose.

The Character of Sir *John Daw* in the same Play, is a Character of Affectation. He every where discovers an Affectation of Learning; when he is not only Conscious to himself, but the Audience
also plainly perceives that he is Ignorant. Of this kind are the Characters of *Thraso* in the Eunuch of *Terence,* and *Pyrgopolinices* in
the *Miles Gloriosus* of *Plautus.* They affect to be thought Valiant,
when both themselves and the Audience know they are not. Now
such a boasting of Valour in Men who were really Valiant, would
undoubtedly be a *Humour;* for a Fiery Disposition might naturally
throw a Man into the same Extravagance, which is only affected in
the Characters I have mentioned.

The Character of *Cob* in *Every Man in his Humour,* and most
of the under Characters in *Bartholomew-Fair,* discover only a Singularity of Manners, appropriated to the several Educations and Professions of the Persons represented. They are not Humours but
Habits contracted by Custom. Under this Head may be ranged all
Country Clowns, Sailers, Tradesmen, Jockeys, Gamesters and such
like, who make use of *Cants* or peculiar *Dialects* in their several
Arts and Vocations. One may almost give a Receipt for the Composition of such a Character: For the Poet has nothing to do, but to
collect a few proper Phrases and terms of Art, and to make the
Person apply them by ridiculous Metaphors in his Conversation,
with Characters of different Natures. Some late Characters of this
kind have been very successful; but in my mind they may be Painted
without much Art or Labour; since they require little more, than a
good Memory and Superficial Observation. But true *Humour* cannot be shewn, without a Dissection of Nature, and a Narrow Search,
to discover the first Seeds, from whence it has its Root and growth.

If I were to write to the World, I should be obliged to dwell longer, upon each of these Distinctions and Examples; for I know that they would not be plain enough to all Readers. But a bare hint is sufficient to inform you of the Notions which I have on this Subject: And I hope by this time you are of my Opinion, that Humour is neither Wit, nor Folly, nor Personal defect; nor Affectation, nor Habit; and yet, that each, and all of these, have been both written and received for Humour.

I should be unwilling to venture even on a bare Description of Humour, much more, to make a Definition of it, but now my hand is in, Ile tell you what serves me instead of either. I take it to be, *A singular and unavoidable manner of doing, or saying any thing, Peculiar and Natural to one Man only; by which his Speech and Actions are distinguish'd from those of other Men.*[4]

Our *Humour* has relation to us, and to what proceeds from us, as the Accidents have to a Substance; it is a Colour, Taste, and Smell, Diffused through all; thô our Actions are never so many, and different in Form, they are all Splinters of the same Wood, and have Naturally one Complexion; which thô it may be disguised by Art, yet cannot be wholly changed: We may Paint it with other Colours, but we cannot change the Grain. So the Natural sound of an Instrument will be distinguish'd, thô the Notes expressed by it, are never so various, and the Divisions never so many. Dissimulation, may by Degrees, become more easy to our practice; but it can never absolutely Transubstantiate us into what we would seem: It will always be in some proportion a Violence upon Nature.

A Man may change his Opinion, but I believe he will find it a Difficulty, to part with his *Humour,* and there is nothing more provoking, than the being made sensible of that difficulty. Sometimes, one shall meet with those, who perhaps, Innocently enough, but at the same time impertinently, will ask the Question; *Why are you not Merry? Why are you not Gay, Pleasant, and Cheerful?* then instead of answering, could I ask such one; *Why are you not handsome? Why have you not Black Eyes, and a better Complexion?* Nature abhors to be forced.

The two Famous Philosophers of *Ephesus* and *Abdera,*[5] have their different Sects at this day. Some Weep, and others Laugh at one and the same thing.

I dont doubt, but you have observed several Men Laugh when they are Angry; others who are Silent; some that are Loud: Yet I cannot suppose that it is the passion of *Anger* which is in it self different, or more or less in one than t'other; but that it is the *Humour* of the Man that is Predominant, and urges him to express it in that manner. Demonstrations of pleasure are as Various; one Man has a Humour of retiring from all Company, when any thing has happen'd to please him beyond expectation; he hugs himself alone, and thinks it an Addition to the pleasure to keep it Secret. Another is upon Thorns till he has made Proclamation of it; and must make other people sensible of his happiness, before he can be so himself. So it is in Grief, and other Passions. Demonstrations of Love and the Effects of that Passion upon several Humours, are infinitely different; but here the Ladies who abound in Servants are the best Judges. Talking of the Ladies, methinks something should be observed of the Humour of the Fair Sex; since they are sometimes so kind as to furnish out a Character for Comedy. But I must confess I have never made any observation of what I Apprehend to be true Humour in Women. Perhaps Passions are too powerful in that Sex, to let Humour have its Course; or may be by Reason of their Natural Coldness, Humour cannot Exert it self to that extravagant Degree, which it often does in the Male Sex. For if ever any thing does appear Comical or Ridiculous in a Woman, I think it is little more than an acquir'd Folly, or an Affectation. We may call them the weaker Sex, but I think the true Reason is, because our Follies are Stronger, and our Faults are more prevailing.

One might think that the Diversity of Humour, which must be allowed to be diffused throughout Mankind, might afford endless matter, for the support of Comedies. But when we come closely to consider that point, and nicely to distinguish the Difference of Humours, I believe we shall find the contrary. For thô we allow every Man something of his own, and a peculiar Humour; yet every Man has it not in quantity, to become Remarkable by it: Or, if many do become Remarkable by their Humours; yet all those Humours may not be Diverting. Nor is it only requisite to distinguish what Humour will be diverting, but also how much of it, what part of it to shew in Light, and what to cast in Shades; how to set it off by preparatory Scenes, and by opposing other humours to it in the same Scene. Thrô a wrong Judgment, sometimes, Mens Humours may be opposed when there is really no specific Difference between them; only a greater proportion of the same, in one than t'other; occasion'd by his having more Flegm, or Choller, or whatever the Constitution is, from whence their Humours derive their Source.

There is infinitely more to be said on this Subject; thô perhaps I have already said too much; but I have said it to a Friend, who I am sure will not expose it, if he does not approve of it. I believe the Subject is intirely new, and was never touch'd upon before; and if I would have any one to see this private Essay, it should be some one, who might be provoked by my Errors in it, to Publish a more Judicious Treatise on the Subject. Indeed I wish it were done, that the World being a little acquainted with the scarcity of true Humour, and the difficulty of finding and shewing it, might look a little more favourably on the Labours of them, who endeavour to search into Nature for it, and lay it open to the Publick View.

I dont say but that very entertaining and useful Characters, and proper for Comedy, may be drawn from Affectations, and those other Qualities, which I have endeavoured to distinguish from Humour: but I would not have such imposed on the World, for Humour, nor esteem'd of Equal value with it. It were perhaps, the Work of a long Life to make one Comedy true in all its Parts, and to give every Character in it a True and Distinct Humour. Therefore, every Poet must be beholding to other helps, to make out his Number of ridiculous Characters. But I think such a One deserves to be broke, who makes all false Musters; who does not shew one true Humour in a Comedy, but entertains his Audience to the end of the Play with every thing out of Nature.

I will make but one Observation to you more, and have done; and that is grounded upon an Observation of your own, and which I mention'd at the beginning of my Letter, *viz*, That there is more of Humour in our English Comick Writers than in any others. I do not at all wonder at it, for I look upon Humour to be almost of English Growth; at least, it does not seem to have found such Encrease on any other Soil. And what appears to me to be the reason of it, is the great Freedom, Privilege, and Liberty which the Common People of *England* enjoy. Any Man that has a Humour, is under no restraint, or fear of giving it Vent; they have a Proverb among them, which, may be, will shew the Bent and Genius of the People, as well as a longer Discourse: *He that will have a May-pole, shall have a May-pole.* This is a Maxim with them, and their Practice is agreeable to it. I believe something Considerable too may be ascribed to their feeding so much on Flesh, and the Grossness of their Diet in general. But I have done, let the Physicians agree that. Thus you have my Thoughts of *Humour,* to my Power of Expressing them in so little Time and Compass. You will be kind to shew me wherein I have Err'd; and as you are very Capable of giving me Instruction, so, I think I have a very Just title to demand it from you; being without Reserve,

> *Your real Friend,*
> *and humble Servant,*
> *W. Congreve.*

EDITIONS: Dennis, pp. 80-96; *Familiar Letters,* Vol. I, pp. 152-163; *Memoirs,* Part II, pp. 41-57; *The Works of Mr. William Congreve,* 3 vols., Birmingham, 1761, Vol. III, pp. 495-514; Summers, Vol. III, pp. 161-168; Dobrée, *Comedies,* pp. 1-11; J. E. Spingarn, *Critical Essays of the Seventeenth Century,* 3 vols., Bloomington, Indiana University Press, 1957, Vol. III, pp. 242-252.

[1] This idea that the English are especially humorous could have been suggested by Ben Jonson in his Prologue to *The Alchemist* or by Sir William Temple in "Of Poetry," Spingarn, *Critical Essays of the Seventeenth Century,* 1957, Vol. III, p. 104.

[2] "Continued" in Dennis; "contain'd" in *Familiar Letters* and in *Memoirs;* "contained" in Birmingham ed. of 1761.

[3] See No. 109, where Dennis does much more than hint a dislike for the characterization of Morose. Congreve is more nearly in agreement with Dryden's opinion of Morose as expressed in his "Essay of Dramatic Poesy," ed. by W. P. Ker, *Essays of John Dryden,* Vol. I, pp. 83, 84.

[4] Cf. Dryden in "Essay of Dramatic Poesy," ed. by W. P. Ker, Vol. I, p. 85. ". . . by humour is meant some extravagant habit, passion, or affection, particular . . . to some one person, by the oddness of which, he is immediately distinguished from the rest of men. . . ." Congreve follows Dryden more closely than he does Jonson in the famous Preface to *Every Man Out of His Humour*.

[5] Heraclitus of Ephesus (*ca.* 540-475 B.C.), called the "Weeping Philosopher"; Democritus of Abdera (fifth century B.C.), called the "Laughing Philosopher."

III   JOHN DENNIS TO CONGREVE

London, August 8. 1695.

DEAR SIR,

Mr. *Moyle* [1] and I have impatiently expected to hear from you. But if the Well which you Drink of had sprung up from *Lethe*, you could not have been more forgetful of us. Indeed, as the *Tunbridge-Water* is good for the Spleen, it may be said in some manner to cause Oblivion. But I will yet a while hope that Mr. *Moyle* and I are not of the Number of things that plague you. However I am so sensible of your being mindful of me in Town, that I should be Ungrateful, if I should complain that you do not remember me where you are. Mr. *Moyle* tells me that you have made a Favourable mention of me, to a certain Lady of your Acquaintance, whom he calls ———— But then to mortifie the Old Man in me, or indeed rather the Young, he assur'd me, that you had given a much better Character of him. However, for that which you gave of me I cannot but own my self obliged to you, and I look upon your Kindness as so much the greater, because I am sensible that I do not deserve it. And I could almost wish that your good Qualities, were not quite so numerous, that I might be able to make you some Return *in specie*. For commending you now, I do you but Justice, which a Man of Honour will do to his Enemy; whereas you, by partial Praise, have treated me like a Friend. I make no doubt, but that you do me the Justice to believe that I am perfectly yours; and that your Merit has engag'd me, and your Favours oblig'd me to be all my Life time,

Dear Sir,
You[r] most Humble
Servant,
John Dennis.

EDITIONS: Dennis, pp. 97-98; *Familiar Letters*, Vol. I, pp. 164-165.

[1] Walter Moyle. See No. 114, note 1.

112   CONGREVE TO JOHN DENNIS

Tunbridge-Wells, August 11. 1695.

DEAR SIR,

It is not more to keep my Word, than to gratifie my Inclination, that I write to you; and thô I have thus long deferr'd it, I was never forgetful of you, nor of my Promise. Indeed I waited in Expectation of something that might enable me to return the Entertainment I received from your Letters: but you represent the Town so agreeable to me, that you quite put me out of Conceit with the Country; and my Designs of making Observations from it.

Before I came to *Tunbridge*, I proposed to my self the Satisfaction of Communicating the Pleasures of the Place to you: But if I keep my Resolution, I must transcribe, and return you your own Letters; since I must own I have met with nothing else so truly Delightful. When you suppose the Country agreeable to me, you suppose such Reasons why it should be so, that while I read your Letter, I am of your Mind; but when I look off, I find I am only Charm'd with the Landskip which you have drawn. So that if I would see a fine Prospect of the Country, I must desire you to send it me from the Town; as if I would eat good Fruit here, Perhaps the best way were, to beg a Basket from my Friends in *Covent-*

Garden. After all this, I must tell you, there is a great deal of Company at *Tunbridge;* and some very agreeable; but the greater part, is of that sort, who at home converse only with their own Relations; and consequently when they come abroad, have few Acquaintance, but such as they bring with them. But were the Company better, or worse, I would have you expect no Characters from me; for I profess my self an Enemy to Detraction; and who is there, that can justly merit Commendation? I have a mind to write to you, without the pretence of any manner of News, as I might drink to you without naming a Health; for I intend only my Service to you. I wish for you very often, that I might recommend you to some new Acquaintance that I have made here, and think very well worth the keeping; I mean Idleness and a good Stomach. You would not think how People Eat here; every Body has the Appetite of an *Oastrich,* and as they Drink Steel [1] in the Morning, so I believe at Noon they could digest Iron. But sure you will laugh at me for calling Idleness a New Acquaintance; when, to your Knowledge, the greatest part of my business, is little better. Ay, But here's the Comfort of the Change; I am Idle now, without taking pains to be so, or to make other People so; for Poetry is neither in my Head, nor in my Heart. I know not whether these Waters may have any Communication with *Lethe,* but sure I am, they have none with the Streams of *Helicon.* I have often wonder'd how those wicked Writers of Lampoons, could crowd together such quantities of Execrable Verses, tag'd with bad Rhimes, as I have formerly seen sent from this place: but I am half of Opinion now, that this Well is an *Anti-Hypocrene.* What if we should get a Quantity of the Water privately convey'd into the Cistern at *Will's* Coffee-House, for an Experiment? But I am Extravagant—Thô I remember *Ben. Johnson* in his Comedy of *Cynthia's* Revels, makes a Well, which he there calls the Fountain of Self-Love, to be the Source of many Entertaining and Ridiculous Humours. I am of Opinion, that something very Comical and New, might be brought upon the Stage, from a Fiction of the like Nature. But now I talk of the Stage, pray if any thing New should appear there, let me have an Account of it: for thô Plays are a kind of Winter-Fruit, yet I know there are now and then, some Windfalls at this time of Year, which must be presently served up, lest they should not keep till the proper Season of Entertainment. 'Tis now the time, when the Sun breeds Insects; and you must expect to have the Hum and Buz about your Ears, of Summer Flies and small Poets. Cuckows have this time allow'd them to Sing, thô they are damn'd to Silence all the rest of the Year. Besides, the approaching Feast of St. *Bartholomew*[2] both creates an Expectation and bespeaks an Allowance of unnatural Productions and Monstrous Births. Methinks the Days of *Bartholomew-Fair* are like so many Sabbaths, or Days of Privilege, wherein Criminals and Malefactors in Poetry, are permitted to Creep abroad. They put me in mind (thô at a different time of year) of the Roman *Saturnalia,* when all the Scum, and Rabble, and Slaves of *Rome,* by a kind of Annual and limited Manumission, were suffer'd to make Abominable Mirth, and Profane the Days of *Jubilee,* with Vile Buffoonry, by Authority. But I forget that I am writing a Post Letter, and run into length like a Poet in a Dedication, when he forgets his Patron to talk of himself. But I will take care to make no Apology for it, lest my Excuse (as Excuses generally do) should add to the Fault. Besides, I would have no appearance of Formality, when I am to tell you, that

I am,
Your real Friend,
and Humble Servant,
W. Congreve.

EDITIONS: Dennis, pp. 99-103; *Familiar Letters,* Vol. I, pp. 165-168; Summers, Vol. I, pp. 94-96; Dobrée, pp. 517-520.

[1] Tunbridge was known for its "steel-waters."

[2] August 24, the time for Bartholomew Fair, less than two weeks after the date of Congreve's letter.

113   JOHN DENNIS TO CONGREVE

[*August, 1695?*]

DEAR SIR.

My Business and my Thanks for your Kindness, you will find in
the enclos'd, which I had sent by the last Post, had not an Accident
hinder'd it. All the Return that I can make you at present is, to
acquaint you with such News as we have. Our Friend, Mr. ——
went last Friday to the *Bath.* He promis'd to write to me from that
place, but it would be unreasonable indeed to expect it. For W——
takes up his Afternoons, and his Mornings, I suppose, are spent in
Contemplation at the *Cross Bath.* Most of your Friends of the
Coffee-House are dispers'd; Some are retreated into the Country
in hopes of some Favours, which they expect from the *Muses:* Two
or Three of them are retir'd in Town to ruminate on some Favours,
which they have receiv'd from their Mistresses.

So that the *Coffee-House* is like to grow into Reputation again.
For if any one gives it the scandalous Denomination of the *Wits
Coffee-House,* he must call it so by Antiphrasis, because there comes
no Wit there. Here are two or three indeed, who set up for Wits
at home, and endeavour to pass for wise at the Coffee-House. For
they hold their Tongues there. Indeed the Coffee-House is generally the Exchange for Wit, where the Merchants meet without
bringing the Commodity with them, which they leave at home in
their Ware-houses, alias their Closets, while they go abroad to take
prudent care for the vending it. But you are of the number of those
happy few, who so abound in Hereditary Possessions and in rich returns from *Greece* and from *Italy,*[1] that you always carry some of
it about you to be liberal to your Friends of that which you sell to
Strangers. Mr. —— babbles eternally according to his old rate, and
as extravagantly as if he talk'd to himself, which he certainly does,
if no body minds him any more than I do. He has been just now
enquiring of me, what sort of Distemper the Spleen is; an infallible
sign that he is the only Man in *Covent-Garden,* who does not know
he is an Ass. To make him sensible what the Spleen is, I could find

in my heart to shew him himself and give it him. If any thing restrains me from being reveng'd of his Impertinence this way, 'tis the Consideration that it will make him wiser. This Coxcomb naturally puts me in mind of the Stage, where they have lately acted some new Plays; but had there been more of them, I would not scruple to affirm, that the Stage is at present a Desart and a barren place, as some part of *Africa* is said to be, though it abounds in Monsters. And yet those prodigious Things have met with Success. For a Fool is naturally fond of a Monster, because he is incapable of knowing a Man. While you drink Steel[2] for your Spleen at *Tunbridge,* I partake of the benefit of the Course. For the gaiety of your Letters relieves me considerably. Then what must your Conversation do? Come up and make the Experiment; and impart that Vigour to me which *Tunbridge* has restor'd to you.

> *I am your most humble*
> *Servant,*
> *John Dennis.*

EDITIONS: Dennis, unnumbered pages (eleventh-thirteenth) following p. 128; *Familiar Letters,* Vol. I, pp. 182-184.

[1] This compliment to Congreve on his classical learning is in keeping with Dryden's opinion (see No. 56), with Riccoboni's (see No. 145), and with the fine collection of Greek and Roman books listed in Congreve's Library. See *Library,* pp. 12-13.

[2] This reference to No. 112, dated 11 August 1695, indicates that No. 113 was a reply written probably during the last half of August, 1695.

114   WALTER MOYLE[1] TO CONGREVE

Bake in Cornwal   *October 7. 1695.*

DEAR SIR,

I Came home from the *Lands-End* Yesterday, where I found Three Letters from Mr. *Dennis,* and one from you with a humerous Description of *John Abassus,* since the dubbing of *Don Quixote;* and

A Country Poet.

the Coronation of *Petrarch* in the *Capitol,* there has not been so
great a Solemnity as the Consecration of *John Abassus.*[2] In all the
Pagan Ritual, I never met with the Form of Poetical Orders; but
I believe the Ceremony of Consecrating a Man to *Apollo,* is the
same with devoting a Man to the *Dii Manes,* for both are Martyrs
to Fame. I believe not a Man of the *Grave-Club*[3] durst assist at this
ridiculous Scene, for fear of laughing out-right. *W.* was in his Kingdom, and for my part I would rather sate there than in the House
of Commons. Would to God I could laugh with you for one hour
or two at all the ridiculous things that have happen'd at *Wills Coffee-
House* since I left it, 'tis the merriest place in the World. Like *Africa,*
every day it produces a Monster; and they are got there just as
Pliny says they are in *Africa,* Beasts of different kinds come to drink,
mingle with one another and beget Monsters. Present my humble
Duty to my new Lord,[4] and tell him, that I am preparing an Address to Congratulate his Accession to the Throne of the Rabble.
Tell the Lady who was the Author of the *Hue* and *Cry* after me,
she might have sent out a hundred *Hues* and *Crys* before she would
have found a Poet. I took an effectual Course not to be apprehended
for a Poet, for I went down clad like a Soldier, with a new Suit of
Cloaths on, and, I think, there could not have been a better Disguise
for a Poet, unless I had stol'n Dr. *B*[*lackmore*]'s[5] Coat. Mr. *Dennis*
sent me down *P*[*eter*] *M*[*otteux*'s][6] Parodie. I can say very little
of the *Poem,* but as for the *Dialogue,* I think, 'twas the first time
that *M*[*otteux*] suffered any body to talk with him, though indeed
here he interrupts Mr. *Boileau* in the midst of the first word. My
humble Service to Mr. *Wycherly,* I desire you would write me some
News of the Stage, and what Progress you have made in your
Tragedy.[7]

> *I am,*
> *Your affectionate Friend*
> *and Servant,*
> *W. Moyle.*

EDITIONS: Dennis, unnumbered pages (first-third) following p. 128; *Familiar
Letters,* Vol. I, pp. 179-180; *The Whole Works of Walter Moyle, Esq; That*

were Published by Himself, London, 1727, pp. 224-226. The text follows Dennis, but the place (*Bake* in *Cornwal*) and the signature (W. Moyle), both lacking in Dennis, are supplied from *The Whole Works*.

[1] Walter Moyle (1672-1721) was born at Bake in Cornwall. After two years at Oxford, he entered the Middle Temple about two months before Congreve. He was also closely associated with Congreve as one of the wits at Will's Coffee-house. Like Congreve, he was a zealous Whig and had gone down to his home in Cornwall to try for a seat in Parliament. See *DNB*.

[2] From *The Whole Works*, p. 224, a note on John Abassus: "A Nickname given to a stupid *Sussex* Squire, fond of Plays and Poems, who came up to Town, as he said, *to see the Poets of the Age*, and was by some of them introduced among the *Wits* of *Will's* Coffee-House in *Covent-Garden* among whom they admitted him, under the form of a Poetical *Consecration*, as a Member of their Society."

[3] The Grave Club and the Rabble (both mentioned in Congreve's reply to Moyle, No. 115) were two of the clubs that were flourishing at Will's Coffee-house in 1695.

[4] A note in *The Whole Works* (published 1727) identifies (p. 225) this lord as Halifax.

[5] Dr. Richard Blackmore (1654-1729), the physician, had published during the preceding spring his *Prince Arthur. An Heroick Poem. In Ten Books.* (See Albert Rosenberg, *Sir Richard Blackmore*, Lincoln, University of Nebraska Press, 1953, p. 23.) Evidently the Wits at Will's Coffee-house had accepted Dr. Blackmore's long, dry poem as proof that he was no poet. In 1728, Pope satirized Blackmore (then Sir Richard Blackmore since he had been knighted in 1697) in his *Dunciad*.

[6] The bracketed parts of No. 114, left blank by Dennis and *Familiar Letters*, were filled out by *The Whole Works*. Peter Anthony Motteux (1660-1718) was born at Rouen and came to England in 1685. As editor of *The Gentleman's Journal: Or The Monthly Miscellany* (1692-1694), he wrote enthusiastically of Congreve's *Old Bachelor*. Motteux was a dramatist, translator, and miscellaneous writer. The *Parodie* referred to was the *Ode De Mr. Boileau Despreaux Sur la Prise de Namur. Avec une Parodie de la Mesme Ode Et Une Parodie d'une Scene du Cid*. Evidently "the *Poem*" referred to the ode and "the *Dialogue*" to the scene from Corneille's *The Cid*.

[7] A note from *The Whole Works*, p. 226, identifies this tragedy as *The Mourning Bride*. The play was not acted until the spring of 1697. See No. 116 and Hodges, p. 58.

115   CONGREVE TO WALTER MOYLE

Wills Coffee-house, [*October*] [1] *13. 1695.*

DEAR SIR,

I Can't but think, that a Letter from me in *London,* to you in *Corn-wal* is like some ancient Correspondence between an Inhabitant of *Rome* and a *Cimmerian.* May be, my way of writing may not be so modestly compared with *Roman* Epistles; but the resemblance of the Place will justify the other part of the Parallel. The Sub-terraneous Habitations of the Miners, and the Proximity of the *Bajæ* help a little; and while you are at *Bake,* let *Bake* be *Cumæ,* and do you supply the Place of *Sybilla.* You may look on this as raillery, but I can assure you, nothing less than Oracles are expected from you, in the next Parliament, if you succeed in your Election,[2] as we are pretty well assured you will. You wish your self, with us at *Wills Coffee-house;* and all here wish for you, from the presi-dent of the Grave Club,[3] to the most puny Member of the Rabble; [3] they who can think, think of you, and the rest talk of you. There is no such Monster in this *Africa,* that is not sensible of your ab-sence; even the worst natured People, and those of least Wit la-ment it, I mean, Half Criticks and Quiblers. To tell you all that want you, I should name all the Creatures of *Covent-Garden,*[4] which like those of *Eden-garden* would want some *Adam* to be a Godfather and give them Names. I can't tell whether I may justly compare our *Covent-garden,* to that of *Eden,* or no; for tho' I be-lieve we may have variety of Strange Animals equal to *Paradise,* yet I fear we have not amongst us, the *Tree* of *Knowledge.* It had been much to the disadvantage of *Pliny,* had the *Coffee-house* been in his days; for sure he would have described some who frequent it; which would have given him, the reputation of a more fabu-lous Writer than he has now. But being in our Age it does him a Service, for we who know it, can give Faith to all his Monsters. You who took care to go down into the Country unlike a Poet, I hope will take care not to come again like a Politician; for then, you will add a new Monster to the *Coffee-house,* that was never seen there before. So you may come back again, in your Soldiers Coat, for in that you will no more be suspected for a Politician, than a Poet. Pray come upon any terms, for you are wished for by every body, but most wanted by your

Affectionate Friend

and Servant,

W. Congreve.

EDITIONS: Dennis, unnumbered pages (fourth-sixth) following p. 128; *Familiar Letters*, Vol. I, pp. 181-182; *The Whole Works of Walter Moyle, Esq; That were Published by Himself*, London, 1727, pp. 227-229; Summers, Vol. I, pp. 93-94; Dobrée, pp. 516-517. The text of No. 115 follows *The Whole Works*.

[1] Dennis gives "August"; *Familiar Letters* and *The Whole Works* omit the date; Dobrée gives "October," which is evidently correct since No. 115 is clearly an answer to No. 114 (as *The Whole Works* says it is).

[2] Moyle won the election and represented Saltash in Parliament from 1695 till 1698. See Luttrell for Saturday, 2 November 1695: "Members of parliament . . . : for Saltash, Mr. Moyle and Mr. Buller. . . ."

[3] See No. 114.

[4] The site of Will's Coffee-house.

116   CONGREVE TO PRINCESS ANNE [1]

[ca. *March 15, 1696/7*] [2]

MADAM,

That high Station, which by Your Birth You hold above the People, exacts from every one, as a Duty, whatever Honours they are capable of paying to Your Royal Highness: But that more exalted Place, to which Your Virtues have rais'd You, above the rest of Princes, makes the Tribute of our Admiration and Praise, rather a Choice more immediately preventing that Duty.

The Publick Gratitude is ever founded on a Publick Benefit; and what is universally Bless'd, is always an universal Blessing. Thus from Your self we derive the Offerings which we bring; and that

Incense which arises to Your Name, only returns to its Original, and but naturally requires [3] the Parent of its Being.

From hence it is that this Poem, constituted on a Moral, whose End is to recommend and to encourage Virtue,[4] of consequence has recourse to Your Royal Highness's Patronage; aspiring to cast it self beneath Your Feet, and declining Approbation, 'till You shall condescend to own it, and vouchsafe to shine upon it as on a Creature of Your Influence.

'Tis from the Example of Princes that Virtue becomes a Fashion in the People, for even they who are averse to Instruction, will yet be fond of Imitation.

But there are Multitudes, who never can have Means nor Opportunities of so near an Access, as to partake of the Benefit of such Examples. And to these, Tragedy, which distinguishes it self from the Vulgar Poetry by the Dignity of its Characters, may be of Use and Information. For they who are at that distance from Original Greatness, as to be depriv'd of the Happiness of Contemplating the Perfections and real Excellencies of Your Royal Highness's Person in Your Court, may yet behold some small Sketches and Imagings of the Virtues of Your Mind, abstracted, and represented on [5] the Theatre.

Thus Poets are instructed, and instruct; not alone by Precepts which persuade, but also by Examples which illustrate. Thus is Delight interwoven with Instruction; when not only Virtue is prescrib'd, but also represented.

But if we are delighted with the Liveliness of a feign'd Representation of Great and Good Persons and their Actions, how must we be charm'd with beholding the Persons themselves? If one or two excelling Qualities, barely touch'd in the single Action and small Compass of a Play, can warm an Audience, with a Concern and Regard even for the seeming Success and Prosperity of the Actor; with what Zeal must the Hearts of all be fill'd, for the continued and encreasing Happiness of those, who are the true and living Instances of Elevated and Persisting Virtue? Even the Vicious themselves must have a secret Veneration for those peculiar Graces and Endowments, which are daily so eminently conspicuous in Your

Royal Highness; and though repining, feel a Pleasure which in spite of Envy they per-force approve.

If in this Piece, humbly offer'd to Your Royal Highness, there shall appear the Resemblance of any one [6] of those many Excellencies which You so promiscuously possess, to be drawn so as to merit Your least Approbation, it has the End and Accomplishment of its Design. And however imperfect it may be in the Whole, through the Inexperience or Incapacity of the Author, yet, if there is so much as to convince Your Royal Highness, that a Play may be with Industry so dispos'd (in spight of the licentious Practice of the Modern Theatre) as to become sometimes an innocent, and not unprofitable Entertainment; it will abundantly gratifie the Ambition, and recompence the Endeavours of,

> *Your Royal Highness's*
> *Most Obedient, and*
> *Most humbly Devoted Servant, —*
> *William Congreve.*

EDITIONS: Dedication to *The Mourning Bride*, London, 1697; *Works* (1710), Vol. II, pp. 499-502; *Works* (1719), Vol. II, pp. 7-9; Summers, Vol. II, pp. 179-181; Dobrée, pp. 77-79. The text for No. 116 follows the *Works* (1710).

[1] Anne Stuart (1665-1714), second daughter of James II by his first wife, Anne Hyde; Queen of England, 1702-1714.

[2] Publication of *The Mourning Bride* was advertised in *The London Gazette* for 11-15 March 1696/7.

[3] "requires," 1710, 1719; "requites," 1697.

[4] Congreve's graceful dedication and his statement that he was writing to encourage virtue was possibly still remembered by Queen Anne when she appointed Vanbrugh and Congreve in 1704 as managers of the new theatre in the Haymarket "for the better reforming the Abuses, and Immorality of the Stage." See No. 70.

[5] "on," 1710, 1719; "in," 1697.

[6] "one," omitted in 1719.

II7   CATHARINE TROTTER [1] TO CONGREVE

[*March, 1697*]

Had heav'n bestow'd on me half Sappho's *flame,*
This noble theme had gain'd me larger fame;
For none can think great Congreve's *to extend,*
Or praising thee, ought but their own intend.
Boundless thy fame does on thy genius flow,
Which spread thus far, can now no limits know:
This only part was wanting to thy name,
That wit's whole empire thou mightst justly claim:
On which so many vain attempts were made,
Numbers pretending right their strength assay'd,
But all alike unfit for the command,
Only defac'd and spoil'd the sacred land;
Which thou, as its undoubted native lord,
Has to its ancient beauty thus restor'd;
Where with amazement we at once may see
Nature preserv'd pure, unconstrain'd, and free,
And yet throughout, each beauty, ev'ry part,
Drest to the strictest forms of gracing art:
Thus perfected, on such a finished piece,
When can my praise begin, or admiration cease!
Sublime thy thoughts, easy thy numbers flow,
Yet to comport with them, majestic too!
But to express how thou our souls do'st move,
How at thy will, we rage, we grieve, we love,
Requires a lofty, almost equal flight,
Nor dare I aim at such a dang'rous height,
A task, which well might Dryden's *muse engage,*
Worthy the first, best poet of the age;
Whose long retreat that we might less bemoan,
He left us thee, his greatest darling son,
Possessor of the stage, once his alone.
Tho' even he gain'd not thy height so soon,
And but the young great Macedonian, *none;*
Alike in youth you both sought early fame,
Both sure to vanquish too where'er you came;
But he by others aid his conquests gain'd,
By others too the fame of them remain'd;

> . *Thou sov'reign o'er the vast poetic land,*
> *Unaided, as unrival'd, do'st command,*
> *And not oblig'd for fame, which records give,*
> *In thy own works thou shalt for ever live.*

EDITION: *The Works of Mrs. Catharine Cockburn, Theological, Moral, Dramatic, and Poetical* . . . Revised and published, With an Account of the Life of the Author, By Thomas Birch, M.A.F.R.S., 2 vols., London, 1751, Vol. II, pp. 564-565. The poetic letter is entitled, "To Mr. *Congreve*, on his Tragedy, the *Mourning Bride*."

[1] Catharine Trotter (1679-1749), only eighteen years old when she wrote the lines to Congreve on *The Mourning Bride*, had already produced one successful tragedy. Sir Edmund Gosse thinks it probable (see "Catharine Trotter, the Precursor of the Bluestockings," *Transactions of the Royal Society of Literature*, Vol. XXXIV, 1916, p. 92) that she met Congreve through Bevil Higgons, who wrote commendatory verses published with Congreve's first comedy. When she was writing her fifth and last play in 1703, a tragedy entitled *The Revolution in Sweden*, she sent a first draft of it to Congreve and received from him a very helpful criticism (see No. 124). In 1708, she married the clergyman Patrick Cockburn.

118   CONGREVE TO CATHARINE TROTTER [1]

[*London?, ca. March 15, 1697*]

I can never enough acknowledge the honour you have done me, nor enough regret the negligence of those, to whom you delivered your valuable Letter. It is the first thing, that ever happened to me, upon which I should make it my choice to be vain. And yet such is the mortification, that attends even the most allowable vanity, that at the same instant I am robb'd of the means, when I am possessed with the inclination. It is but this moment, that I received your verses; and had scarce been transported with the reading them, when they brought me the play from the press printed off.[2] I hope you will do me the justice to believe, that I was not so insensible, as not to be hartily vexed; and all the satisfaction, that I can take, and all the sacrifice that I make to you, is only to stifle some verses on the same barren subject, which were printed with it, and now, I assure you, shall never appear, whatever apology I am forced to make to the authors. And since I am deprived of the recommendation you designed me, I will be obliged to no other, till I have some future opportunity of preferring yours to every body's else. In the mean time, give me leave to value myself upon the favour you have done me; and to assure you, it was not wanting to make me more ready, than I have been, in my inclinations of waiting on all your commands: and if Mr *Betterton's* [3] business does not very speedily disengage him, I will not wait for his being a witness of my professing myself, your

admirer,
and obliged humble servant,
W. Congreve.

I know not what time the princess will give me leave to present her with the play, it being dedicated to her; [4] but as soon as that form is over, I will make bold to send you one.

EDITIONS: *The Works of Mrs. Catharine Cockburn* . . . 1751, Vol. I, pp. vi-vii; Summers, Vol. I, p. 102; Dobrée, pp. 528-529.

[1] See No. 117.

[2] Evidently the play here referred to, *The Mourning Bride*, was then being printed but still only in proof since Congreve goes on to say that he is stifling "some verses" already printed. No verses appeared with the play as it was published.

[3] Apparently Congreve was planning to go with Thomas Betterton, who had just acted the leading part in *The Mourning Bride*, to wait on Catharine Trotter.

[4] For Congreve's dedication of *The Mourning Bride* to Princess Anne, see No. 116.

119   CHARLES HOPKINS [1] TO CONGREVE

[ca. *November, 1697*]

Let other Poets other Patrons Chuse,
Get their best Price, and prostitute their Muse
With flattering hopes, and fruitless labour wait,
And Court the slippery Friendship of the Great:
Some trifling Present by my Lord is made,
And then the Patron thinks the Poet paid.
On you, my surer, nobler Hopes depend,
For you are all I wish; you are a Friend.
From you, my Muse her Inspiration drew,
All she performs, I Consecrate to you.
You taught me first my Genius and my Power,
Taught me to know my own, but gave me more,
Others may sparingly their Wealth impart,
But he gives Noblest, who bestows an Art.
Nature, and you alone, can that confer,
And I owe you, what you your self owe her.
O! Congreve, *could I write in Verse like thine,*
Then in each Page, in every Charming Line,
Should Gratitude, and Sacred Friendship shine.
Your Lines run all on easie, even Feet;
Clear is your Sense, and your Expression sweet.
Rich is your Fancy, and your Numbers go
Serene and smooth, as Crystal Waters flow.
Smooth as a peaceful Sea, which never rolls,
And soft, as kind, consenting Virgins Souls.
Nor does your Verse alone our Passions move,
Beyond the Poet, we the Person Love.
In you, and almost only you; we find
Sublimity of Wit, and Candour of the Mind.
Both have their Charms, and both give that delight,
'Tis pity that you should, or should not Write;
But your strong Genius Fortune's power defies,
And in despight of Poetry, you rise.
To you the Favour of the World is shown,
Enough for any Merit, but your own.
Your Fortune rises equal with your Fame,
The Best of Poets, but above the Name.

O! may you never miss deserv'd success,
But raise your Fortunes 'till I wish them less.

Here should I, not to tire your patience, end,
But who can part so soon, with such a Friend
You know my Soul, like yours, without design,
You know me yours, and I too know you mine.
I owe you all I am, and needs must mourn,
My want of Power to make you some return.
Since you gave all, do not a part refuse,
But take this slender Offering of the Muse.
Friendship, from servile Interest free, secures
My Love, sincerely, and entirely, yours,
                                        Charles Hopkins.

EDITION: Dedication to *Boadicea, Queen of Britain. A. Tragedy, As it is Acted by His Majesty's Servants at the Theatre in Lincolns-Inn-fields. Written by Mr. Charles Hopkins,* London, 1697.

[1] Charles Hopkins (1664?-1700?) was, like Congreve, taken by his father (later Bishop of Derry) to Ireland and educated partly at Trinity College, Dublin. Congreve wrote the prologue for his first play, acted in 1695, and Hopkins in turn dedicated his next play, *Boadicea, Queen of Britain,* to Congreve. A copy of the *Boadicea* was item No. 51 in Congreve's library.

120   JOSEPH ADDISON[1] TO CONGREVE

Paris August 1699

DEAR SIR

You must excuse me if I take the Liberty to trouble you with a Long Letter for to tell you truly I have at present a need to Speak English and meet with so very few here that understand it that I find it some ease to converse with a countryman tho at this Distance.

Since I had the happiness to see you last I have encountered as many misfortunes as a Knight-Errant. I had a fall into the water at Callice and since that several Bruises upon the Land, lame post-horses by Day and hard Beds at night with many other dismal Adventures.

> *Quamquam animus meminisse horret luctuque refugit.*[2]

My arrival at Paris was at first no less uncomfortable where I could not see a face nor hear a Word that I ever met with before: so that my most agreeable companions have bin statues and Pictures which are many of them very extraordinary but what particularly recommends them to me is that they dont Speak French and have a very good quality, rarely to be met with in this Country of not being too Talkative.

I cou'd have wisht for your company last night at the Opera where you would have seen paint enough on the actors Faces to have Dawbed a whole street of sign-posts. Every man that comes upon the Stage is a Beau: the Shepherds are all Embroiderd, Pluto has his Valet de chambre, and a couple of Riders appears in Red Stockins. Alpheus throws aside his Sedge and makes Love in a Fair periwig and a plume of Feathers but with such a horrid voice that [one] woud think the murmurs of a Country-Brook much better music. It is as ridiculous to criticise an opera as a puppet-show or I could send you over a Long Catalogue of the like Indecencys: but since I have mention'd Musick I can't forbear telling you that Corelli[3] has a very mean opinion of Harry Purcell's[4] works as a gentleman told me that presented them to him, which I suppose Will be no Small Mortification to You Tramontane composers. I am etc

MANUSCRIPT: *Addison's Letter Book* (some thirty letters copied by Addison), also called *Tickell Letter Book,* owned by the Tickell Family. EDITIONS: *The Guardian,* No. 101, July 7, 1713 (in part); *The Letters of Joseph Addison,* ed. by Walter Graham, Oxford, 1941, pp. 3-4. The text for Nos. 120, 121, 123 follows Graham's edition of Addison's holograph copy of the letters to Congreve but marks the paragraphs in Nos. 120, 121 as in *The Guardian.* The *Letter Book* puts each of the letters in a single paragraph.

[1] Addison was traveling on the Continent in 1699 to fit himself for the diplomatic service. With this in mind, Charles Montagu (later Lord Halifax) had induced Addison to give up his plans to enter the Church and to accept a yearly pension of £300 to make possible his foreign travel. Addison was still on the

Continent as late as 1 July 1703, when Congreve (No. 69) asked Tonson, in Amsterdam, to give "my humble service to Mr: Addison." See also No. 28.

[2] Virgil's *Aeneid*, Vol. II, p. 12, translated by W. Glynn Williams: ". . . though my mind shudders to remember, and has recoiled in grief . . ."

[3] Arcangelo Corelli (1653-1731), the famous Italian violinist and composer.

[4] Henry Purcell (1659-1695), the great English composer, wrote music for operas and for incidental songs in many plays, including Congreve's.

121   JOSEPH ADDISON TO CONGREVE

Blois.[1] *December 1699.*

DEAR SIR

I was very Sorry to hear in your Last Letter that you were so terribly afflicted with the gout tho For your comfort I believe you are the first English poet that has been complemented with the Distemper: I was myself at that time sick of a Feaver which I believe proceeded From the same Cause; But at present I am so well Recoverd that I can Scarce Forbear beginning my Letter with Tully's preface

Si vales Bene est Ego quidem Valeo.[2]

You must excuse me for giving you a Line of Latin now and then since I find my self in some danger of Losing the Tongue, for I perceive a new Language, like a New Mistress, is apt to make a man forget all his old ones. I assure you I met with a very Remarkable Instance of this Nature at Paris, in a poor Irish-man that had lost the little English he brought over with him without being able to learn any French in its stead. I askt him what Language he spoke, he very innocently answer'd me no Language Monsieur: which as I afterwards found were all the words he was Master of in both Tongues. I am at present in a Town where all the Languages of Europe are spoken except English, which is not to be heard I believe within fifty miles of the place. My greatest diversion is to run over in my Thoughts the Variety of noble scenes I was entertain'd with before I came hither.

I dont believe, as good a poet as you are, that you can make finer landskips than those about the Kings houses or with all your descriptions build a more magnificent palace than Versailles. I am however so singular as to prefer Fontaine-bleau to all the rest. It is situated among rocks and woods that give you a fine varietie of Savage prospects. The King has Humourd the Genius of the place and only made use of so much Art as is necessary to Help and regulate Nature without reforming her too much. The Cascades seem to break through the Clefts and cracks of Rocks that are cover'd over with Moss and look as if they were pil'd upon one another by Accident. There is an Artificial Wildness in the Meadows Walks and Canals and the Garden instead of a Wall is Fenc'd on the Lower End by a Natural mound of Rock-work that strikes the Eye very Agreeably. For my part I think there is something more charming in these rude heaps of Stone than in so many Statues and woud as soon see a River winding through Woods and Meadows as it dos near Fountain-bleau than as when it is toss'd up in such a Variety of figures at Versailles. But I begin to talk like Dr Lister.[3] To pass from Works of Nature to those of Art. In my opinion the pleasantest part of Versailles is the Gallery. Evry one sees on each side of it something that will be sure to please him, for one of them commands a View of the finest Garden in the World and the other is wainscoted with Looking-Glass. The History of the present King till the year 16— is painted on the Roof by LeBrun,[4] so that his Majesty has now Actions enough by him to Furnish another Gallery much Larger than the first.

He is represented with all the Terrour and Majesty that you can Imagine in ev'ry part of the picture and sees his Young face as perfectly drawn in the Roof as his present one in the Side. I believe by this time you are affraid I shall carry you from room to room and lead you through the whole palace and truly if I had not tir'd you already I coud not Forbear Showing you a Stair-case that they say is the noblest in its kind; but after so tedious a letter I shall conclude with a petition to you that you woud deliver the enclos'd to Mr Montague,[5] for I am affraid of interrupting him with my Impertinence when he is Engaged in more serious Affairs.

Tu faciles aditus et mollia tempora noris,[6]

I am, etc.

The painter has represented His Most Christian Majesty under the Figure of Jupiter throwing thunderbolts all about the Ceiling, and Striking terror into the Danube and Rhine that lie astonished and blasted with Lightning a little above the cornice.

MANUSCRIPT: *Addison's Letter Book.* EDITIONS: *The Guardian*, No. 101, 7 July 1713 (in part); *Life of Joseph Addison*, by Lucy Aikin, 2 vols., London, 1843, Vol. I, pp. 76-79; *Works*, ed. by Richard Hurd, 6 vols., London, 1856, Vol. V, pp. 326-327; *Letters*, ed. by Walter Graham, Oxford, 1941, pp. 10-12.

[1] Although Addison is now at Blois, a hundred miles south of Paris, he is still writing chiefly about what he had seen in the vicinity of the French capital.

[2] Cicero often began his letters with the first four of these Latin words, "If you are well, all is right." In the full quotation of seven words, less commonly used by Cicero, Addison adds, "I too am well." See No. 42 for Congreve's use of the same quotation.

[3] Dr. Martin Lister (1638?-1712), the zoologist, had published his very popular *Journey to Paris* in 1698.

[4] Charles LeBrun (1619-1690), the French historical painter, had worked for eighteen years on the decorations of the palace at Versailles.

[5] Addison's patron, Charles Montagu. See No. 120, note 1.

[6] Professor Walter Graham thinks Addison had in mind Virgil's *Aeneid*, Vol. IV, p. 423, "*sola viri mollis aditus et tempora noras*" ("alone thou knowest the hour for easy access to him"—H. Rushton Fairclough).

122   CONGREVE TO RALPH MONTAGU,[1] FIRST EARL OF MONTAGU

[*March, 1700*]

MY LORD,

Whether the World will arraign me of Vanity, or not, that I have presum'd to Dedicate this Comedy to Your Lordship, I am yet in Doubt: Tho' it may be it is some degree of Vanity even to doubt of it. One who has at any time had the Honour of Your Lordship's Conversation, cannot be suppos'd to think very meanly of that which he wou'd prefer to Your Perusal: Yet it were to incur the Imputation of too much Sufficiency, to pretend to such a Merit as might abide the Test of Your Lordship's Censure.

Whatever Value may be wanting to this Play while yet it is mine, will be sufficiently made up to it, when it is once become Your Lordship's; and it is my Security, that I cannot have over-rated it more by my Dedication, than Your Lordship will dignifie it by Your Patronage.

That it succeeded on the Stage, was almost beyond my Expectation; for but little of it was prepar'd for that general Taste which seems now to be predominant in the Pallats of our Audience.

Those Characters which are meant to be ridicul'd[2] in most of our Comedies, are of Fools so gross, that in my humble Opinion, they shou'd rather disturb than divert the well-natur'd and reflecting Part of an Audience; they are rather Objects of Charity than Contempt; and instead of moving our Mirth, they ought very often to excite our Compassion.

This Reflection mov'd me to design some Characters, which shou'd appear ridiculous not so much thro' a natural Folly (which is incorrigible, and therefore not proper for the Stage) as thro' an affected Wit; a Wit, which at the same time that it is affected, is also false. As there is some Difficulty in the Formation of a Character of this Nature, so there is some Hazard which attends the Progress of its Success, upon the Stage: For many come to a Play, so over-charg'd with Criticism, that they very often let fly their Censure, when thro' their Rashness they have mistaken their Aim. This I had Occasion lately to observe: For this Play had been acted two or three Days, before some of these hasty Judges cou'd find the leisure to distinguish betwixt the Character of a *Witwoud* and a *Truewit.*

I must beg Your Lordship's Pardon for this Digression from the true Course of this Epistle; but that it may not seem altogether impertinent, I beg, that I may plead the Occasion of it, in part of that Excuse of which I stand in need, for recommending this Comedy to Your Protection. It is only by the Countenance of Your Lordship, and the *Few* so qualify'd, that such who write with Care and Pains can hope to be distinguish'd: For the Prostituted Name of *Poet* promiscuously levels all that bear it.

Terence,[3] the most correct Writer in the World, had a *Scipio* and a *Lelius*, if not to assist him, at least to support him in his Reputation: And notwithstanding his extraordinary Merit, it may be, their Countenance was not more than necessary.

The Purity of his Stile, the Delicacy of his Turns, and the Justness of his Characters, were all of them Beauties, which the greater Part of his Audience were incapable of Tasting: Some of the coursest Strokes of *Plautus*, so severely censur'd by *Horace*, were more likely to affect the Multitude; such, who come with expectation to laugh at[4] the last Act of a Play, and are better entertain'd with two or three unseasonable Jests, than with the artful Solution of the *Fable.*

As *Terence* excell'd in his Performances, so had he great Advantages to encourage his Undertakings; for he built most on the Foundations of *Menander:* His Plots were generally modell'd, and his Characters ready drawn to his Hand. He copied *Menander;* and *Menander* had no less Light in the Formation of his Characters, from the Observations of *Theophrastus*, of whom he was a Disciple; and *Theophrastus* it is known was not only the Disciple, but the immediate Successor of *Aristotle*, the first and greatest Judge of Poetry. These were great Models to design by; and the further Advantage which *Terence* possess'd, towards giving his Plays the due Ornaments of Purity of Stile, and Justness of Manners, was not less considerable, from the Freedom of Conversation, which was permitted him with *Lelius* and *Scipio*, two of the greatest and most polite Men of his Age. And indeed, the Privilege of such a Conversation, is the only certain Means of attaining to the Perfection of Dialogue.

If it has happen'd [5] in any Part of this Comedy, that I have gain'd a Turn of Stile, or Expression more Correct, or at least more Corrigible than in those which I have formerly written, I must, with equal Pride and Gratitude, ascribe it to the Honour of Your Lordship's admitting me into Your Conversation, and that of a Society where every body else was so well worthy of You, in Your Retirement last Summer from the Town: For it was immediately after, that this Comedy was written. If I have fail'd in my Performance, it is only to be regretted, where there were so many, not inferior either to a *Scipio* or a *Lelius*, that there shou'd be one wanting, equal in Capacity to [6] a *Terence*.

If I am not mistaken, Poetry is almost the only Art, which has not yet laid Claim to your Lordship's Patronage. Architecture, and Painting, to the great Honour of our Country, have flourish'd under Your Influence and Protection. In the mean time, Poetry, the eldest Sister of all Arts, and Parent of most, seems to have resign'd her Birth-right, by having neglected to pay her Duty to Your Lordship; and by permitting others of a later Extraction, to prepossess that Place in Your Esteem, to which none can pretend a better Title. Poetry, in its Nature, is sacred to the Good and Great; the Relation between them is reciprocal, and they are ever propitious to it. It is the Privilege of Poetry to address to them, and it is their Prerogative alone to give it Protection.

This receiv'd Maxim is a general Apology for all Writers who Consecrate their Labours to great Men: But I could wish, at this time, that this Address were exempted from the common Pretence of all Dedications; and that as I can distinguish Your Lordship even among the most Deserving, so this Offering might become remarkable by some particular Instance of Respect, which should assure Your Lordship, that I am, with all due Sense of Your extream Worthiness and Humanity,

My LORD,
Your Lordship's most Obedient
and most Oblig'd Humble Servant,
Will. Congreve.

EDITIONS: Dedication to *The Way of the World*, London, 1700; *Works* (1710), Vol. II, pp. 605-611; *Works* (1719), Vol. II, pp. 99-103; Summers, Vol. III, pp. 9-11; Dobrée, *Comedies*, pp. 336-339. The text for No. 122 follows the *Works* (1710).

¹ Ralph Montagu (1638?-1709) succeeded his father as third Baron Montagu in 1684. He was created Earl of Montagu in 1689 and Duke of Montagu in 1705.

² "ridicul'd," 1710, 1719; "ridiculous," 1700.

³ Congreve had a special interest in Terence. By 1700, if we may judge by the publication dates in his books, he already had in his library a folio edition of the six comedies, Paris, 1642, and an English translation, London, 1694. In 1701, he added the fine large-paper quarto edition published by subscription at Cambridge; then in 1706 the three-volume French translation by Madame Dacier; and finally, in 1713, an edition published by Jacob Tonson. See *Library*, Nos. 191, 592, 593, 594, 595.

⁴ "at," 1710, 1719; "out," 1700.

⁵ "happen'd," 1710, 1719; "hapned," 1700.

⁶ "to," 1710, 1719; "of," 1700.

123   JOSEPH ADDISON TO CONGREVE

[Switzerland, Sunday, August 1, 1702]

DEAR SIR

I believe this is the first letter that was ever sent you from the middle Region where I am at this present writing. Not to keep you in suspense it comes to you from the top of the highest mountain in Switzerland where I am now shivering among the Eternal frosts and snows. I can scarce forbear dating it in December tho they call it the first of August at the bottome of the hill. I assure you I can hardly keep my Ink from Freezing in the middle of the Dog-days. I am here entertained with the prettiest variety of snow-prospects that you can Imagine, and have several pits of it before me that are very near as old as the mountain it-self: for in this country 'tis as hard and as lasting as marble. I am now upon a Spot of it that must have falln about the Reign of Charlemain or King Peppin. The Inhabitants of the country are as great Curiosities as the country it-self. They generally hire themselves out in their youth, and if they are musquet-proof till about Fifty, they bring home the money they have got and the Limbs they have left to pass the rest of their time among their Native mountains. One of the gentlemen of the place, that is come off with the Loss of an Eye only, told me by way of Boast that there were now seavn wooden Legs in his Family, and that for these four generations there had not bin one in his line that carryd a whole Body with him to the grave. I believe you will think the stile of this Letter a little extraordinary, but the Rehersal will tell you that people in clouds must not be confined to Speak sense [1] and I hope we that are above them may claim the same privilege.

Where'er I am I shall always be
Dear Sir
Your etc.

MANUSCRIPT: *Addisons Letter Book.* EDITIONS: *The Tatler*, No. 93, 12 November 1709; *The Letters of Joseph Addison*, ed. by Walter Graham, London, 1941, pp. 34-35.

[1] The reference is to *The Rehearsal*, Act V, Scene 1 (pp. 47-48 of the Fifth Edition, London, 1687, which Congreve had in his library, item No. 406), to the following passage:

> *Smith.* Well, but methinks the Sense of this Song is not very plain.
> *Bayes.* Plain? why did you ever hear any People in Clouds speak plain? They must be all for flight of Fancy, at its full Range, without the least Check, or Controul upon it. When once you tie up Spirits, and People in Clouds to speak plain, you spoil all.

124   CONGREVE TO CATHARINE TROTTER [1]

London November 2, 1703.

MADAM,

I had sooner acknowledged the favour of your letter, together with
the agreeable entertainment of the scheme you were pleased to send
with it, if I had not been unavoidably engaged in business. But at
this time I can hardly complain of a great cold, which has confined
me, and given me an opportunity to obey your commands. I think
the design in general very great and noble; the conduct of it very
artful, if not too full of business, which may either run into length
or obscurity; but both those, as you write, you have skill enough to
avoid. You are the best judge, whether those of your own sex will
approve as much of the heroic virtue of *Constantia* and *Christina*,
as if they had been engaged in some *belle passion:* for my part, I
like them better as they are. In the second act, I would have that
noise, which generally attends so much fighting on the stage, provided against; for those frequent alarms and excursions do too much
disturb an audience. The difficulty in the third act is as well solved
by you as possible; and certainly you can never be too careful not to
offend probability, in supposing a man not to discover his own wife.

In the fourth act, it does not seem to me to be clear enough, how
Constantia comes to be made free, and to return to *Gustavus;* the
third act intimating so strongly, why we might expect to have her
continued in the viceroy's power. This act is full of business; and
intricacy, in the fourth act, must by all means be avoided.

The last act will have many harangues in it, which are dangerous in a catastrophe, if long, and not of the last importance. To conclude, I approve extremely of your killing *Fredage* and *Beron.*
Poetical justice requires him; and for her you may easily drop a
word, to intimate her delivering of *Gustavus* to have proceeded
from some spark of love, which afterwards she may repent of, and
her character remain as perfect as nature need require. One thing
would have a very beautiful effect in the catastrophe, if it were

possible to manage it thro' the play; and that is to have the audience kept in ignorance, as long as the husband (which sure they
may as well be) who *Fredage* really is, till her death.

You see, Madam, I am as free as you command me to be; and
yet my objections are none but such, as you may provide against, even
while you are writing the dialogue.

I wish you the success, which you can wish, and that, I think,
will hardly be so much as you deserve, in whatever you undertake.
I am, with all acknowledgments for your too favourable opinion
of me,

Madam,
Your most obedient
humble servant,
W. Congreve.

EDITIONS: *The Works of Mrs. Catharine Cockburn* . . . 1751, Vol. I, pp.
xxii-xxiii; Summers, Vol. I, pp. 102-103; Dobrée, pp. 529-530.

[1] See No. 117, note 1. For a long note on Congreve's valuable criticism in this
letter, see Summers, Vol. I, pp. 242-243.

125 A DISCOURSE ON THE PINDARIQUE ODE

1706

The following Ode is an Attempt towards restoring the Regularity
of the Ancient Lyrick Poetry, which seems to be altogether forgotten or unknown by our *English* Writers.

There is nothing more frequent among us, than a sort of Poems
intituled Pindarique Odes; pretending to be written in Imitation
of the Manner and Stile of *Pindar,* and yet I do not know that
there is to this Day extant in our Language, one Ode contriv'd
after his Model. What *Idea* can an *English* Reader have of *Pindar,*
(to whose Mouth, when a Child, the Bees [1] brought their Honey,

in Omen of the future Sweetness and Melody of his Songs) when he shall see such rumbling and grating Papers of Verses, pretending to be Copies of his Works?

The Character of these late Pindariques, is, a Bundle of rambling incoherent Thoughts, express'd in a like Parcel of irregular Stanza's, which also consist of such another Complication of disproportion'd, uncertain and perplex'd Verses and Rhimes. And I appeal to any Reader, if this is not the Condition in which these Titular Odes appear.

On the contrary, there is nothing more regular than the Odes of *Pindar*, both as to the exact Observation of the Measures and Numbers of his Stanza's and Verses, and the perpetual Coherence of his Thoughts. For tho' his Digressions are frequent, and his Transitions sudden, yet is there ever some secret Connexion, which tho' not always appearing to the Eye, never fails to communicate it self to the Understanding of the Reader.

The Liberty which he took in his Numbers, and which has been so [2] misunderstood and misapply'd by his pretended Imitators, was only in varying the Stanza's in different Odes; but in each particular Ode they are ever Correspondent one to another in their Turns, and according to the Order of the Ode.

All the Odes of *Pindar* which remain to us,[3] are Songs of Triumph, Victory or Success in the *Grecian* Games: They were sung by a Chorus, and adapted to the *Lyre*, and sometimes to the *Lyre* and *Pipe*;[4] they consisted oftnest of Three Stanza's, the first was call'd the *Strophé*, from the Version or circular Motion of the Singers in that Stanza from the Right Hand to the Left.[5] The second Stanza was call'd the *Antistrophé*, from the Contraversion of the *Chorus*; the Singers, in performing that, turning from the Left Hand to the Right, contrary always to their Motion in the *Strophé*. The Third Stanza was called the *Epode*, (it may be as being the After-song) which they sung in the middle, neither turning to one Hand nor the other.

What the Origin was of these different Motions and Stations in singing their Odes, is not our present Business to enquire. Some have thought that by the Contrariety of the *Strophé* and *An-*

tistrophé, they intended to represent the Contrarotation of the *Primum Mobile,* in respect of the *Secunda Mobilia;* and that by their standing still at the *Epode,* they meant to signifie the Stability of the Earth. Others[6] ascribe the Institution to *Theseus,* who thereby expressed the Windings and Turnings of the Labyrinth in celebrating his Return from thence.

The Method observ'd in the Composition of these Odes, was therefore as follows. The Poet having made Choice of a certain Number of Verses to constitute his *Strophé* or first *Stanza,* was oblig'd to observe the same in his *Antistrophé,* or second *Stanza;* and which accordingly perpetually agreed whenever repeated, both in number of Verses and quantity of Feet: He was then again at Liberty, to make a new choice for his third *Stanza,* or *Epode;* where, accordingly, he diversify'd his Numbers as his Ear or Fancy led him; composing that *Stanza* of more or fewer Verses than the former, and those Verses of different Measures and Quantities, for the greater Variety of Harmony, and Entertainment of the Ear.

But then this *Epode* being thus form'd, he was strictly oblig'd to the same Measure,[7] as often as he should repeat it in the Order of his Ode, so that every *Epode* in the same Ode is eternally the same in Measure and Quantity, in respect to it self; as is also every *Strophé* and *Antistrophé,* in respect to each other.

The *Lyrick* Poet *Stesichorus* (whom *Longinus*[8] reckons amongst the ablest Imitators of *Homer,* and of whom *Quintilian*[9] says, that if he could have kept within Bounds, he would have been nearest of any Body, in Merit, to *Homer*) was, if not the Inventer of this Order in the Ode, yet so strict an Observer of it in his Compositions, that the Three *Stanza*'s of *Stesichorus* became a common Proverb to express a thing universally known, *ne tria quidem Stesichori nosti;* so that when any one had a mind to reproach another with excessive Ignorance, he could not do it more effectually than by telling him, *he did not so much as know the Three Stanza's of* Stesichorus; that is, did not know that an Ode ought to consist of a *Strophé,* an *Antistrophé,* and an *Epode.* If this was such a mark of Ignorance among them, I am sure we have been pretty long liable to the same Reproof; I mean, in respect of our Imitations of the Odes of *Pindar*.

My Intention is not to make a long Preface to a short Ode, nor to enter upon a Dissertation of Lyrick Poetry in general: But thus much I thought proper to say, for the Information of those Readers whose Course of Study has not led them into such Enquiries.

I hope I shall not be so misunderstood, as to have it thought that I pretend to give an exact Copy of *Pindar* in this ensuing Ode; or that I look upon it as a Pattern for his Imitators for the future: Far from such Thoughts, I have only given an Instance of what is practicable, and am sensible that I am as distant from the Force and Elevation of *Pindar*, as others have hitherto been from the Harmony and Regularity of his Numbers.

Again, we having on *Chorus* to sing our Odes, the Titles, as well as Use of *Strophe, Antistrophe,* and *Epode,* are Obsolete and Impertinent: And certainly there may be very good *English* Odes, without the Distinction of *Greek* Appellations to their Stanza's. That I have mention'd them here, and observ'd the Order of them in the ensuing Ode, is therefore only the more intelligibly to explain the extraordinary Regularity of the Composition of those Odes, which have been represented to us hitherto, as the most confus'd Structures in Nature.

However, though there be no necessity that our Triumphal Odes should consist of the Three afore-mentioned Stanza's; yet if the Reader can observe that the great Variation of the Numbers in the Third Stanza (call it *Epode,* or what you please) has a pleasing Effect in the Ode, and makes him return to the First and Second Stanza's, with more Appetite, than he could do if always cloy'd with the same Quantities and Measures, I cannot see why some Use may not be made of *Pindar's* Example, to the great Improvement of the *English* Ode. There is certainly a Pleasure in beholding any Thing that has Art and Difficulty in the Contrivance; especially, if it appears so carefully executed, that the Difficulty does not shew it self, 'till it is sought for; and that the seeming Easiness of the Work, first sets us upon the Enquiry. Nothing can be call'd Beauti-

ful without Proportion. When Symmetry and Harmony are wanting, neither the Eye nor the Ear can be pleas'd. Therefore certainly *Poetry*, which includes Painting and Musick, should not be
destitute of them; and of all *Poetry*, especially the *Ode*, whose End
and Essence is Harmony.

Mr. *Cowley*, in his Preface to his Pindarique Odes, speaking of
the Musick of Numbers, says, *which sometimes (especially in Songs
and Odes) almost without any thing else makes an Excellent Poet.*

Having mention'd Mr. *Cowley*, it may very well be expected,
that something should be said of him, at a time when the Imitation
of *Pindar* is the Theme of our Discourse. But there is that great
Deference due to the Memory, great Parts, and Learning of that
Gentleman, that I think nothing should be objected to the Latitude
he has taken in his Pindarique Odes. The Beauty of his Verses, are
an Attonement for the Irregularity of his Stanza's; and though he
did not imitate *Pindar* in the Strictness of his Numbers, he has very
often happily copy'd him in the Force of his Figures, and Sublimity
of his Stile and Sentiments.

Yet I must beg leave to add, that I believe those irregular
Odes of Mr. *Cowley*, may have been the principal, though innocent
Occasion, of so many deformed Poems since, which instead of being
true Pictures of *Pindar*, have (to use the *Italian* Painters Term)
been only *Caricatura's* of him, Resemblances that for the most part
have been either Horrid or Ridiculous.

For my own part I frankly own my Error, in having heretofore
mis-call'd a few irregular *Stanza's* a Pindarique Ode; [10] and possibly, if others, who have been under the same Mistake, would ingenuously confess the Truth, they might own, that never having
consulted *Pindar* himself, they took all his Irregularity upon trust;
and finding their Account in the great Ease with which they could
produce Odes without being oblig'd either to Measure or Design,
remain'd satisfy'd; and it may be were not altogether unwilling
to neglect being undeceiv'd.

Though there be little (if any thing) left of *Orpheus* but his
Name, yet if *Pausanias* was well inform'd, we may be assur'd that
Brevity was a Beauty which he most industriously labour'd to pre-

serve in his *Hymns*, notwithstanding, as the same Author reports, that they were but few in Number.[11]

The Shortness of the following Ode will, I hope, attone for the Length of the Preface, and in some measure for the Defects which may be found in it. It consists of the same Number of Stanza's with that beautiful Ode of *Pindar*, which is the first of his *Pythicks;* and though I was unable to imitate him in any other Beauty, I resolv'd to endeavour to Copy his Brevity, and take the Advantage of a Remark he has made in the last *Strophé* of the same Ode, which take in the Paraphrase of *Sudorius*.[12]

> *Qui multa paucis stringere Commode*
> *Novere, morsus hi facile invidos*
> *Spernunt, & auris mensq; pura*
> *Omne supervacuum rejectat.*

EDITIONS: *A Pindarique Ode, Humbly Offer'd to the Queen . . . To which is prefix'd, A Discourse on the Pindarique Ode* (folio), London, 1706; *Works* (1710), Vol. III, pp. 1073-1082; *Works* (1719), Vol. II, pp. 429-436; Summers, Vol. IV, pp. 82-86; Dobrée, pp. 329-335.

[1] Pausanias, IX (*Boeotica*), xxiii, 2. For Congreve's 1613 folio edition of Pausanius, see *Library*, No. 457.

[2] "For certainly they have utterly misunderstood *Horace*. L. 4. *Ode* 2. who have apply'd *numerisq; fertur lege solutis*, to all the Odes of *Pindar;* which, there, expresly relates only to his Dithyrambicks, and which are all entirely lost. Nothing is plainer, than the Sense of *Horace* in that Place. He says, *Pindar* deserves the Lawrel, let him write of what, or in what manner soever, *viz.* first, whether he writes *Dithyrambicks*, which *break through the Bounds prescrib'd to other Odes;* Or, secondly, whether he writes of Gods and Heroes, their Warlike Atchievements, *&c.* Or, thirdly, whether he sings of the Victors in the *Grecian* Games: Or, lastly, whether he sings in Honour of the Dead, and writes Elegies, *&c.*" Congreve's note, added 1710.

[3] "which remain to us," added in 1710.

[4] "*Pind. Olymp.* 10. and *Horace L. 4. Ode* 1. *mistis Carminibus non sine fistula.* and *L. 3. Ode* 19. *cur pendet tacita fistula cum Lyra?*" Congreve's note.

[5] "Or from the Left to the Right, for the *Scholiasts* differ in that, as may be seen in *Pind. Schol. Introduc. ad Olymp.* And *Alex. ab Alexandro, L. 4. c. 17.* speaking of the Ceremony of the Chorus, says, *Cursum auspicati a Lœva dextrorsum . . . mox a dextra Lœvorsum.* But the Learned *Schmidius* takes part with the first Opinion, as more consistent with the Notions of the Ancients

concerning the Motions of the Heavenly Spheres, and agreeable to *Homer* there cited by him. See *Eras. Schmid. Prolegom. in Olymp. & de Carmin. Lyric.*" Congreve's note. It is interesting that Congreve had in his library the works of Pindar edited by Erasmus Schmid, "the Learned Schmidius" of Congreve's note. See *Library*, No. 464.

6 "*Pind. Schol. & Schmid.* ibid." Congreve's note.

7 "*Vid. Jul. Scal. Poetic. ad Fin. Cap.* 97. *l.* 3." Congreve's note. For Congreve's copy of Julius Caesar Scaliger, see *Library*, No. 559.

8 "*Longin. de Sub. c.* 13." Congreve's note. For Congreve's copy of Longinus, see *Library*, No. 351.

9 "*Quint. Inst. l.* 10. *c.* 1." Congreve's note. For Congreve's copy of Quintilian, see *Library*, No. 493.

10 "Upon a Lady's Singing," 1692 ("On Mrs. Arabella Hunt, Singing," 1693) and "To the King, on His Taking Namure," 1695, were first called "Pindarick" or "Pindarique" odes but "Irregular" odes in the 1710 *Works*, Vol. III, pp. 847, 875.

11 See *Boeotica*, Vol. XXX, p. 12.

12 Nicholas Lesueur (Sudorius) (*ca.* 1545-1594) translated Pindar into Latin.

126 RICHARD STEELE TO CONGREVE

[*December 29, 1713*] [1]

SIR,

My Name, as Publisher of the following Miscellanies, I am sensible, is but a slight Recommendation of them to the Publick; but the Town's Opinion of them will be raised, when it sees them address'd to Mr. *Congreve*. If the Patron is but known to have a Taste for what is presented to him, it gives an hopeful Idea of the Work; how much more, when He is an acknowledg'd Master of the Art He is desired to Favour? Your just Success in the various Parts of Poetry, will make Your Approbation of the following Sheets a Favour to many Ingenious Gentlemen, whose Modesty wants the Sanction of such an Authority. Men of your Talents oblige the World, when they are studious to produce in others the Similitude of their Excellencies. Your great Discerning in distinguishing the Characters of Mankind, which is manifested in Your Comedies, renders Your good Opinion a just Foundation for the Esteem of other Men. I know, indeed, no Argument against these Collections, in Comparison of any other *Tonson* has heretofore Printed; but that there are in it no Verses of Yours: That gentle, free, and easie Faculty, which also in Songs, and short Poems, You possess above all others, distinguishes it self wher-ever it appears. I cannot but instance Your inimitable *DORIS*,[2] which excels, for Politeness, fine Raillery, and courtly Satyr, any Thing we can meet with in any Language.

Give me leave to tell You, that when I consider Your Capacity this Way, I cannot enough Applaud the Goodness of Your Mind, that has given so few Examples of these Severities, under the Temptation of so great Applause, as the ill-natured World bestows on them, tho' addressed without any Mixture of Your Delicacy.

I cannot leave my Favourite *DORIS*, without taking Notice how much that short Performance discovers a True Knowledge of Life. *DORIS* is the Character of a Libertine Woman of Condition, and the Satyr is work'd up accordingly: For People of Quality are seldom touched with any Representation of their Vices, but in a Light which makes them Ridiculous.

As much as I Esteem You for Your Excellent Writings, by which You are an Honour to our Nation; I chuse rather, as one that has passed many Happy Hours with You, to celebrate that easie Condescention of Mind, and Command of a pleasant Imagination, which give You the uncommon Praise of a Man of Wit, always to please and never to offend. No one, after a joyful Evening, can reflect upon an Expression of Mr. *Congreve*'s, that dwells upon him with Pain.

In a Man capable of Exerting himself any Way, this (whatever the Vain and Ill-natured may think of the Matter) is an Excellence above the brightest Sallies of Imagination.

The Reflection upon this most equal, amiable, and correct Behaviour, which can be observed only by your intimate Acquaintance, has quite diverted me from acknowledging your several Excellencies as a Writer; but to dwell particularly on those Subjects, would have no very good Effect upon the following Performances of my Self and Friends: Thus I confess to You, your Modesty is spared only by my Vanity, and yet I Hope You will give me leave to indulge it yet further, in telling all the World, I am, with great Truth,

> Sir,
>
> *Your most Obedient, and most Humble Servant,*
> *Richard Steele.*

EDITIONS: Dedication to *Poetical Miscellanies, Consisting of Original Poems and Translations. By the Best Hands. Publish'd by Mr. Steele,* London, 1714; *The Correspondence of Richard Steele,* ed. by Rae Blanchard, London, 1941, pp. 472-475.

[1] Steele's *Miscellany* was advertised as published "this day" in *Englishman,* No. 37, for 29 December 1713. For Steele's dedication of Addison's *Drummer* to Congreve, see No. 139.

[2] Congreve's satirical poem "Doris," printed in the collected *Works* (1710), Vol. III, pp. 992-995, is mentioned as "a Master-piece in its kind" in Steele's *Spectator,* No. 422. The character of Doris was possibly drawn by Congreve from the actress Mrs. Elizabeth Barry. See Summers, Vol. IV, p. 215.

127   POPE TO CONGREVE

[Binfield],[1] *January 16, 1714-15.*
Methinks when I write to you, I am making a confession, I have got (I can't tell how) such a custom of throwing my self out upon paper without reserve. You were not mistaken in what you judg'd of my temper of mind when I writ last. My faults will not be hid from you, and perhaps it is no dispraise to me that they will not. The cleanness and purity of one's mind is never better prov'd, than in discovering its own faults at first view: as when a Stream shows the dirt at its bottom, it shows also the transparency of the water.

My spleen was not occasion'd however, by any thing an abusive, angry Critick[2] could write of me. I take very kindly your heroick manner of congratulation upon this scandal; for I think nothing more honorable, than to be involved in the same fate with all the great and the good that ever lived; that is, to be envy'd and censur'd by bad writers.

You do no more than answer my expectations of you, in declaring how well you take my freedom in sometimes neglecting as I do, to reply to your Letters so soon as I ought; those who have a right taste of the substantial part of friendship, can wave the ceremonial. A friend is the only one that will bear the omission; and one may find who is not so, by the very trial of it.

As to any anxiety I have concerning the fate of my *Homer*, the care is over with me. The world must be the judge, and I shall be the first to consent to the justice of its judgment, whatever it be. I am not so arrant as Author, as even to desire, that if I am in the wrong, all mankind should be so.

I am mightily pleas'd with a saying of Monsieur *Tourreil:* "When a Man writes, he ought to animate himself with the thoughts of pleasing all the world: but he is to renounce that desire or hope, the very moment the Book goes out of his hands."[3]

I write this from *Binfield*, whither I came yesterday, having past a few days in my way with my Lord *Bolingbroke:*[4] I go to *London* in three days time, and will not fail to pay a visit to Mr. M———,[5] whom I saw not long since at my Lord *Halifax*'s.[6] I hoped from thence he had some hopes of advantage from the present administration: for few people (I think) but I, pay respects to great Men without any prospects. I am in the fairest way in the world of being not worth a groat, being born both a *Papist* and a *Poet*. This puts me in mind of reacknowledging your continued endeavours to enrich me:[7] But I can tell you 'tis to no purpose, for without the *Opes*, *Æquum animum mi ipse parabo*.[8]

> *I am your, &c.*

EDITIONS: *Letters of Mr. Pope, and Several Eminent Persons. In the Years 1705, Sc. to 1717*. London: J. Roberts, 1735, pp. 88-90 of the second section of numbered pages; Sherburn, Vol. I, pp. 274-275.

[1] Binfield, near Ockingham in Berkshire, was the residence of Pope and his parents from 1700 till 1716.

[2] In a note, Pope explains that the critic was "*Dennis*, who writ an abusive Pamphlet this Year, intitled, *Remarks on Mr. Pope's Homer*." But Pope seems to forget that his letter is dated months before his first volume of Homer appeared and thus before Dennis could have written his *Remarks*. This inconsistency suggests that No. 127 was not an actual letter written on 16 January 1714/15 but something composed many years later to fill out a correspondence with Congreve. See Sherburn, Vol. I, p. 274.

[3] A translation of the last sentence of the "Préface historique" to the French translation of Demosthenes by Jacques de Tourreil.

[4] See No. 45, note 4.

[5] "Possibly Mr. (later Sir) Paul Methuen, who in 1716 as Secretary of State forwarded letters from Pope or from Congreve to Lady Mary Wortley Montagu in Constantinople." Sherburn, Vol. I, p. 275.

[6] See No. 6, note 7.

[7] Perhaps a reference to Congreve's efforts to secure subscriptions for Pope's translation of Homer.

[8] Horace, *Epistolae*, I. xviii. 112.

128   POPE TO CONGREVE

March 19, 1714/15.

The Farce of the *What-d'ye-call-it*,[1] has occasioned many different speculations in the town. Some look'd upon it as meer jest upon the tragic poets, others as a satire upon the late war. Mr. *Cromwell* [2] hearing none of the words, and seeing the action to be tragical, was much astonished to find the audience laugh; and says, the Prince and Princess [2] must doubtless be under no less amazement on the same account. Several templers, and others of the more vociferous kind of criticks, went with a resolution to hiss, and confest they were forced to laugh so much, that they forgot the design they came with. The Court in general has in a very particular manner come into the jest, and the three first Nights, (notwithstanding two of them were court-nights) were distinguish'd by very full audiences of the first quality. The common people of the pit and gallery, receiv'd it at first with great gravity and sedateness, some few with tears; but after the third day they also took the hint, and have ever since been very loud in their claps. There are still some sober men who cannot be of the general opinion, but the laughers are so much the majority, that one or two criticks seem determined to undeceive the town at their proper cost, by writing grave dissertations against it: To encourage them in which laudable design, it is resolv'd a *Preface* shall be prefixt to the *Farce,* in vindication of the nature and dignity of this new way of writing.

Yesterday Mr. *Steele*'s affair was decided:[3] I am sorry I can be of no other opinion than yours, as to his whole carriage and writings of late. But certainly he has not only been punish'd by others, but suffer'd much even from his own party in the point of character, nor (I believe) receiv'd any amends in that of interest, as yet; whatever may be his Prospects for the future.

This Gentleman, among a thousand others, is a great instance of the fate of all who are carried away by party-spirit, of any side. I wish all violence may succeed as ill: but I am really amazed that so much of that sower and pernicious quality shou'd be joyned with so much natural good humour as I think Mr. *Steele* is possess'd of.

I am, &c.

EDITIONS: *Letters of Mr. Pope* . . . London: J. Roberts, 1735, pp. 90-92 of the second section of numbered pages; Sherburn, Vol. I, pp. 285-286. "The first paragraph of this letter is taken from that found among the Caryll transcripts dated 3 Mar. 1714 [1715] and sent to Caryll. It was used practically without change. The two paragraphs about Steele were borrowed from Pope's letter to Caryll of 19 Mar. 1714: whence Pope's date for his fabrication." Sherburn, Vol. I, p. 285.

[1] By John Gay, acted with great applause on 23 February 1714/15.

[2] Henry Cromwell, Pope's friend, was too deaf to hear the words and the Prince and Princess, only recently from Hanover, could not yet understand English.

[3] Steele's expulsion from the House of Commons on 18 March 1713/14 is correctly referred to as happening "yesterday" in Pope's letter to Caryll dated

19 March 1713/14 but not in the composite letter to Congreve dated 19 March 1714/15.

129   GAY AND POPE TO CONGREVE

[*London*] *April 7, 1715.*

Mr. *Pope* is going to Mr. *Jervas*'s,[1] where Mr. *Addison* is sitting for his picture; in the mean time amidst clouds of tobacco at a coffee-house I write this letter. There is a grand revolution at *Will*'s, *Morrice*[2] has quitted for a coffee-house in the city, and *Titcomb*[3] is restor'd to the great joy of *Cromwell*,[4] who was at a great loss for a person to converse with upon the fathers and church-history; the knowledge I gain from him, is entirely in painting and poetry; and Mr. *Pope* owes all his skill in astronomy to him and Mr. *Whiston*,[5] so celebrated of late for his discovery of the longitude in an extraordinary copy of Verses. Mr. *Rowe*'s *Jane Gray* is to be play'd in *Easter-week*,[6] when Mrs. *Oldfield*[7] is to personate a character directly opposite to female nature; for what woman ever despis'd Sovereignty? You know *Chaucer* has a tale where a knight saves his head, by discovering it was the thing which all women most coveted. Mr. *Pope*'s *Homer* is retarded by the great rains that have fallen of late, which causes the sheets to be long a drying; this gives Mr. *Lintot*[8] great uneasiness, who is now endeavouring to corrupt the Curate of his parish to pray for fair weather, that his work may go on. There is a six-penny *Criticism*[9] lately publish'd upon the Tragedy of the *What-d'ye-call-it*, wherein he with much judgment and learning calls me a blockhead, and Mr. *Pope* a knave. His grand charge is against the *Pilgrims Progress* being read, which he says is directly level'd at *Cato*'s reading *Plato*; to back this censure, he goes on to tell you, that the *Pilgrims Progress* being mention'd to be the eighth edition, makes the reflection evident, the Tragedy of *Cato* having just eight times (as he quaintly expresses it) *visited the Press*. He has also endeavoured to show, that every particular passage of the play alludes to some fine part of Tragedy, which he says I have injudiciously and profanely abused. Sir *Samuel Garth*'s Poem upon my Lord *Clare*'s house,[10] I believe will be publish'd in the *Easter-week*.

Thus far Mr. *Gay*—who has in his letter forestall'd all the subjects of diversion; unless it should be one to you to say, that I sit up till two a-clock over *Burgundy* and *Champagne;* and am become so much a rake, that I shall be ashamed in a short time to be thought to do any sort of business. I fear I must get the gout by drinking, purely for a fashionable pretence to sit still long enough to translate four books of *Homer*. I hope you'll by that time be up again, and I may succeed to the bed and couch of my predecessor: Pray cause the stuffing to be repaired, and the crutches shortned for me. The calamity of your gout is what all your friends, that is to say all that know you, must share in; we desire you in your turn to condole with us, who are under a persecution, and much afflicted with a distemper which proves grievous to many poets, a *Criticism.* We have indeed some relieving intervals of laughter, (as you know there are in some Diseases;) and it is the opinion of divers good guessers, that the last fit will not be more violent than advantageous; for poets assail'd by critics, are like men bitten by *Tarantula*'s, they dance on so much the faster.

Mr. *Thomas Burnet* hath play'd the precursor to the coming of *Homer*, in a treatise call'd *Homerides.* He has since risen very much in his criticism, and after assaulting *Homer*, made a daring attack upon the *What-d'ye-call-it.*[11] Yet is there not a proclamation issued for the burning of *Homer* and the *Pope* by the common hangman; nor is the *What-d'ye-call-it* yet silenc'd by the Lord-Chamberlain. They shall survive the conflagration of his father's works, and live after they and he are damned; (for that the B—p of S. already is so, is the opinion of Dr. *Sacheverel* and the Church of *Rome.*)

I am, &c.

EDITIONS: *Letters to Mr. Pope* . . . London: J. Roberts, 1735, pp. 92-95 of the second section of numbered pages; Sherburn, Vol. I, pp. 290-291. "This letter is taken from two letters to Caryll here dated [*c.* 19 Mar. 1714/15] and [Apr. 1715]." Sherburn, Vol. I, p. 290.

[1] Charles Jervas (1675?-1739), the portrait painter, at whose house in Cleveland Court Pope stayed when he was in London. Professor Sherburn suggests (Vol. I, p. 290) that Jervas could have been trying to reconcile Pope and Addison.

[2] Perhaps William Morice, the High Bailiff of Westminster, frequently mentioned in Pope's correspondence.

[3] See No. 37, note 5.

[4] Henry Cromwell. See No. 128.

[5] William Whiston (1667-1752) issued many publications on religious and mathematical subjects. His "Ode on the Longitude" appeared in Swift and Pope's *Miscellanies in Prose and Verse.* See No. 420 in Congreve's *Library.*

[6] Acted on 20 April 1715.

[7] See No. 19, note 4.

[8] Bernard Lintot then had in press the first volume of Pope's Homer, which was published the following June. See No. 100, note 8.

[9] "This curious Piece was entitled, *A Compleat Key to the What-d'ye-call-it.* It was written by one *Griffin,* a Player, assisted by *Lewis Theobald.*" Pope's note.

[10] "Garth's *Claremont,* published 2 May, contained a fine compliment to *Windsor Forest.*" Sherburn's note, Vol. I, p. 289. Sir Samuel Garth (1661-1719) was an able physician and one of the literary members of the Kit-Cat Club. See *DNB.*

[11] "In one of his Papers call'd *The Grumbler;* long since dead." Pope's note.

130   CHARLES BECKINGHAM [1] TO CONGREVE

[*December 26, 1718?*] [2]

SIR,

The only Hope I have of obtaining Your Pardon for prefixing Your Name to these Sheets, is, from their being an Attempt to preserve the Memory of a Person,[3] who, when Living, was so nearly allied to You, by the most sincere Endearments of a mutual, extensive, and disinterested Friendship.

Tho' I am an absolute Stranger to Your Person, I cannot be so to Your Character, and must be allowed to say, That as You were distinguished for so uncommon a Union in Affections, You were equally celebrated for as extraordinary a Superiority in Genius; and the declining Stage may now justly complain of a Double Loss in their most substantial Entertainments, by the Death of Mr. Rowe, and Your Own voluntary Retirement. But I am afraid I transgress the Bounds I prescribed my self for this short Address, and shall therefore wave any Freedoms of this Nature (however due to Merit) which may prove the least disagreeable to a Person placed so happily above them. And if the Authors of the following Poems are so fortunate as to have contributed any thing worthy the Character of the Deceased, and the Patronage of his Living Friend, it will answer the utmost Wishes of, *Sir, Your most Obedient, Humble Servant,*

Ch. Beckingham.

EDITION: The Epistle Dedicatory to *Musarum Lachrymæ; or, Poems to the Memory of Nicholas Rowe, esq; By Several Hands* [ed. by Charles Beckingham], London, Printed for E. Curll, MDCCXIX.

[1] Charles Beckingham (1699-1731) was mentioned very favorably by Giles Jacob (*Poetical Register*, 1719, reissued, 1723, Vol. I, p. 281, Vol. II, p. 288) for his two tragedies and for his "Poem on the Death of N. Rowe, Esq." See also *DNB*.

[2] The introductory letter to Mr. Curll is dated 26 December 1718.

[3] Nicholas Rowe (1674-1718) had been, like Congreve, a member of the Middle Temple and, again like Congreve, had abandoned the law for the theatre. Congreve's two references to Rowe's plays in letters to Keally (Nos. 7 and 19) indicate no special interest in Rowe as a dramatist. But Congreve admired him as a writer:

> *If* Addison, *or* Rowe, *or* Prior *write,*
> *We study 'em with Profit and Delight.*
> —"Of Pleasing," *Works*
> (1710), Vol. III, p. 1066.

Congreve had in his library Rowe's translations of Dacier's *Pythagoras* (1707), Quillet's *Callipædia* (1712), and Lucan's *Pharsalia* (1718), the last being Tonson's large-paper edition in which Congreve is listed as one of the subscribers. Congreve also had Rowe's edition of Shakespeare, one of the six large-paper copies very specially bound in nine instead of the regular six volumes. See *Library*, Nos. 89, 343, 365, 544.

131   RICHARD BOYLE, VISCOUNT SHANNON (FOR CONGREVE) TO
       POPE

Ashley [1] *Thursday* [*1719?*]

SIR

By Candle light Mr Congreve wants a Scribe.[2] He has not been well indeed, but will take the air your way to morrow morning. Don't let this be any restraint on you, for he is not Qualified for long visits. Since you were so kind to mention me in your letter, I hope you'll keep your promiss, and let me have the pleasure of seeing you here what day is most Convenient for you next weeke, and it will be a very great Satisfaction to Sir

your most humble
servant Shannon

Address: *To Mr Pope*

MANUSCRIPT: British Museum Add. 4808. EDITIONS: *Supplemental Volume to the Works of Alexander Pope, Esq.*, London, 1825, pp. 51-52; Hodges, p. 104; Sherburn, Vol. II, p. 12.

[1] Lord Shannon's seat at Ashley was not far from Twickenham, where Pope had taken a villa about March, 1719. See Sherburn, Vol. II, p. 1. For other letters written from Ashley, see Nos. 54, 83, 133. The date of No. 131 could not be earlier than 1719, the year when Pope moved to Twickenham.

[2] This is one of many references to Congreve's defective eyesight. See especially No. 41. Congreve had been the guest of Lord Shannon at Ashley as early as 5 October 1717. See No. 83.

132   CONGREVE TO GILES JACOB [1]

Surrey-street, July 7, 1719.

SIR,

I much approve the Usefulness of your Work; any Morning, about Eleven, I shall be very ready to give you the Account of my own poor Trifles and Self, or any thing else that has fallen within the compass of my Knowledge, relating to any of my Poetical Friends.

I am, Sir,
Your Humble Servant,
William Congreve.

EDITIONS: *Memoirs*, pp. xv–xvi; Summers, Vol. I, p. 104; Dobrée, pp. 531–532.

[1] The author of the *Memoirs* says in his Preface, p. xv, that Congreve sent this letter when Mr. Curll was printing the first volume of *The Poetical Register*, thus implying that the letter was sent to Edmund Curll. The friendly tone of the letter suggests that it was written to the editor of *The Poetical Register*, Giles Jacob, rather than to the unprincipled publisher. Giles Jacob (1686–1744) compiled not only the two volumes of *The Poetical Register*, 1719, but also the very popular *New Law Dictionary*, 1729. See *DNB*.

133   CONGREVE TO POPE

Ashley Monday. [Late Summer, 1719] [1]

SIR

I had designd to have waited on you to day but have been out of order since Saturday as I have been most of the Summer. And as the days are now unlesse I am able to rise in a Morning, it will be hard to go and come and have any pleasure between the whiles. The next day after I had known from you where Lady Mary [2] was, I sent to know how she did but by her answer I perceive she has the goodnesse for me to believe I have been all this summer here, tho' I had been here a fortnight when you came to see me. Pray give her my most humble service. If I can I will wait on you. I am Your

Most Obedient
humble Servant
Wm Congreve

MANUSCRIPT: British Museum Add. 4808. EDITIONS: *The Works of Alexander Pope*, ed. by Whitwell Elwin, London, 1871, Vol. VI, p. 416; Dobrée, pp. 534, 535; Sherburn, Vol. II, pp. 12-13.

[1] Profesesor Sherburn (Vol. I, p. 12) has placed this letter late in the summer, 1719. Perhaps it followed by a few weeks letter No. 131, which was also written from Lord Shannon's seat at Ashley.

[2] Lady Mary Wortley Montagu was living in Twickenham during the summer of 1719. See Sherburn, Vol. II, p. 1.

134   CONGREVE TO THOMAS PELHAM-HOLLES, DUKE OF NEW-CASTLE [1]

[ca. *November, 1719*]

MY LORD

By Your Graces direction, Mr Southern [2] has don me the honour to read his tragedy [3] to me. I cannot but think that it has been a wrong to the town, as well as an injury to the Author, that such a work has been so long withheld from the Publick. This I say with respect to it as a Play.

Whatever may have been supposed or suggested against it on the score of Politicks is in my Opinion absolutely groundlesse. I can see no shadow of an Objection to it upon that account; tho I have attended to it very precisely even in regard to that particular in Justice to Mr Southern and in Obedience to Your Graces Commands. I am thus plain in my thoughts on this Occasion. I am allways with the greatest respect

My Lord
Your Graces most Obedient
humble servant
Wm CONGREVE

MANUSCRIPT: British Museum Add. MS. 32685, ff. 49-50; reproduced in Garnett and Gosse, *English Literature*, Vol. III (1903), p. 165. EDITIONS: Summers, Vol. I, p. 97; Dobrée, p. 521.

[1] For Congreve's dedication of his edition of Dryden's *Dramatick Works*, 1717, to the Duke of Newcastle, see No. 84. In his capacity as Lord Chamberlain, the Duke had the responsibility of authorizing the production of plays.

[2] See No. 102, note 1.

[3] *The Spartan Dame*, a tragedy which Southerne had begun more than thirty years earlier while he was actively writing for the stage. The play had been withheld because it was suspected of a political meaning. After Southerne had deleted nearly four hundred lines and the play had been approved by Congreve as unobjectionable politically, it was acted with great success at Drury Lane on 11 December 1719. The printed play restored the lines that had been deleted from the acting version. See Summers, Vol. I, pp. 241-242.

135   CONGREVE TO POPE

                      Surry street   January 20 [*1719/20?*] [1]
I return you a Thousand thanks for your letter about spaw water.[2] Dr Arbuthnot [3] has orderd me at present to drinke bathe water. So I cannot expressly say when I shall want the spaw but if the person mentiond by you imports any quantity for himself at any time I shall be glad to know of it. I am sorry You did not keep Your Word in letting me see You a second time.[4] I am
                allways Dear Sir Your most Obedient
                humble servant
                Wm Congreve

Address: *To Mr Pope at his house in Twit'nam*
Postmark: *20/IA Peny Post Payd*

MANUSCRIPT: British Museum Add. 4808. EDITIONS: Dobrée, p. 535; Sherburn, Vol. II, pp. 27-28.

[1] The year 1719/20 is suggested by Pope's use of the verso of Congreve's note in translating Book XXIV of the *Iliad*. Pope was completing his translation of the *Iliad* early in 1720. See Sherburn, Vol. II, p. 27.

² For Congreve's receipt of a case of spa water from Pope, see No. 137.

³ Dr. John Arbuthnot (1667-1735) was Congreve's physician as late as September, 1726, when Arbuthnot wrote to Swift: "I have been for near three weeks together every day at the Duchess of Marlborough's [at her Lodge in Windsor Park], with Mr. Congreve, who has been likely to die with a fever, and the gout in his stomach; but he is better, and likely to do well." See Swift, Vol. III, p. 343. Dr. Arbuthnot wrote many miscellaneous essays, two of which Congreve had in his library (see *Library*, Nos. 34, 35). Congreve also owned Dr. Arbuthnot's satirical "History of John Bull," which was included in Pope's and Swift's *Miscellanies in Prose and Verse*, London, 1727 (see *Library*, No. 420).

⁴ Probably while Congreve was at Ashley late in the summer of 1719. See No. 133.

136   POPE TO CONGREVE

March 25. 1720.

For what remains, I beg to be excused from the ceremonies of taking leave at the end of my work; and from embarrassing my self, or others, with any defenses or apologies about it. But instead of endeavouring to raise a vain monument to my self, of the merits or difficulties of it (which must be left to the world, to truth, and to posterity) let me leave behind me a memorial of my friendship, with one of the most valuable men as well as finest writers, of my age and country: One who has try'd, and knows by his own experience, how hard an undertaking it is to do justice to *Homer:* And one, who (I am sure) sincerely rejoices with me at the period of my labours. To him therefore, having brought this long work to a conclusion, I desire to *dedicate*¹ it; and to have the honour and the satisfaction of placing together, in this manner, the names of Mr. *CONGREVE*, and of

A. POPE.

EDITIONS: *The Iliad of Homer.* Translated by Mr. *Pope.* Vol. VI. London: Printed by W. Bowyer, for Bernard Lintot between the Temple-Gates. 1720, pp. 220-221; Vol. VI. London: Printed for Henry Lintot. MDCCXLIII, p.

194. The text follows the edition of 1743 (the last during Pope's lifetime), which has the wording of the first edition, 1720, but omits most of the capitalization.

[1] Pope apparently decided to dedicate his *Iliad* to Congreve as early as 1 October 1719. On the back of a letter from James Craggs bearing that date Pope wrote: "End the notes with a dedication to Mr. Congreve, as a memorial of our friendship occasioned by his translation of this last part of Homer." See Sherburn, Vol. II, p. 16.

137   CONGREVE TO POPE

June 23 [*1720?*] [1]

DEAR SIR

I am very sorry to hear you have been ill. It has not been my fault that I have not been to wait on you. I shall think it very long till I hear you are better. I am my selfe but upon a very indifferent foot. I thank you a thousand times for your Case of the Spaw water. I have sent this morning to the Custom house about them. I believe I shall not need quite so many but some friends may be glad of some of them. I am Dear Sir ever your most Obedient
                              humble servant
                              Wm Congreve

MANUSCRIPT: In the Locker-Lamson Album, Harvard Library. EDITION: Sherburn, Vol. V, p. 4.

[1] The year 1720 is indicated by Congreve's thanks for the "Case of Spaw water" sent by Pope. In No. 135, apparently dated in January of 1720, Congreve had given Pope "a Thousand thanks" for recommending spa water and had shown an interest in using it at some later time.

138   JOHN DENNIS TO CONGREVE

August 1, 1721.[1]

SIR,

I have lately heard, with some Indignation, that there are Persons who arraign the ridiculous Characters of our late Friend Mr. *Wycherley,* for being forsooth too witty; mov'd, I suppose, by the wise Apprehension that they may be of dangerous Example, and spread the Contagion of Wit in this Witty and Politick Age; an Age so very Witty, and so very Politick, that it is always like to be an undetermin'd Question, whether our Wit has the Advantage of our Politicks, or our Politicks of our Wit.

As soon as I heard of this Accusation, I resolved to write a Defence of Mr. *Wycherley,* and to direct this Defence to you, for the following Reasons: Because you had a true Esteem for Mr. *Wycherley*'s Merit, as well as had your humble Servant; Because you are allow'd by all to be an undoubted Judge of the Matter in debate; and Because an express Vindication of Mr. *Wycherley*'s ridiculous Characters, is an implicite one of some of your own. . . .[2]

Thus, Sir, I have endeavour'd to defend the *Plain-dealer* against the foresaid Accusation, as far as my present Avocations would give me leave. If it appears to you, who are so great a Judge of these matters, that I am in the right in what I have said, I make no doubt but I have done an agreeable thing to you, in doing Justice to the Merit of our deceased Friend, and setting it in a true Light. But if I happen to be mistaken, which yet I will not believe, till I hear from you, that I am so, I will make no Excuse for my self but what one whom you have the greatest Regard for has already made to my Hand.

> *Vellem in amicitia sic erraremus, et isti*
> *Errori, virtus nomen posuisset honestum.*[3]
>   Hor.

At the same time I am very far from believing that the *Plain-dealer* is a faultless Play, for where is the Play or the Poem that is without

Fault? But since these People have not hit on the true Faults, it becomes his Friends to say nothing at all concerning them.

I am, Sir,
Yours, &c.

EDITIONS: "Letters on Milton and Wycherley," pp. 21-32, attached to *Proposals for Printing by Subscription, in Two Volumes in Octavo, the Following Miscellaneous Tracts, Written by Mr. John Dennis,* London, 1721-1722; Hooker, Vol. II, pp. 230-235.

[1] This is the date given by Dennis for the last of four letters attached to his *Proposals.* The letter is entitled "A Defense of Mr. *Wycherley's* Characters in the *Plain-dealer.* To *William Congreve,* Esq."

[2] For Dennis' defense of Wycherley, here omitted, see Hooker, Vol. II, pp. 230-234. For Congreve's earlier correspondence with Dennis, see Nos. 108-113.

[3] Horace, *Sermones,* I. iii. 41-42.

139   RICHARD STEELE TO CONGREVE

[*December 22, 1721*] [1]

SIR,

This is the second [2] time that I have, without your leave, taken the Liberty to make a publick Address to you. However uneasy you may be for your own sake in receiving Compliments of this nature, I depend upon your known Humanity for Pardon, when I acknowledge, that you have this present Trouble for mine. When I take my self to be ill-treated with regard to my Behaviour to the Merit of other Men, my Conduct towards you is an Argument of my Candour that way, as well as that your Name and Authority will be my Protection in it. You will give me leave therefore, in a matter that concerns us in the Poetical World, to make you my Judge, whether I am not injur'd in the highest manner; for with Men of your Taste and Delicacy, it is a high Crime and Misdemeanour to be guilty of any thing that is disingenuous: but I will go into the matter. . . .[3]

When he [Tickell] [4] speaks of Mr. *Addison*'s declining to go into Orders, his way of doing it is, to lament that his Seriousness and Modesty, which might have recommended him, *proved the chief Obstacles to it; it seems, these Qualities, by which the Priesthood is so much adorn'd, represented the Duties of it as too weighty for him, and rendred him still more worthy of that Honour which they made him decline.* These, you knew very well, were not the Reasons which made Mr. *Addison* turn his thoughts to the civil World: and as you were the Instrument of his becoming acquainted with my Lord *Halifax*,[5] I doubt not but you remember the warm Instances that Noble Lord made to the Head of the College not to insist upon Mr. *Addison*'s going into Orders; his Arguments were founded upon the general Pravity and the Corruption of Men of Business, who wanted liberal Education. And I remember, as if I had read the Letter yesterday, that my Lord ended with a Compliment, that however he might be represented as no Friend to the Church, he never would do it any other Injury than keeping Mr. *Addison* out of it. . . .[3]

I must conclude without satisfying as strong a Desire as ever Man had of saying something remarkably handsome to the Person to whom I am writing; for you are so good a Judge, that you would find out the Endeavourer to be witty: and therefore as I have tir'd you and my self, I will be contented with assuring you, which I do very honestly, I had rather have you satisfied with me on this Subject, than any other Man living.

You will please to pardon me, that I have, thus, laid this nice Affair before a Person who has the acknowledg'd Superiority to all others, not only in the most excellent Talents, but possessing them with an Æquanimity, Candour and Benevolence, which render those Advantages a Pleasure as great to the rest of the World, as they can be to the Owner of them. And since Fame consists in the Opinion of wise and good Men, you must not blame me for taking the readiest way to baffle an attempt upon my Reputation, by an Address to one whom every wise and good Man looks upon with the greatest Affection and Veneration. I am,

> Sir,
>
> Your most oblig'd,
> most obedient and
> most humble Servant,
> Richard Steele.

EDITIONS: Dedication to *The Drummer*, London, 1722, pp. iii-xxiii; Rae Blanchard, *Correspondence of Richard Steele*, London, 1941, pp. 505-518.

[1] *The Drummer* was advertised as published "this day" by *The Daily Post* for 22 December 1721.

[2] For the "first" time, nearly eight years earlier, see Steele's dedication of his *Poetical Miscellanies* to Congreve, No. 126.

[3] Steele's detailed argument (here omitted) for including *The Drummer* among Addison's works is given by Rae Blanchard, *The Correspondence of Richard Steele*, pp. 506-517.

[4] Thomas Tickell (1686-1740) had offended Steele by omitting *The Drummer* from Addison's *Works*.

[5] See Nos. 6, 24, 28.

140   POPE TO GAY (OR CONGREVE)

London, Sept. 11, 1722.

DEAR GAY,—I thank you for remembring me. I would do my best to forget my self, but that I find your Idea is so closely connected to me, that I must forget both together, or neither. I'm sorry, I could not have a glympse either of you, or of the Sun (your Father) before you went for *Bath*. But now it pleases me to see him, and hear of you. Pray put Mr. *Congreve* in mind that he has one on this side of the World who loves him; and that there are more Men and Women in the Universe, than Mr. *Gay* and my Lady Dutchess of *M*.[1] There are Ladies in and about *Richmond* that pretend to value him and yourself; and one of them at least may be thought to do it without Affectation, namely Mrs. *Howard.* . . .² Pray tell Dr. *Arbuthnot* ³ that even Pigeon-pyes and Hogs-puddings are thought dangerous by our Governors; for those that have been sent to the Bishop of *Rochester*,⁴ are open'd and prophanely pry'd into at the *Tower:* 'Tis the first time dead Pigeons have been suspected of carrying Intelligence. To be serious, you, and Mr. *Congreve* (nay and the Doctor if he has not dined) will be sensible of my concern and surprize at the commitment of that Gentleman, whose welfare is as much my concern as any Friend's I have. I think my self a most unfortunate wretch; I no sooner love, and, upon knowledge, fix my esteem to any man; but he either dies like Mr. *Craggs* ⁵ or is sent to Imprisonment like the Bishop. God send him as well as I wish him, manifest him to be as Innocent as I believe him, and make all his Enemies know him as well as I do, that they may love him and think of him as well!

If you apprehend this Period to be of any danger ⁶ in being address'd to you; tell Mr. *Congreve* or the Doctor, it is writ to them. I am Your, &c.

EDITIONS: *Letters of Mr. Pope* . . . London: J. Roberts, 1735, Vol. II, pp. 134-137; Sherburn, Vol. II, pp. 133-134.

¹ Henrietta, Duchess of Marlborough, was with Congreve and Gay at Bath during the summer of 1722.

² Henrietta Howard (1681-1767), later Countess of Suffolk, had a house at Marble Hill, Twickenham. Richmond and Twickenham were adjoining suburbs of London on opposite banks of the Thames River about eight miles west of Congreve's lodgings in the Strand.

³ See No. 135.

⁴ Francis Atterbury, Bishop of Rochester (1662-1732), was imprisoned in the Tower in August of 1722 for alleged conspiracy with the Pretender. Next year he was deprived of his offices and banished.

⁵ James Craggs, the younger (1686-1721), Secretary of State and good friend and neighbor to Pope in Twickenham, had died of smallpox on 16 February 1720/21. See Sherburn, Vol. II, p. 73.

[6] The danger, if any, would apparently lie in the references to the imprisoned Bishop Atterbury.

141   GAY, SWIFT, AND POPE ON CONGREVE

Gay to Swift, London, 3 February 1722/23: Mr. Congreve I see often. He always mentions you with the strongest expressions of esteem and friendship. He labours still under the same afflictions, as to his sight and gout, but in his intervals of health, he has not lost anything of his cheerful temper. I passed all the last season with him at the Bath, and I have great reason to value myself upon his friendship; for I am sure he sincerely wishes me well.

Swift to Pope, Dublin, 20 September 1723: You must remember me with great affection to Dr. Arbuthnot,[1] Mr. Congreve, and Gay.

Gay to Swift, Bath, 6 July 1728: Mr. Congreve and I often talk of you, and wish you health and everything good thing; but often, out of self-interest, we wish you with us.

Swift to Pope, Dublin, 13 February 1728/9: But this renews the grief for the death of our friend Mr. Congreve, whom I loved from my youth, and who surely, beside his other talents, was a very agreeable companion. He had the misfortune to squander away a very good constitution in his younger days, and I think a man of sense and merit like him, is bound in conscience to preserve his health for the sake of his friends, as well as of himself. Upon his own account I could not much desire the continuance of his life, under so much pain, and so many infirmities. Years have not yet hardened me, and I have an addition of weight on my spirits since we lost him, though I saw him so seldom, and possibly if he had lived on, should never have seen him more.

Pope to Gay [*1728/29*]: I never pass'd so melancholy a time, and now Mr. *Congreve*'s death touches me nearly. It is twenty years that I have known him. Every year carries away something dear with it, till we outlive all tenderness, and become wretched Individuals again as we begun.

Pope to Edward Harley, second Earl of Oxford, 21 January 1728/29: Mr Congreves death was to me sudden, and strook me through. You know the Value I bore him and a long 20 years friendship.

EDITIONS: Ball, Vol. III, p. 153; Ball, Vol. III, p. 176, and Sherburn, Vol. II, p. 200; Ball, Vol. IV, p. 37; Ball, Vol. IV, p. 58, and Sherburn, Vol. III, pp. 15-16; Sherburn, Vol. III, p. 3; Sherburn, Vol. III, p. 10.

[1] See No. 135.

142   PETER DAVALL [1] TO CONGREVE

Middle Temple, March 1, 1722/23

TO WILLIAM CONGREVE, ESQ;

SIR,

I should never have thought of Publishing the following Translation, if I had not been in some measure encourag'd to it, by the Approbation You seem'd to express for some Part of it, when my Father took the Liberty to communicate it to You. If the Stile in which it is written is in any manner tolerable, it is chiefly owing to your kind and useful Instructions. You know, Sir, that I was inclined to have kept this Translation by me, for a longer Time, during which I might possibly have brought it somewhat nearer Perfection: And You likewise know the Reasons which have prevailed upon me to venture it Abroad, sooner than I intended. Such as it is, I hope You will excuse the Freedom which I have taken in Addressing it to You;

and the Regard I have had for my Self, in making use of the Name of Mr. *Congreve,* which alone is sufficient to bespeak the good Opinion of the Publick, or to excite, at least, a Curiosity of reading a Book, which has that Name prefixt to it. I am, Sir,

> *Your most Humble, and most Obedient Servant,*
> *P. Davall.*

EDITION: Dedicatory letter to *Memoirs of the Cardinal de Retz,* 4 vols., London, 1723.

[1] ". . . Peter Daval, esq. of the Middle Temple, a barrister at law, afterwards master in Chancery, and at the time of his death, January 8, 1763, accomptant general of that court. He, at an early period of life, translated the Memoirs of Cardinal De Retz, which were printed in 12mo, 1723, with a dedication to Mr. Congreve, who encouraged the publication. He was Fellow of the Royal Society, and an able Mathematician." John Nichols, *Literary Anecdotes of the Eighteenth Century,* Vol. II, p. 372.

143   VOLTAIRE ON CONGREVE

[*1726(?)*] [1]

The late Mr. *Congreve* rais'd the Glory of Comedy to a greater Height than any English Writer before or since his Time. He wrote only a few Plays, but they are all excellent in their kind. The Laws of the Drama are strictly observ'd in them; they abound with Characters all which are shadow'd with the utmost Delicacy, and we don't meet with so much as one low, or coarse Jest. The Language is every where that of Men of Honour, but their Actions are those of Knaves; a Proof that he was perfectly well acquainted with human Nature, and frequented what we call polite Company. He was infirm, and come to the Verge of Life when I knew him. Mr. *Congreve* had one Defect, which was, his entertaining too mean an Idea of his first Profession, (that of a Writer) tho' 'twas to this he ow'd his Fame and Fortune. He spoke of his Works as of Trifles [2] that were beneath him; and hinted to me in our first

Conversation, that I should visit him upon no other Foot than that of a Gentleman, who led a Life of Plainness and Simplicity. I answer'd, that had he been so unfortunate as to be a mere Gentleman I should never have come to see him; and I was very much disgusted at so unseasonable a Piece of Vanity.

Voltaire, *Letters Concerning the English Nation*, No. XIX, London, 1733, pp. 188-189.

¹ François Marie Arouet (1694-1778), better known as Voltaire, probably visited Congreve early during his stay in London from 1726 to 1729 and made the notes later used in his *Letters.* Congreve was one of the subscribers to Voltaire's *La Henriade,* published in London in 1728 in quarto. Congreve had also a copy of the second edition, in octavo, and a copy of Voltaire's *An Essay upon the Civil Wars in France,* London, 1728. See *Library,* Nos. 648, 649, 650.

² Congreve had modestly referred to his works as "Trifles" throughout his life (see Nos. 103, 104, 107, 132), and only Voltaire, of all Congreve's contemporaries, interpreted the expression as evidence of vanity. See John C. Hodges, "Saint or Sinner: Some Congreve Letters and Documents," *Tennessee Studies in Literature,* Vol. III (1958), pp. 11-15.

144   CONGREVE TO POPE

[Bath], May 6 [*1727*] ¹

I have the pleasure of your very kind letter. I have always been obliged to you for your friendship and concern for me, and am more affected with it, than I will take upon me to express in this letter. I do assure you there is no return wanting on my part, and am very sorry I had not the good luck to see the Dean before I left town: it is a great pleasure to me, and not a little vanity to think that he misses me. As to my health, which you are so kind to enquire after, it is not worse than in London: I am almost afraid yet to say that it is better, for I cannot reasonably expect much effect from these waters in so short a time: but in the main they seem to agree with me. Here is not one creature that I know, which next to the few I would chuse, contributes very much to my satisfaction.

At the same time that I regret the want of your conversation, I please my self with thinking that you are where you first ought to be, and engaged where you cannot do too much. Pray give my humble service, and best wishes to your good mother. I am sorry you don't tell me how Mr. Gay does in his health; I should have been glad to have heard he was better. My young Amanuensis,[2] as you call him, I am afraid will prove but a wooden one: and you know *ex quovis ligno,* &c.[3] You will pardon Mrs. R——'s [4] Pedantry, and believe me to be

Yours, &c.

P.S. By the inclosed you will see I am like to be impress'd, and enroll'd in the lists of Mr. Curll's [5] Authors; but I thank God I shall have your company. I believe it is high time you should think of administring another *Emetick.*[6]

EDITIONS: *The Works of Alexander Pope, Esq.;* Vol. V. Containing an Authentic Edition of his Letters. The Second Edition, Corrected. London: Printed for T. Cooper, in Pater-noster-Row. MDCCXXXVII, pp. 239-240; Dobrée, pp. 535-536; Sherburn, Vol. II, pp. 433-434.

[1] The year could be either 1726 or 1727 in so far as Congreve's reference to Dean Swift is concerned, for Swift was visiting Pope during both of those years. In addition to several reasons given by Professor Sherburn (Vol. II, p. 433) for considering 1727 "far more probable," it should be noted that Congreve's letter, written from Bath on 6 May, is probably the letter from Congreve mentioned by Pope in writing to his publisher Benjamin Motte on 30 June [1727]: "You shall begin printing the next Volume of Prose, when you will . . . I am very sincerely, (& so is the Dean) Your affect. Servant A. Pope. I'm afraid you have not sent the Books to Mr. Congreve at Bath, for I recd a letter from him without mention of them. Pray enquire about it." Sherburn, Vol. II, p. 439. The "Books" were apparently the first two of the three volumes of *Miscellanies in Prose and Verse* that were issued during 1727 and appear in Congreve's *Library* as No. 420.

[2] Possibly the assistant who prepared Congreve's manuscript book list about 1726. See *Library,* p. 9.

[3] "The full adage seems to be: *Ex quovis ligno Mercurius non fingitur.*" Sherburn, Vol. II, p. 434.

[4] Possibly the Mrs. Deborah Rooke to whom Congreve willed "one hundred pounds with all my Linnen and apparel." See No. 148.

[5] Edmund Curll (1675-1747), the unprincipled publisher, had apparently advertised without authorization the publication of some work by Congreve just as he had done earlier for Pope.

[6] A vomit administered to Curll in 1716 for publishing Pope's *Court Poems* without authorization. See Sherburn, Vol. I, p. 326.

145   LOUIS RICCOBONI [1] ON CONGREVE

[*1727*]

Amongst the Crowd of *English* Poets, Mr. *Congreve* is most esteemed for Comedy. He was perfectly acquainted with Nature; and was living in 1727, when I was in *London;* I conversed with him more than once, and found in him Taste joined with great Learning. It is rare to find many Dramatic Poets of his Stamp.

Louis Riccoboni, *An Historical and Critical Account of the Theatre in Europe,* London, 1744, p. 175.

[1] Louis (Lodovico) Riccoboni (1674?-1753), actor and playwright, was born in Italy but made a great reputation in Paris and was naturalized as a French citizen. In 1727, he published in Paris an octavo volume entitled *Histoire du Théâtre Italien depuis la décadence de la comédie latine.* A copy of this work in Congreve's library was possibly the gift of Riccoboni when he visited Congreve in London in 1727. See *Library,* No. 314.

Three Women

All his life Congreve was attentive to women. He gave special attention to three. The first of these was the lovely singer and lutenist Arabella Hunt, for whom the twenty-two-year-old poet wrote his ode "Upon a Lady's Singing" (1692). From Windsor he wrote her, two years later: "Angel, There can be no stronger Motive to bring me to *Epsom,* or to the North of *Scotland,* or to Paradise, than your being in any of those places; for you make every Place alike Heavenly wherever you are" (No. 146). After Arabella's untimely death in 1705, he penned this epigram under a painting by Kneller:

> *Were there on Earth another Voice like thine,*
> *Another Hand so blest with Skill Divine!*
> *The late afflicted World some Hopes might have,*
> *And Harmony retrieve thee from the Grave.*[1]

[1] *Works* (1710), Vol. III, p. 917; Dobrée, p. 245.

Possibly Congreve's attention to Arabella Hunt was only a gallant expression of interest in a beautiful and gifted woman. For the charming Anne Bracegirdle, creator of the heroines in his comedies, he had a far deeper feeling. About the time Congreve met Anne, so her fellow actor tells us, she was just "blooming to her Maturity . . . the Darling of the Theatre . . . the Universal Passion." [2] Is it any wonder that the susceptible young dramatist entirely lost his heart as he composed his heroine's parts for Anne and then watched her perform them "to a miracle," as he wrote his friend Keally (No. 8)? We cannot be sure just what her response was to Congreve's ardent wooing. For a period she was certainly no more than his "Pious Selinda," [3] on whom he could only look and sigh. As a member of an old county family and jealous of his rank as a gentleman, Congreve could hardly have thought seriously of allying himself by marriage with an actress. It would certainly not have been the way of his world, even if his cousin Robert Leke, third Earl of Scarsdale, had not become infatuated with Anne about 1703, and she had never given the poet occasion to write "False tho' you've been to me and Love." [4]

Congreve's attachment to Henrietta, later known as the "young Duchess" of Marlborough, was the one enduring passion of his life. Lady Henrietta Churchill, oldest daughter of the great Duke of Marlborough, had married Francis Godolphin, son of Sidney, first Earl of Godolphin, in 1698, when she was only eighteen. Congreve probably knew her by 1705, when he and Vanbrugh opened their fine new theatre in the Haymarket with a special prologue that mentioned Henrietta Godolphin as "the learn'd Minerva." [5] It was said that she had "a great mind to be thought a Wit," and she was flattered to have Congreve at Godolphin House in St. James's or at her little lodge in Windsor Park, or to be with him at one of the

---

[2] Cibber, Vol. I, pp. 170-172.

[3] *Works* (1710), Vol. III, p. 918; Dobrée, p. 245.

[4] See Hodges, pp. 87, 88.

[5] See *The History of the English Stage* by Thomas Betterton. Revised, with additional notes, by Charles L. Coles, Boston, 1814, p. 105.

watering places.[6] During the summer of 1722, Congreve was devoting himself so exclusively to her at Bath that Pope asked John
Gay, who was also at Bath, to "put Mr. *Congreve* in mind that he
has one on this side of the World who loves him; and that there
are more Men and Women in the Universe, than Mr. *Gay* and
my Lady Dutchess of *M[arlborough]*" (see No. 140). As Congreve
became more infirm during his last years, the young Duchess became
more attentive. Early in the summer of 1728, she went with him to
Bath and stayed late in a vain effort to help him regain his health.
When he died on 19 January 1728/9, she arranged a dignified
funeral in Westminster Abbey (see Nos. 149, 150, 151), erected a
monument to his memory (No. 152), and tried unsuccessfully to
buy from old Jacob Tonson a Congreve portrait that she admired
(No. 153).

No doubt Congreve's long attachment to Anne Bracegirdle and
then to the young Duchess of Marlborough produced an extensive
correspondence, but it is not surprising that so intimate a correspondence should have been carefully guarded at first and apparently destroyed entirely later. At any rate, not a single note or letter is
now to be found.

Gossip and Interlocking Wills.

Interest in Congreve's will (No. 148) began with his death. It has
continued ever since. The day following Congreve's elaborate funeral in Westminster Abbey, old Jacob Tonson wrote from his
country estate to inquire of his nephew in London "how Mr Congreves Circumstances were at his Death. I beleive they must be
considerable . . ." and he wondered about Congreve's "executors"
and "to whom" he had "left" his property (No. 99). Four days later,
on 1 February 1728/9, Lady Irwin wrote from London to her
father in the country that Congreve had made the young Duchess of
Marlborough "executrix, by which she gets 7000 pounds, in wrong,

[6] See Hodges, pp. 112, 115, 120, 121.

I think one may say, to a great many poor relations he had, and some say a son by Mrs. Bracegirdle" (No. 151). Thus began more than two centuries of gossipy criticism of a will that seemed strange and inexplicable.

Congreve's true motives in leaving his property to the wealthy Duchess can best be understood when read with the interlocking will of the Duchess (No. 154). But this will was not written until 1733, shortly before the Duchess died, and it was not made public. Years elapsed, perhaps intentionally, before the will was even probated. Congreve's will, on the contrary, was pried into immediately —witness Tonson's inquiry and Lady Irwin's remarks above mentioned. The will was published during the year of Congreve's death and again the following year. The will of the Duchess is here published for the first time.

It should be noted that her will made sure that her body would be buried, not at Blenheim, but in Westminster Abbey "in the very same place with the Right honourable Sidney late Earl of Godolphin"; *i.e.*, in the same part of the Abbey where, according to *The Daily Journal* for the 27 January 1728/9, she had buried Congreve. In the remainder of the will, the Duchess concerned herself chiefly with her "Dearly beloved Daughter Mary Godolphin," to whom she left specifically "all Mr Congreves Personal Estate that he left me" and her plate engraved "with Mr. Congreves Armes"; the "Three thousand pounds" that her husband Francis, Earl of Godolphin, Congreve's executor, was holding for her (drawn from Congreve's account at the Bank of England on 12 February 1728/9, as shown by No. 90); and the famous diamond necklace and earrings which had cost £7,500. These, presumably, were the jewels costing "seven thousand pounds" that the Duchess showed to Dr. Young when she told him they had been "purchased with the money Congreve left her." [7]

When her daughter Mary Godolphin was born in 1723, the year after Pope had noticed Congreve's attentiveness to the Duch-

[7] Joseph Spence, *Anecdotes*, ed. by S. W. Singer, London, 1820, p. 376. The £3,000 from the Bank of England plus the £7,000 or £7,500 for the jewels approximate the £10,000 Congreve is reputed to have left the Duchess.

ess, there was gossip about the young girl's parentage. But most of this was forgotten when it developed that Congreve's will named as his sole executor the Duchess' husband and she appointed him one of Congreve's pallbearers. As the years passed, it came to be widely accepted that the relationship between Congreve and the Duchess had been merely platonic, and consequently his will seemed eccentric. Contemporaries, or near contemporaries, of Congreve who still believed that Mary Godolphin was the natural daughter of Congreve are represented by the authors of *Phino-Godol* (No. 155), *The Secret History of Henrada Maria Teresa* (No. 156), and the *London Journal, 1762-1763* (No. 157).

One of the four codicils to Congreve's will referred to a will dated 6 February 1725/6 and twice mentioned the young Duchess of Marlborough as "sole Executrix." Elsewhere the will, under date of 26 February 1725/6, named the husband, Francis, Earl of Godolphin, "sole Executor," and it was certainly he who served as executor. Evidently Congreve did, at one stage in the preparation of his will, name the Duchess as his executrix. If Mary Godolphin was his daughter, he naturally wanted her to have his personal things, his plate engraved with the Congreve arms, and the choice collection of books he valued so highly. And all this he wanted to pass along quietly, without scandal or embarrassment. He would hardly have considered naming Mary directly as his heir. To do so would multiply gossip without end. He could depend on the mother, as sole executrix, to care for his property and pass it along in her will to Mary. But on second thought, Congreve apparently realized that he could accomplish his purpose regarding his property and at the same time help to quiet gossip by naming the husband of the Duchess as his sole executor. The will, it should be noted, was carefully drawn to restrict the powers of the husband and to leave the Duchess entirely free to transmit Congreve's property (as she did) to Mary.

Somewhere out of the early gossip, and without any substantial evidence, came the story that the Duchess, in doting upon the memory of Congreve, secured an image of him which she worshipped or treated in some unnatural way. Perhaps the image story had its beginning in 1732 with the publication of the poem *Phino-Godol* (No. 155). The Duchess did erect a statue to Congreve in Westminster Abbey, as the poem points out, and the *Daily-Post* for 15 July 1732 reports that she had secured at a cost of £200 a fine waxen image of Congreve that was broken in moving. That she worshipped this image seems to be only a figment of the imagination, as the satirist implies by citing the paragraph in the *Daily-Post* as his source. This source, it will be noted (No. 155), does not justify the satirist's imaginative story. Next year the image story was further publicized when the lampoon was issued again under the title, *The Amorous D[uc]h[ess]: or, Her G[race] Grateful*. But in this same year, it should be noted, the image story was ignored by the detailed and much more factual *Secret History of Henrada Maria Teresa*. Before the end of the century, however, the tale had been so often repeated that the image became either an ivory automaton bowing to the Duchess[8] or a waxen figure to be served food and to be attended by a physician.[9] It remained for Macaulay in the nineteenth century to provide the Duchess with *two* images, one of ivory and one of wax.[10]

146   CONGREVE TO MRS. ARABELLA HUNT

Windsor, July 26, 1694.

ANGEL,

There can be no stronger Motive to bring me to *Epsom*,[1] or to the North of *Scotland*, or to Paradise, than your being in any of those Places; for you make every Place alike Heavenly where-ever you are. And I believe if any thing could cure me of a natural Infirmity, seeing and hearing you would be the surest Remedy; at least, I

[8] Thomas Davies, *Dramatic Miscellanies*, 1784, Vol. III, p. 372.

[9] *Biographia Britannica*, 1789, Vol. IV, p. 79.

[10] *Edinburgh Review* for January, 1841.

should forget that I had any thing to complain of, while I had so much more Reason to rejoice. I should certainly (had I been at my own Disposal) have immediately taken Post for *Epsom,* upon Receipt of your Letter: But I have a Nurse here, who has Dominion over me; a most unmerciful She-Ass. *Balaam* [2] was allow'd an Angel to his Ass; I'll pray, if that will do any good, for the same Grace. I would have set out upon my Ass to have waited upon you, but I was afraid I should have been a tedious while in coming, having great Experience of the Slowness of that Beast: For you must know, I am making my Journey towards Health upon that Animal, and I find I make such slow Advances, that I despair of arriving at you, or any great Blessing, till I am capable of using some more expeditious means. I could tell you of a great Inducement to bring you to this Place, but I am sworn to Secrecy; however, if you were here, I would contrive to make you of the Party. I'll expect you, as a good Christian may every thing that he devoutly prays for. I am

> *Your everlasting Adorer,*
> *W. Congreve.*

EDITIONS: *Familiar Letters of Love, Gallantry, and several occasions,* London, printed for Sam Briscoe, 1718, pp. 82-83; *Memoirs of the Life, Writings, and Amours of William Congreve, Esq;* Compiled by Charles Wilson, London, *1730,* pp. 63-64 (Part II); Summers, Vol. I, p. 104; Dobrée, pp. 530-531.

[1] The mineral springs discovered at Epsom about 1618 made the town a popular watering place during the seventeenth century. Congreve valued the waters at Epsom but disliked its "noisy pleasures." See No. 58.

[2] For the Biblical story of Balaam and his ass, see Numbers, 22:21-33.

147   HENRIETTA, DUCHESS OF MARLBOROUGH, TO LADY MARY
       WORTLEY MONTAGU [1]

                                                    [ca. *1722*]

I am sure you won't dislike to have Mr. Congreve tomorrow if you can get him, for he is like all good things hard to come at. And though I shan't add to the company I have wit enough not to spoil it, which you must allow is being tolerable. What hour would you have me come?

MANUSCRIPT: Wortley MSS., IV, f. 185. EDITIONS: George Paston [Emily Morse Symonds], *Lady Mary Wortley Montagu and Her Times*, London, 1907, p. 310; Hodges, p. 114; Robert Halsband, *The Life of Lady Mary Wortley Montagu*, Oxford, 1956, p. 116.

[1] For the coolness between the Duchess and Lady Mary Wortley Montagu, see Hodges, pp. 113-116.

148   WILL AND CODICILS OF WILLIAM CONGREVE

Westminster, 26 February 1725[6]

In the Name of God Amen. This is the last Will of mee William Congreve of the parish of St. Clement Danes Westminster in the County of Middlesex Esqr. made the Twenty Sixth day of February Anno Domini 1725. And first I desire and direct that my Funerall shall bee privately performed without the least Ostentation and the place where, I refer to my Executor to appoint. I give to the Severall persons herein after named the respective Legacyes following (That is to say) To

[First Codicil or Testamentary Schedule]

My intention is that the following Legacys be given to the respective persons herein named as if they were insert in the blank Space left in this Will for that purpose. Imprimis I give and bequeath to Ann Jellet [1] twenty pounds a Year during her life. Item to William Congreve [2] Son to Coll: Willm Congreve of Highgate and my Godson three hundred pounds. To Mrs. Ann Congreve Daughter to my late Kinsman Coll: Ralph Congreve [3] of Clarges Street, two hundred pounds. To Mrs. Ann Bracegirdle of Howard Street two hundred pounds. To Mrs. Frances Porter Fifty pounds. Item to Mrs. Deborah Rooke one hundred pounds with all my Linnen and apparel. For other lesse legacys I leave them as Specified in a Codicill enclosed in the duplicate of this Will and left in the Custody of the Dutchess of Marlborough.

[Continuation of the Will]

All the rest and residue of my Estate the same consisting in personall things only (not having any Lands or other Reall Estate) I give and bequeath to the Dutchess of Marlborough the now Wife of Francis Earl of Godolphin of Godolphin in the County of Cornwall But not soe as to vest in him the said Earl of Godolphin the Equitable right and Interest of such rest and residue But that the same and every part thereof and the Interest produce and benefitt thereof shall and may at all times from and after my Decease bee had and received by her the said Dutchess, Namely Henrietta Dutchess of Marlborough to her Sole and Seperate [*sic*] use and wherewith her said Husband or any after taken Husband of her the said Dutchess of Marlborough shall not intermeddle or have any controuling power over, nor shall the said rest and residue or the Interest and produce thereof bee lyable to the Debts and Incumbrances of the said Earl of Godolphin or of any after taken Husband of her the said Dutchess of Marlborough in any Wise But shall be had and received Issued and payd as Shee the said Dutchess of Marlborough Shall by Writeing under her hand from time to time Direct and appoint and her owne acquittance shall bee a Sufficient discharge for all or any part of the Estate soe given to her as aforesaid and in Confidence of the honesty and Justice of him the said Francis Earl of Godolphin I do hereby Constitute and Appoint him the Sole Executor of this my Will in Trust for his said Wife as aforesaid. In Witness whereof I have hereunto Subscribed my name and Sett my Seale the day and Yeare aforesaid. William Congreve Signed Sealed and Declared by the said William Congreve the Testator to bee his last Will in the presence of us Timo: Kiplin Thos. Swan.   [End of the Will]

[The Duplicate Will, which counts as the second codicil, repeats the will but with different witnesses: William Humpstone, George Thorpe, and Jonathan White.]

[Third Codicil (Second Testamentary Schedule)]

Legacys intended to be inserted in Blank Space of this Will and which I desire may be payd tho any thing should prevent my inserting them with my own hand in manner as I have filled up the other Blanks in the same. Imprimis to Ann Jellet twenty pounds a Year for her Life. Item to my Godson William Congreve Son of Coll Wm. Congreve of Highgate three hundred pounds. Item to Ann Congreve daughter of the Late Coll Ralph Congreve of Clarges Street two hundred pounds. Item to Mrs Ann Congreve [4] her Mother and to Coll Willm. Congreve of Highgate each twenty pounds. Item to Mrs Ann Bracegirdle of Howard Street two hundred pounds. Item to Mrs. Deborah Rook one hundred pounds and all my wearing apparel and Linnen of all Sorts. Item to Mrs. Frances Porter [5] fifty pounds. Item to Peter Walter Esqr. of St. Margets Westminster twenty pounds. Item to Richard Lord Viscount Cobham [6] and Richard Lord Viscount Shannon [7] twenty pounds each. Item to Charles Mein Esqr. [8] and Mr. Edward Porter [5] and Mr. Joshua White [9] twelve pounds each. Item to her Grace Henrietta Dutchess of Newcastle [10] I give and bequeath the Dutchess of Marlboroughs picture by Kneller. Item to the Lady Mary Godolphin [11] Youngest Daughter to the Dutchess of Marlborough I give and bequeath her Mothers picture Ennamelld in Miniature together with my white brilliant Diamond Ring. Item to Coll. Charles Churchill [12] twenty pounds together with my gold headed Cane. Item to all and each of my Domestick Servants a years Wages and proper Mourning. Item to the poor of the parish ten pounds.

[Fourth Codicil]

Whereas I William Congreve did by my last Will and Testament bearing date the Sixth [13] day of February 1725 affix a Schedule of Legacys written in my own hand over a blank space left for that purpose in the said Will I do hereby revoke and annull those Legacys excepting such as are bequeath'd to persons related to me and bearing my own name as also what is therein Bequeath'd to Mrs. Ann Jellet and Mrs. Ann Bracegirdle which said Legacys I do hereby Confirm and do hereby revoke and annull all other Legacys therein

mention'd or in the Counterpart of the said Will more at large Set
down which Counterpart is by me left in the Custody of her Grace
Henrietta Dutchess of Marlborough my Sole Executrix as is Specified in the said Will and Counterpart thereof. Be it understood that
my intention is by this Writing to revoke those Legacys not herein
Confirm'd as above mention'd, in such manner onely as to leave them
absolutely in the power and determination of the abovenamed Henrietta Dutchess of Marlborough, my Sole Executrix, either to pay
or refuse to pay them, to take from them or add to them as She
shall Judge the persons therein named especially my Domestick
Servants therein mention'd or not mention'd may have merited of
me William Congreve. Signed and Sealed in the presence of Joseph
Lee William Humpstone.

29° Januarij 1728°. [1729]

Which day appeared personally Thomas Snow of Saint Clements
Danes in the County of Middlesex Goldsmith and John Paltock of
the same parish Goldsmith and by virtue of their Oaths Deposed
that they Severally knew and were well acquainted with William
Congreve late of the parish of St. Clements Danes in the County
of Middlesex Esqr. deceased and with his handwriting Character
and manner of Writing having Severall times Seen him Write, and
having Seen and perused a Codicil annexed to the last Will and
Testament of the said deceased beginning thus (my intention is that
the following Legacys be given to the respective persons herein
named) and ending thus (and left in the Custody of the Dutchess of
Marlborough) and having also Seen and perused another Codicil
enclos'd in the Duplicate of the said Will beginning thus (Legacys
intended to be inserted in Blank Space of this Will) and ending thus
(Item to the poor of the parish Ten pounds) these Deponents do
beleive that the said Codicills and each of them were totally wrote
by and are the proper handwriting of the said William Congreve
deceased Tho Snow. John Paltock. Eodem die Dicti Thomas Snow
et Johannes Paltock Jurati fuerunt Super veritate premissorum
Coram me G Paul Sur. prsen. Tho: Tyllott Notario Publico.

Probatum Londini cum quatuor Codiciliis sive Schedulis Testamentis annex Tertio die Mensis Februarii 1728. . . .

Received this Twenty first day of February 1728 of Mr. Linthwaite Farrant Deputy Register assumed of the prerogative Court of Canterbury the Original Will and four Codicills or Testamentary Schedules of the above named William Congreve Esqr. deceased of which the above written is a true copy. I say received the said Originall Will and Codicills or Testamentary Schedules as Proctor and for the Use of the Right Honourable Francis Earl of Godolphin the Sole Executor therein named pursuant to an Order or Decree of the Judge of the said Court bearing date the Seventeenth day of this Instant February.

Per me
Robt Rous

Witnesses
  L. Farrant.
  Jo: Taylor
  Tho Lort.

MANUSCRIPTS: Somerset House, London, Prerogative Court of Canterbury, Brook 135 (the official transcript and also a separate copy of Congreve's holographic will). The copy was left on 21 February 1728/9 when the "Original Will and four Codicills or Testamentary Schedules," as stated in the receipt (see p. 258), were taken out for the use of the executor, Francis, Earl of Godolphin. These four codicils or testamentary schedules were mentioned also when the will was proved on 3 February 1728/29. But five days earlier, Thomas Snow and John Paltock, in swearing to Congreve's handwriting, mentioned only two codicils, one "annexed" to the will and the other "enclosed in the Duplicate of the said Will" (see p. 257), and they made each codicil unmistakable by pointing out its beginning and its ending. They made no mention of the very important codicil beginning "Whereas I William Congreve did by my last Will" and ending "may have merited of me" (see pp. 256-257). Three codicils are easily identified, but not the fourth unless the duplicate will is counted as a codicil. EDITIONS: *A True Copy of the Last Will and Testament of William Congreve, Esq*; London, 27 May 1729; included with *Memoirs of the Life, Writings, and Amours of William Congreve Esq*; London, 12 August 1730.

[1] Henrietta, Duchess of Marlborough, left Ann Jellett an annuity of £45. See No. 154.

[2] Congreve's godson, born about 1695, was an officer in the army. For Colonel William Congreve, see No. 93, note 4.

[3] Ralph Congreve had died about three months before Congreve made his will. Ralph's will (see No. 93), dated 8 November 1725 and proved 3 December 1725, named the dramatist as one of the executors. See No. 94 for a document signed by Congreve as executor. The "Mrs. Anne Congreve" mentioned here was evidently still a very young girl since her parents had been married less than nine years.

[4] Ralph Congreve had married Ann Hanmer in October, 1717.

[5] Sister of Anne Bracegirdle and wife of Edward Porter, with whom Congreve had lodgings in Surrey Street from 1706 till his death.

[6] See No. 51 for Congreve's letter to Edward Porter written from Lord Cobham's country estate at Stowe, Buckinghamshire.

[7] Richard Boyle, Viscount Shannon, had a country seat at Ashley near London, where Congreve was a frequent visitor. Letters Nos. 54, 83, 131, and 133 were written from Ashley.

[8] See No. 3, note 5.

[9] Congreve's deputy as undersearcher of the customs.

[10] The Duchess of Newcastle was the oldest daughter of Henrietta, Duchess of Marlborough.

[11] Lady Mary Godolphin is the "Connelia" of *Phino-Godol* (No. 155) and the "young daughter" of *The Secret History* (No. 156).

[12] Remembered also in the will of Henrietta, Duchess of Marlborough, No. 154.

[13] The date mentioned in this codicil, "the Sixth," might be considered an error for "the Twenty Sixth," which appears in both the original will and the duplicate will, if the codicil did not mention (twice, it will be noted) Henrietta, Duchess of Marlborough, as "Sole Executrix," whereas the wills name the husband, Francis, Earl of Godolphin, as "Sole Executor." And certainly it was the Earl of Godolphin who was the sole executor when the will was probated on 3 February 1728/9. Evidently this last codicil refers to an earlier will in which Congreve did name the Duchess of Marlborough as his "Sole Executrix."

149   HENRIETTA, DUCHESS OF MARLBOROUGH, TO GEORGE
BERKELEY [1]

January ye. 22d. [*1728/9*].

SIR

I must desire you to be one off the Six next Sunday upon this very
mellancholley occation. I allways used to think you had a respect for
him and I woud not have any there that had not. I am your most
Humble servant.

Marlborough

MANUSCRIPT: British Museum Add. 22,628, f. 88. EDITIONS: *Letters To and
From Henrietta, Countess of Suffolk, and Her Second Husband, The Hon.
George Berkeley; From 1712 to 1767,* London, 1824, Vol. I, pp. 330-331;
Hunt, p. xxxi; Hodges, p. 122.

[1] This note requesting George Berkeley to be one of six pallbearers at Congreve's
funeral was written on Wednesday after Congreve had died the preceding Sunday. For George Berkeley (1693-1746), youngest son of Charles, second Earl
of Berkeley, see *DNB*. Congreve's death and funeral were thus reported by a
contemporary:

> Mr. Congreve died about five o'Clock, on *Sunday* Morning, *January* the
> 19th 1728-9, at his House in *Surrey-street* in the *Strand*, in the 57th Year
> of his Age; and on the *Sunday* following, *January* 26th, his Corps lay in
> State in the *Jerusalem* Chamber; from whence, the same Evening, between
> the Hours of Nine and Ten, it was carried, with great Decency and
> Solemnity, into King HENRY the VIIth's Chapel in *Westminster-Abbey*,
> and Interred near the late Earl of *Godolphin*. The PALL was supported
> by, I. the Duke of *Bridgewater*. II. Earl of *Godolphin*. III. Lord *Cobham*.
> IV. Lord *Wilmington*. V. The Honourable *George Berkeley*, Esq; VI.
> Brigadier-General *Churchill*. And Colonel *Congreve* followed the Corps as
> Chief Mourner. [From *Memoirs*, p. 17 of addenda, separately paged.]

Henrietta, the Young Duchess of Marlborough

150   HENRIETTA, DUCHESS OF MARLBOROUGH,
TO GEORGE BERKELEY [1]

January ye. 28th. 1728[29].

SIR

The last letter I writ to you was upon allways having thought that
you had a respect and a kind one, for Mr. Congreve. I dare Say
you believe I could Sooner think off doing the most monstrous thing
in the world, then Sending any thing that was his, where I was
not perswaded it would be valued. The number off them I think so
off, are a mighty few indeed. Therefore must allways be in a particular manner your most Humble servant.

Marlborough

MANUSCRIPT: British Museum Add. 22,628, f. 87. EDITIONS: *Letters To and
From Henrietta, Countess of Suffolk, and Her Second Husband, The Hon.
George Berkeley; From 1712 to 1767*, London, 1824, I, 330-331; Hunt, p.
xxxi; Hodges, p. 123.

[1] This letter, dated two days after George Berkeley had served as one of the six
pallbearers at Congreve's funeral, was evidently written to accompany something
of Congreve's as a remembrance.

151   ANNE, VISCOUNTESS OF IRWIN,[1] TO HER FATHER, CHARLES
HOWARD, THIRD EARL OF CARLISLE

1 February [1728/9]

. . . The old Duchess of Marlborough [2] is very ill, and likely soon
to make her heirs happy. The young Duchess has made herself very
particular upon Mr. Congreve's death: he left her executrix,[3] by
which she gets 7000 pounds, in wrong, I think one may say, to a
great many poor relations he had, and some say a son by Mrs.
Bracegirdle. The Duchess buried him very handsomely, and showed
so great an affection for his dead body that she quitted her house
and sat by his corpse till he was interred. . . .

MANUSCRIPT: Carlisle MSS. at Castle Howard. EDITION: Historical Manuscripts Commission *Fifteenth Report*, Appendix, Part VI, 1897, pp. 56-57, from which No. 151 is reprinted.

[1] The Viscountess of Irwin was lady-in-waiting to Princess Augusta, the wife of Crown Prince Frederick.

[2] Sarah Jennings, Duchess of the first Duke of Marlborough, was called the "old Duchess" after his death in 1722 to distinguish her from the Duke's oldest daughter, Henrietta, who succeeded to her father's title by special act of Parliament. In spite of the severe illness of the old Duchess in 1729, she lived on till 1744, eleven years longer than the "young Duchess," Henrietta.

[3] Although the young Duchess was named executrix in one draft of Congreve's will (see No. 148), her husband, Francis, second Earl of Godolphin, was made executor by another draft and actually served as such. No doubt Congreve's naming the husband as executor, and his participation as one of the pallbearers, hushed much of the gossip about Congreve's association with the young Duchess.

152   CONGREVE'S EPITAPH,[1] BY HENRIETTA, DUCHESS
       OF MARLBOROUGH

Mr. William Congreve,
Dyed *jan* the 19th 1728 Aged 56.[2] And was buried near this place,
To whose most Valueable Memory this Monument is Sett up by
HENRIETTA *Dutchess* of MARLBOROUGH as a mark how
    dearly,
She remembers the happiness and Honour She enjoyed in
the Sincere Friendshipp of so worthy and Honest a Man,
Whose Virtue Candour and Witt gained him the love and
Esteem of the present Age and whose Writings will be the
        Admiration of the Future.

ENGRAVING: On the statue of Congreve in Westminster Abbey. EDITION: Lord Killanin, *Sir Godfrey Kneller and His Times, 1646-1723*, London, 1948, opposite p. 78.

[1] This epitaph in Westminster Abbey is engraved under a portrait medallion carved by Francis Bird after a painting by Sir Godfrey Kneller. The painting is now in the Kit-Cat Collection of the National Portrait Gallery, London.

[2] The age should be fifty-eight, since Congreve lacked just five days of reaching his fifty-ninth birthday. See Hodges, p. 6.

153 HENRIETTA, DUCHESS OF MARLBOROUGH, TO JACOB TONSON II [1]

November ye. 29th. 1729

SIR

I know 'tis only the Sett [2] off those pictures that your Uncle values and not that that I would give the world for. Therefore Sure except 'tis purely out off ill nature and having no respect for that picture he would change with me for an originall one off Sir Godfrey Knellars [3] just the same size off the Kittcat ones. I wish this was in your own power. I am sir your Humble servant.

Marlborough

MANUSCRIPT: Tonson MSS., Folger Shakespeare Library. EDITIONS: *Country Life*, 24 June 1925; Lord Killanin, *Sir Godfrey Kneller and His Times, 1646-1723*, London, 1948, p. 77. Lord Killanin thinks this letter probably refers to the Kit-Cat portrait of Congreve by Kneller. The statue in Westminster Abbey was carved from the Kneller portrait. See No. 152.

[1] This Jacob Tonson was the nephew, not the son, of Congreve's old publisher Jacob Tonson, but he was often called "Junior" to distinguish him from the older man. About 1720, old Jacob turned over to his nephew the active management of his fine publishing business and retired to his country estate in Herefordshire about one hundred miles northwest of London. Some seventy letters of his nephew covering the period 1727-1735 have been preserved at the Bodleian Library and the University of Texas Library, and others are among the Tonson papers in the British Museum. Four of these letters mentioning Congreve are reproduced in part as Nos. 98-101.

[2] During the period 1700-1720 Tonson had induced Sir Godfrey Kneller to paint for him in uniform size the portraits of the forty-odd persons who made up the famous Kit-Cat Club. He built a special room for these portraits at his home in Barn Elms near London and hoped at one time to move the portraits to his Herefordshire country estate. Evidently he did not part with Congreve's portrait since it is now with the Kit-Cat Collection in the National Portrait Gallery, but he probably loaned it for the making of the portrait medallion in

Westminster Abbey. Old Tonson also loaned the picture, at the request of the dramatist (see No. 91), to the dramatist's cousin Colonel William Congreve of Highgate to have a copy made. Henrietta had no more success in getting permanent possession of one of Tonson's precious Kit-Cat paintings than Tonson did in having his nephew buy Congreve's choice library just after Congreve's death (see No. 99). The library stayed with Henrietta, to be handed on to Mary and thus to become the property of the Leeds family into which Mary married in 1740.

[3] This original by Kneller was willed to the Duchess of Newcastle. See No. 154.

154   INTERLOCKING WILL OF HENRIETTA, DUCHESS
OF MARLBOROUGH

11 July 1732

In the Name of God Amen. This eleventh day of July in the Year of our Lord One thousand seven hundred and Thirty two I the most Noble Henrietta Dutchess of Marlborough with the full consent and approbation of the Right honourable Francis Earl of Godolphin testified by his being a Witness hereunto and on his solemn promise to permit the same to be proved in the proper Ecclesiastical Court and as much as in him lyes to see the same performed Do make this my last Will and Testament in manner and form following Vid First and principally I recommend my Soul to the Infinite Mercy of God my Body to the Earth to be Buried in Westminster Abby in the very same place with the Right honourable Sidney late Earl of Godolphin [1] Deceased and tis my Desire and express Will that my Body be not at any time hereafter or on any pretence whatsoever carried to Blenham. [2]

And as to my Temporall Estate First I direct all my just Debts to be paid. I Bequeath to my Daughter the Dutchess of Newcastle my Yellow Brilliant Diamond Ring and Mr. Congreves Picture by Knellar. I Give and Devise to the said Francis Earl of Godolphin my Husband my Gold Snuf Box with his Fathers Picture in it. Item I Give my Seal of Cæsars Head to Mr Charles Churchill.

I Devise to Mrs. Anne Jellet during her naturall Life one Annuity or Yearly sume of Forty and five Pounds. I Bequeath to Mary Spencer and Jane Barbar that wait on me if they are in my Service at the time of my Death all my wearing Apparell of all sorts Except Jewells and the like which I wear as Ornaments and also to each of them the sume of Fifty pounds and in case there shou'd be but one of them in my Service at the time of my Death then my Will is that she shall have all my wearing Apparell as aforesaid. I Bequeath to Sir John Evelyn Baronet, Mr Andrew Carletone, Mr Edwards three of my Executors and Trustees herein after named Two hundred pounds apeice.

I Give Devise and Bequeath to my Dearly beloved Daughter Mary Godolphin all my other Rings and all my other Seal's All my Watches Diamonds Pearles Jewells of all sorts Gold Medalls all my Plate with my own Armes on it my Two large Japan Cabinets my fine Japan Chest my Japan Scrutoir my fine Japan Skreen with four Leaves and all my Scrutoir's Cabinets Cubboards and Boxes and all that is in them my Gilt Twylett of Plate and five fine Japan Tables under Glasses. I also give to my said Daughter Mary all Mr Congreves Personal Estate that he left me and all my own money or which I Enjoy'd as such and whatever is put out or shall be put out either in Government or other Securities in my own or in any other Name or Names And the Three thousand pounds which is mine and is now in the Hands of the said Francis Earl of Godolphin my Husband.[3] And I do also give to my said Daughter Mary all arrears whatever that is Due to me from my Father's the Duke of Marlboroughs Estate and all other my Real and Personal Estate of what nature or kind soever which was reputed or used as mine or which I can any ways with the consent of my said Husband give to her. And my Will and Desire is and I request my Executors and Trustees hereafter named that the Money and other things hereby given to my Daughter Mary may be safely kept and the Money from time to time improved to the best advantage by adding and making the Interest from time to time Principal. And when my said Daughter Mary shall attain the Age of Thirteen Year's my Will is and I Do hereby direct that my said Daughter Mary shall have and receive out of the Interest of her Fortune and what is given her as aforesaid the Annual sume of One Hundred Pounds for Pocket Money and at her Age of Sixteen the Annual sume of Two hundred pounds And at her Age of one and Twenty Years if she shall not then be Married All her Portion and Fortune and I direct the same to be Paid and delivered to her my said Daughter accordingly. And I direct the said Annual Sumes hereby provid'd for my said Daughters Pocket Money to be paid Quarterly at Christmass Lady day Midsummer and Michaelmass without any Deduction or abatement for Taxes or any other matter or thing whatsoever. And I Do hereby impower my said Daughter from time to time at her Will and pleasure to change and alter any of her Trustees, that shall be negligent in performance of the Trust in them reposed. And in case my said Daughter shall not think fit to Marry then and in such case I do hereby impower her to Leave her said Fortune to such Person and Persons as she shall think fit to give the same by her Last Will and Testament Except the Widow of the late Marquiss of Blanford[4] or any of her familly or Relations. And it is my Will and Desire that the said Earl of Godolphin Do pay for all his and my said Daughters Cloaths Servants Wages and whatever else is suitable for the Education of a Person of her Quality untill she attains the Age of One and Twenty Years or Marries.

Item my Will is that if my said Daughter Marries then and in such case I hereby Order and Direct my Executors to Assign my Fine Brilliant Diamond Neck-lace which cost Five Thousand Three hundred Pounds And also the fine Diamond Ear-Rings with Diamond Drop's to them which cost Two thousand Pounds[5] and all other my Jewells and also all my Plate both Gold and Silver of what Nature or kind soever as well that with my own Armes as that with Mr Congreves Armes to proper Persons to be Named by my Executors In Trust for the Sole seperate Personal and peculiar use of my said Daughter Mary Exclusive of her Husband or any other Husband she shall or may hereafter Marry. Neither are the same or any part thereof to be subject to the disposition Intermedling Debts or Incumberances of any Husband she shall Marry. And Upon further

Trust that my said Daughter Mary shall and may notwithstanding her Coverture and Without the consent of her Husband and as fully as if she were Sole and Unmarried and independent of her Husband Give the said Diamond Neck-lace Diamond Ear-Rings Drop's and other Jewells together with all the said Plate or any part thereof to which ever Child she has as she Pleases and if she has no Child to leave the same to any other Person she thinks fit Except the Widdow of the late Marquiss of Blanford or any of her familly or Relations.

And it is my Will that after my Death my said Daughter Mary may go and Live with her Sister the Dutchess of Newcastle the Earl of Godolphin my Husband paying what he thinks fit for her little familly And that Mary Ierland may be always her Nersery Maid. And of this my last Will and Testament I Ordain constitute and appoint my said Husband Francis Earl of Godolphin Sir John Evelyn Mr Andrew Charlton and Mr Samuell Edwards Executors In Trust for the Sole benefit of my said Daughter Mary Godolphin Witness my Hand and Seal the Day and Year above Written.

Marlborough

Signed Sealed Published and Declared by the said Dutchess of Marlborough as and for her last Will and Testament in the Presence of

> *Godolphin*
> *Joseph Doyly*
> *Jno. Owen*

19th. of May 1736.

The Right Honourable Francis Earl of Godolphin the Husband of the deceased, Sir John Evelyn Baronet and Andrew Charlton Esquire three of the Executors within named were duly sworn (power being reserved to Samuel Edwards Esquire the other Executor when he shall apply for the same) before me

> *J. Andrew*
> *Surrogate*

Proved at London before the Worshipfull John Andrew Doctor of Laws and Surrogate the nineteenth day of May in the year of our Lord 1736 by the Oaths of the Right Honourable Francis Earl of Godolphin the husband of the deceased, Sir John Evelyn Baronet and Andrew Charlton Esquire three of the Executors To whom Administration was granted being first sworn duly to administer (power reserved of making the like Grant to Samuel Edwards Esquire the other Executor named in the said Will when he shall apply for the same).

MANUSCRIPT: Somerset House, London, Prerogative Court of Canterbury, 113 Derby. A copy of the will is in the British Museum Add. MSS. 28,071, ff. 34-39. The original will is on a single sheet of parchment in one paragraph.

[1] The Duchess had buried Congreve near Sidney, Earl of Godolphin, and was now arranging to be buried in the same place.

[2] Evidently the young Duchess wished to be buried in Westminster Abbey near Congreve, but the long feud between her and her old mother could also account for Henrietta's not wanting to be buried at Blenheim. See Lynch, pp. 76-81.

[3] This £3,000, left to the Duchess in Congreve's account at the Bank of England, had been drawn out by the Earl of Godolphin as executor. See the account, No. 90.

[4] William Godolphin, Marquis of Blandford, was the oldest child of Henrietta. For years before his death in 1731, he had been on bad terms with his mother. He had especially antagonized her by insisting on a marriage which she strenuously opposed.

[5] This was evidently the diamond necklace the Duchess showed to Joseph Spence "that cost seven thousand pounds and was bought with the money Congreve left her." (Spence, *Anecdotes*, ed. by Singer, p. 376). These £7,000, plus the £3,000 in the Earl's hands, account for the total estate of £10,000 thought to have been left by Congreve. The diamond necklace is mentioned prominently in the marriage settlement between Mary Godolphin and the fourth Duke of Leeds, 1740. This lengthy document on the original parchment is preserved among the Leeds Papers by the Yorkshire Archaeological Society in the City of Leeds. In reporting the wedding, which occurred on 26 June 1740, Mrs. Elizabeth Montagu wrote her mother: "The Duchess had a diamond necklace from her Mother worth £10,000, she was very fine in cloaths and jewels." See *Elizabeth Montagu, The Queen of the Blue Stockings*, ed. by E. J. Climenson, London, 1906, Vol. I, p. 51. *The Private Letter-Books of Sir Walter Scott* (ed. by Wilfred Partington, London, 1930, p. 345) records this story about

the famous necklace: "Congreve's contemporaries . . . were far from thinking the Duchess of Leeds (at least) no relation to him. The Duchess of Portland once borrowed her jewels to wear at a masquerade, and as they were examining them together, the other taking up this massive necklace, asked her whether she could guess why the letters W. C. were engraved upon the back of every collet? 'I have often puzzled myself to divine what could be my mother's meaning in it,' said she, 'do you think it was the name of the jeweler?' 'Oh yes, it must have been so,' replied the Duchess of Portland, well knowing the cypher meant William Congreve, and in a hurry to get rid of the subject." Evidently the Duchess of Marlborough had caused "W. C." to be engraved on the silver links between the diamonds but had told Mary nothing about it. Mary was not yet ten years old when her mother died.

155 PHINO-GODOL. A POEM. IN HUDIBRASTICK VERSE.[1] (EXCERPTS)

[*London, August 11, 1732*]

We hear that the Effigies of the late ingenious WILLIAM CONGREVE, *Esq; done in Wax-Work, at the Expence of* 200£. *and which was kept at a Person of Quality's in St.* James's,[2] *was broke to Pieces by the Carelessness of a Servant in bringing it down Stairs last* Monday *Night*. Daily-Post. Numb. 3997. [Saturday, 15 July 1732]

> *Thus, to a* single *Paragraph,*
> (*A simple Thing to make one laugh*)
> *I' th'* Daily-Post, *a while ago,*
> *The World th' ensuing Work does owe* . . . (ll. 43-46)
> *Examine we that Fabrick* dread,
> *The* Noblest *Store-House of the Dead,*
> *And 'mong the sev'ral Regions,*
> *You'll find a Tomb of* Comick Con's,
> *Erected to his Memory*
> *By Great Hotonta*[3] *worthily;*
> *Not* undeserv'd—*such Excellence*
> *Most* justly *claims that Deference* . . . (ll. 121-128)
> Pictures *and* Prints *she now possesses,*
> *And oft ingenious Conny blesses;*

But long nor this, nor that contents;
She something more of Substance wants;
Something that she might, with her Arm,
Stroke o'er, and Finger ev'ry Charm . . . (ll. 135-140)
    She now, judicious, gives a Plan
To raise in Wax the God-like Man.
She shews his Statue, how't must be;
Assigns the Limbs their Symmetry. . . . (ll. 150-153)
    The Figure form'd, with lively Grace,
Having for Niche, a curious Case,
She visits oft the dear-lov'd Place.
Breaths out her soft Desires, some say,
Full Half a Dozen Times a Day;
And thus, for Years, she has gone—on,
As if she never meant t' have done
Lamenting for Apollo's Son. . . . (ll. 157-164)
    It happen'd, O! the fatal Day!
That Tom was order'd to convey
The Relick to another Room,
(Perhaps it better wou'd become.)
Poor Tom, being aukward, let it fall . . . (ll. 177-181)
It came with such a Swank to th' Ground,
That scarce a Morsel whole is found.
He strives to patch it up again,
But all his Labour is in vain . . . (ll. 185-188)
            —he was turn'd away . . . (l. 248)
'Tis sure Hotonta, if she cou'd,
Wou'd have exacted Blood for Blood;
At least, his Sight she wou'd not bear,
Who'd been her Conny's Murderer.
    And now sh' indulges wild Dispair,
And frets, and fumes, and rends her Hair.
No Victuals wou'd she eat that Day,
And, tho' she fasted, cou'd not pray.
Her House, a House of Lamentation,
Where every thing's in Fermentation;
No Peace, or Quiet, find you there;
Both High and Low the Sorrow share. . . . (ll. 250-262)
    And is the dear, good Man, then lost?
And am I to be always crost? . . . (ll. 271-272)
Ye Gods! ye Trees! ye murmuring Brooks!
Be ye my Comfort, with my Books.[4]

Henceforth, Hotonta, Man detest,
No longer with thy Conny blest;
Henceforth renounce the worthless Sex,
Nor let 'em more thy Peace perplex;
But use the Slaves, that prostrate fall,
As thou wert wedded to them all.
  O, dearest Conny! for thy Sake,
This Resolution sad I make.
O, Shade immortal! (does she cry)
Twice it was given to Thee to die.
A second Burial thou shalt have;
Nobler shall be thy second Grave;
Encircled with the Muses Nine,
Their darling Friend, as well as mine.
  Come, dear Connelia,⁵ come, my Love,
Help me the Manes to remove.
Let 'em no longer on the Floor
Be strew'd about, or trampled o'er;
Let us collect them, and bemoan;
For thou must give me Groan for Groan. . . . (ll. 277-298)

EDITION: *Phino-Godol. A Poem. In Hudibrastic Verse.* London: Printed for J. Towers, near Charing-Cross; and Sold by the Booksellers of London and Westminster. MDCCXXXII. Price One Shilling.

[1] This mock heroic poem of some three hundred lines in the style of Pope's *Rape of the Lock* was published in a sixteen-page quarto three years after Congreve's death and a year before the Duchess' death (advertised as "This Day is Published" by *The Daily Journal* for Friday, 11 August 1732). On the title page of the quarto appears, evidently as the inspiration for the poem, the news item from the *Daily-Post*, No. 3997 (for Saturday, 15 July 1732).

[2] Henrietta, the young Duchess of Marlborough, lived at Godolphin House in St. James's.

[3] The young Duchess, called Hotonta in this poem, had erected a statue to Congreve's memory in Westminster Abbey. See No. 152.

[4] When the Haymarket Theatre was opened in 1705, the Prologue referred to the young Duchess as "the learn'd Minerva." See Thomas Betterton, *The History of the English Stage*, revised by Charles L. Coles, Boston, 1814, p. 105. When Congreve died in 1729, the Duchess inherited his fine collection of books (see Congreve's Will, No. 148), which old Jacob Tonson described as "genteel and wel chosen," and suggested that his nephew try to buy them

(see No. 99). But of course the Duchess would part with nothing that had been Congreve's.

[5] To London readers in 1732, the connection between "Comick Con" or "Conny" and "Connelia" (Mary Godolphin, then about nine years old) was evident, and also the implication in the last line, "For thou must give me Groan for Groan."

156   THE SECRET HISTORY OF HENRADA MARIA TERESA

1733

Henrada Maria Teresa,[1] was descended from a very ancient and honourable Family, on her Father's Side, but her Mother was of low Extraction. This Gentleman,[2] having but a small Estate of paternal Inheritance, was obliged to cut out his Fortune with his Sword, which was the Fate of many others; he was a Person of great Conduct and Courage, and his gallant Behaviour soon rendered him conspicuous in the Eyes of the World. He had a lively and enterprizing Genius, was tall, well-shaped, and his Complexion was so fair mixed with a due Proportion of red, and there was such a Symmetry of Parts in his Face, that he obtained the Name of *Fair*.

In his younger Years he married *Jenina*,[3] whose Mother had but an indifferent Character; but the Daughter had a plentiful Fortune, was a Woman of a deep Penetration, an aspiring Nature, and always pushed herself forward, hoping that she should thereby be one Day advanced, and her Husband promoted to some considerable Post in the Army: Nor was she deceived in her Expectation, for she had wormed herself into the Affection and good Graces of the Empress's Sister,[4] who gave her not only a Place under her at Court, but made her (as it were) her Companion, and intrusted her with all her Secrets.

She soon gained the Ascendant over this Royal Lady, and nothing was transacted without her Consent and Approbation. She was a Woman of so much Policy that she prevailed with the Emperor [5] to make her Husband a *Count*, and indeed his Conduct and personal

Bravery rendered him worthy of that Title. He commanded in Chief the Confederate Forces, when the Empire was threatened with a total Destruction upon an Invasion of their Enemies, whom he frequently routed, and at last forced them to quit the Country, and in the most supplicant Manner to sue for Peace. Having preserved the Empire from the impending Ruin that was over its Head, and compelled the Enemy to retire shamefully into their own Country, having suffered many ignominious Defeats, he had several Places of great Profit and Honour given to him, and was advanced to a higher Degree of Dignity. The Income of the many Posts he enjoy'd, together with the Advantages that accrued from the War, rendered him the most wealthy Person in the Empire. As there is no Man without one Fault or another, so the greatest Imperfection this Nobleman had, was Coveteousness; but in reality he was not so very penurious as People represented him, nor indeed so liberal as his Wealth and Dignity required. He considered that he had several Daughters, and as he did intend to match them with Families of high Rank, so he resolved to give them Portions adequate to his own and their Husbands Qualities.

Henrada was his Eldest Daughter, whose Wit and Beauty attracted the Hearts of many Noblemen, particularly of the young Count *Adolphus*,[6] the Eldest Son of Count *Gustains Adolphus*.[7] This young Nobleman had all the Qualifications necessary to form a complete Gentleman; but above all he was singularly remarkable for the noble Endowments of the Mind, he was strictly Virtuous, and strictly Chaste; Charitable, Even-temper'd, Good-natur'd, and a most kind and indulgent Husband. He esteemed himself extreamly happy in his Marriage with *Henrada*, and she was well pleased with her Felicity of having espoused a young Nobleman, who had so many shining Excellencies, and manifested such conjugal Tenderness, that she was sensible of her being the only Object of his Desire. Thus they lived for many Years; and indeed might have lived many more in the same State had *Henrada* been so prudent to have adhered to virtuous Principles.

As she was a Lady of Wit and Spirit, she took a secret Pleasure in reading Poetry, of which she was a good Judge; but the Works of *Congravino*,[8] gave her the greatest Satisfaction. To give him what is due to his Character, he was one of the best of the Age, and a peculiar Talent in writing Comedies, wherein he never failed of some double *Entendre's,* to raise a becoming Blush in the Fair Sex: And when he made Love his Subject, he writ such Softness, that he made a deep Impression in their Hearts. This was the Fate of *Henrada,* who was captivated with his Poems. If, says she, the bare Reading of the Works of this Gentleman, can have such an Effect upon our Minds, what Wonders must he needs be capable of performing, when we hear the Words from his own Mouth? From that Day she studied how there might be an Interview between them; and as Secrecy was a material Point in this Case, it was some time before she could accomplish her Design: At last she determined to write to him, which she did to the following Effect.

Signior Congravino,

If you have the Spirit of an English-man, *you will not refuse a Woman's Challenge; meet me therefore this Evening in the* Inamorate's *Grove at the Back of the Palace.*　　　*Adieu.*

She sent this Letter by a trusty Servant, with Orders to deliver it into *Congravino's* own Hand, who as soon as he had read it, said, Give my humble Service to the Lady, and let her know that her Commands shall be punctually obey'd.

This was acceptable News to *Henrada,* who, in reading her Favourite's Poems, had let the Time pass away imperceptibly 'till it was almost Six o'Clock. She then began to prepare herself for a Sally, and disguising herself in the best Manner she was able, and yet not to appear as a Person of the inferior Sort, she hasten'd to the Place of Rendezvous, accompanied by the Female Servant whom she intrusted with the Secret.

In a few Minutes after she came thither, she saw *Congravino* coming towards the Grove, upon whose Approach the Servant retired, and play'd the Part of a Centinel to give an Alarm, if any Person approached to interrupt their Conversation. As soon as he had the Honour of comming up to the Lady, whose Face was covered with a Veil, he said, Madam, if you are the Heroine, who sent

me a Challenge this Day to meet you at this Place, I desire to know
your Commands; but if you are some other Lady, who have made
an Assignation here, I will instantly withdraw: For as you have the
Right of Possession, as being the First, it would be indecent, as well
as injust, to interrupt you.— Sir, answered *Henrada*, I flatter myself
in saying, that the Conversation of so polite a Gentleman as the
celebrated *Congravino*, cannot fail of a kind Reception from me,
who am the Person that sent you the Challenge. They then seated
themselves on a Green Bank, and when they had talked half an
Hour about one Affair or another, she pulled out of her Pocket a
Volume of his Writings, and turning to a particular Page, which
treated of Love, told him, that she had read that Piece with an in-
expressible Pleasure, but desired she might hear it repeated by him,
for then she was sure it would receive an Addition of many Beauties,
which she had not Sense enough to discover. He readily complied
with her Request, and laying every Emphasis in its proper Place,
raised such an Emotion in the young Countess,⁹ that she could not
refrain from squeezing his Hand, and thereby letting him know
what an Extacy she was in. To work up her Imagination to the
Height, hoping thereby to gratify his Inclinations, he turned to some
other Parts of the Book, which he read with such a Grace, that she
had certainly yielded to any thing he would desire, if they had not
been interrupted by the sudden Approach of her Servant, who nevertheless hem'd and coughed twenty times before she enter'd the
Grove. She went directly to her Lady, and whispering said, Madam,
I perceive a Gentleman steering his Course this Way, and by his
Stature, Air, and Mien, I am persuaded that he is my Lord the
Count. Go back, says the Lady, and bring the best Intelligence you
can; then turning to *Congravino*, she said, Sir, I have too much
Reason to apprehend a Discovery, and therefore must retreat in
Time, but as a Signal of the Value I have for you, I request you
to wear this for my Sake. She then took a Diamond Ring off her
Finger, which she presented to him, and which he received upon his
Knees, and begg'd the Favour of kissing her Hand. My Hand, said
she! there is but little Satisfaction in such a Trifle: And thereupon
she unveiled her Face. By all the Saints above, Madam, said he, if

I were to draw the Picture of *Venus* to the utmost Perfection, I
wou'd only aim to copy from such a beautiful Original. Upon this
he embraced her, kissed her with Extacy, and vow'd eternal Fidelity.
The young Countess promised he should hear quickly from her,
and upon her Servant's Return, she went out at a private Part of
the Grove, and was not detected by her Lord.

Contrary to the Practise of most Persons of Quality, *Henrada*
performed her Promise, for the very next Day she sent him a
Letter, wherein she acquainted him, that she would be at his House
in cog that Afternoon. She came punctual to the Time appointed,
and was received with all the tender Respect imaginable. They pass'd
the Evening in Gallantry, and before they parted, they had the
Satisfaction of revelling together for the space of two Hours. The
Countess in a short Time perceived the blooming Hopes of their
unlawful Pleasures, which prov'd to be a Pregnancy, and thereupon
having a Meeting to consult what was proper to be done, they concluded to go to *Aix le Chapele*,[10] where there was not so great a
Probability of their being discovered, as there might be if they went
to the *Spaw*. However they did not think it convenient to travel together, and therefore concluded that the Countess should set out
first, and her Lover follow her the next Day. *Henrada* travelled by
slow Stages on purpose to give *Congravino* an Opportunity of over-
taking her, which he did in about two Days Journey from *Aix le
Chapele;* they dined together, and in the Afternoon he took his leave
and set forward. When he had arrived at *Aix,* he hired a first Floor
consisting of six Rooms, and going to meet the Countess, he seperated her trusty Servant from the rest, and slipt a Letter into her
Hand, directed for her Lady, wherein he acquainted her with what
Steps he had taken; and advised what Method to pursue. In the
Evening *Henrada* arrived at the Lodgings, but was informed that
a Gentleman had taken the first Floor: The young Countess seemed
surprised, but on a sudden, with a smiling Countenance, she said,
If he be a true *Chevaliere,* he will surrender five Rooms to a Lady
in my Distress, and thereupon she took Possession of them. *Congravino* being informed by the Mistress of the House of what had
passed, and that she could not possible refuse a Lady of her Quality,

to whose Family she was under many Obligations, he said, He would be content with the single Room, and hoped the Countess would permit him to acknowledge the Honour she had done him in accepting the Lodgings. He was introduced immediately, and after mutual Complements, they passed the Time away in discoursing on various Subjects, 'til Supper was laid upon the Table. When the Cloth was removed, *Henrada* told him, That there was a greater Conveniency in the Lodgings, than he was aware of; for a Door opened out of her Bed-chamber upon the Stair-Case, opposite to his, whereby they might have an Opportunity of conversing together without Suspicion.

They continued here the whole Season, to the great Joy and Satisfaction of each other; and tho' they were known by several Persons of Quality, yet they carried on their Intrigue with such Subtlety, that they did not give the least Occasion for Censure. They now prepared to return home, and began their Journey after the same Manner as when they set out.

The Kind, the Tender, and the Affectionate *Adolphus* received his Lady with open Arms; whether he had received any Information of her Behaviour, is what History does not mention; however he was so cautious, that he did not give his Domesticks any Umbradge to suspect his Uneasiness. A little before Bed-time, looking very intently upon the young Countess, he said, Either my Eyes deceive me, or your Ladyship is with Child. Your Lordship is much in the Right, she replied, without shewing any Manner of Concern. Then, Madam, said the young Count, I hope your Ladyship will give me the Satisfaction of knowing the Father's Name. As she would not comply with his Desire, they were seperated by Consent from Bed, and in that State they continued for twelve Years, and kept a constant Correspondence with *Congravino*. At length *Henrada* was delivered of a Daughter,[11] of whom all the Care imaginable was taken; and she was brought up in the House with her Mother. Much about this Time the Countess's Father died, whereby his Titles descended to her,[12] and with them, a large Estate to support the Dignity. Little Miss, encreasing in Years, had the Happiness of pleasing her Mother, who perceived in her the Wit and Sprightliness of the Father, who dying a few Years after, placed such an entire Confidence in *Henrada,* that he made her his sole Heiress and Executrix,[13] not in the least doubting but she would take care of his Daughter. 'Tis true, he did not recommend the Child to her, which he imagined would be fruitless, being persuaded that *Henrada* would always look upon her with an Eye of Tenderness and Affection. She took as much Care of her Education, as if she had been her Legitimate-Daughter, and no Pains or Cost were spared to make her an accomplished young Woman. She would not permit her to be called by any other Name than her Father's, for whom she retained a grateful Remembrance, and, as it is said, shed many Tears, when she looked earnestly upon Miss: She took Care to have her imbibe the most virtuous Principles, and to be instructed in the strictest Rules of Morality, that her Mind might not be formed only with an Idea of what was Good, but cultivated with the Practice of it; and also to have an Abhorrence of entertaining a Notion of any thing tending to Vice or Dishonesty, even in the most minute Point. A Mind thus framed in its tender Years, must render the Person the Delight of Mankind, especially when arrived to Maturity.[14]

Whether *Henrada* laid too much too Heart the Death of *Congravino,* I cannot take upon me to determine; she did not survive him above five Years; at last being seized with a lingring Distemper, she was advised to take the Country Air, but relapsing several times, and her Constitution being greatly impaired by her Sickness, she was at last constrained to pay the last Debt to Nature.[15]

When she was sensible of the Approach of Death, she called for Miss, gave her her Blessing, and having made her Will, left her all her Father's Estate, by whom she was impowered to leave it to whom she pleased,[16] and made a very large Addition to it. She died a Penitent, and was sorry she had wronged so good a Husband as *Adolphus.*

EDITION: *The Court Parrot. A New Miscellany, in Prose and Verse,* London printed; Sold by F. Dormer, 1733.

[1] Henrietta Churchill, the young Duchess of Marlborough (1680-1733).

[2] John Churchill, first Duke of Marlborough (1650-1722).

[3] Sarah Jennings, Duchess of Marlborough (1660-1744).

[4] Princess Anne, later Queen Anne (1665-1714).

[5] King William III (1650-1702).

[6] Francis Godolphin, later second Earl of Godolphin (1678-1766).

[7] Sidney Godolphin, first Earl of Godolphin (1645-1712).

[8] William Congreve.

[9] The implication is that the meeting took place not earlier than 1712, when Henrietta became Countess Godolphin on the death of her husband's father. She was then about thirty-one years old.

[10] Bath.

[11] Lady Mary Godolphin, later Duchess of Leeds (1723-1764). See Lynch, pp. 91-109.

[12] On the death of the first Duke of Marlborough in 1722, Henrietta became Duchess of Marlborough by a special act of Parliament.

[13] See Congreve's will (No. 148), in which Henrietta was named heiress and (in one codicil) sole executrix.

[14] This flattering promise for Lady Mary Godolphin was justified, as shown by Boswell's report twenty years later that she "has turned out extremely well." (See No. 157.)

[15] Henrietta died on 24 October 1733 (Lynch, p. 89), about four years and nine months after Congreve. She did die of a "lingring Distemper" and in the country, at Harrow.

[16] Congreve's will (No. 148) did empower Henrietta to leave Congreve's property to whom she pleased, and she left it specifically to her daughter Mary.

157   FROM BOSWELL's *London Journal, 1762-1763*

London, Thursday, 20 January 1763

Mrs. Douglas, who has a prodigious memory and knows a thousand anecdotes, especially of scandal, told me that Congreve the poet lived in the family of old Lord Godolphin, who is yet alive,[1] and that Lady Godolphin was notoriously fond of him. In so much that her lord having gone abroad upon an embassy for two years, on his return she presented him with a fine girl by the author of *Love for Love*, which he was so indulgent as to accept of; nay, after Congreve's death, he joined with her in grief, and allowed her to have an image of him in wax daily set at table and nightly in her bedchamber, to which she spoke, believing it through heat of fancy, or believing it in appearance, to be Congreve himself. The young lady was most tenderly educated, and it is a certain fact that she was never suffered to see the moon for fear she should cry for it.[2] She is now Duchess of Leeds, and has turned out extremely well.[3]

MANUSCRIPT: Boswell Papers, Yale University Library. EDITION: *Boswell's London Journal, 1762-1763*, ed. by Frederick A. Pottle, William Heinemann, London, 1950, pp. 156-157.

[1] Francis Godolphin, second Earl of Godolphin, died in 1766. See the sketch of his life in *DNB*. For his indulgent treatment of his wife, the young Duchess of Marlborough, and her daughter, born on 23 November 1723, see Lynch, pp. 91-108. Professor Lynch suggests (p. 91) that the child "was named Mary, possibly in memory of Congreve's mother."

[2] This story about the young girl's not being allowed to see the moon for fear she might want it was told as early as 1730, when Mary Godolphin was only seven years old, in the *Memoirs of the Life, Writings, and Amours of William Congreve Esq*; (London, 1730, Part II, p. 125) compiled by someone who gave his name as Charles Wilson and pretended to have been acquainted with Congreve:

> Now, since *Love* is our *present Topic*, I will venture to relate an Instance of the most uncommon Affection, which I was an Ear-witness of at the *Bath*. A Gentleman asking a certain Lady, why she did not bring Miss abroad for an Airing, considering the Fineness of the Weather: No, says the indulgent Mother, *Miss is very much indispos'd, and has got the Vapours most inordinately, and if she should go abraoad, perhaps she might fancy the* SUN *or the* MOON, *and those are Things she can't have; but every thing that is under them, she may, and shall have.*
> Thus spoke the Mother most magnificent.

[3] She was married to Thomas Osborne, fourth Duke of Leeds on 26 June 1740 and died suddenly on 3 August 1764. See Lynch, pp. 94-107.

SELECTED BIBLIOGRAPHY

(Arranged Chronologically)

I. CONGREVE'S PLAYS—FIRST EDITIONS IN QUARTO

The Old Batchelour. London: Peter Buck, 1693.
The Double-Dealer. London: Jacob Tonson, 1694.
Love for Love. London: Jacob Tonson, 1695.
The Mourning Bride. London: Jacob Tonson, 1697.
The Way of the World. London: Jacob Tonson, 1700.

II. SOME COLLECTED EDITIONS—POEMS AND PLAYS
(*Later Editions Including the Essay on Humor,* Incognita, *and Letters*)

The Works of Mr. William Congreve, 3 vols. London: Jacob Tonson, 1710. Reprinted, 1717, as the second edition.
The Works of Mr. William Congreve, 2 vols. The third edition, revis'd by the author. London: Jacob Tonson, 1719-1720.
The Works of Mr. William Congreve, 3 vols. The fourth edition. London: Jacob Tonson, 1725.
The Works of Mr. William Congreve, 3 vols. The fifth edition. London: Jacob Tonson, 1730.
The Works of Mr. William Congreve, 2 vols. Dublin: Theo. Jones, 1736.
The Works of Mr. William Congreve, 3 vols. Birmingham: John Baskerville, for J. and R. Tonson, 1761. (The first edition to include Congreve's essay on humor.)
The Complete Works of William Congreve, 4 vols. Edited by Montague Summers, the plays from the first quartos. London: The Nonesuch Press, 1923. (The first edition to include the novel *Incognita* and a collection of letters.)
Comedies by William Congreve and *The Mourning Bride, Poems, & Miscellanies by William Congreve,* 2 vols. Edited by Bonamy Dobrée, the plays from the 1710 *Works.* London: Oxford University Press, The World's Classics, 1925, 1928. (The most complete and satisfactory edition of Congreve's collected works.)
The Works of Congreve. Edited by F. W. Bateson. New York: Minton, Balch & Company, 1930. (Scholarly but not complete.)

III. BIOGRAPHICAL STUDIES

Charles Gildon. *The Lives and Characters of the English Dramatick Poets. First begun by Mr. Langbain.* London, 1699.

Giles Jacob. *The Poetical Register: or, The Lives and Characters of the English Dramatick Poets.* London, 1719.
Charles Wilson. *Memoirs of the Life, Writings, and Amours of William Congreve Esq.* London, 1730.
Edmund Gosse. *Life of William Congreve.* London, 1888. Revised, 1924.
D. Schmid. *William Congreve, Sein Leben und Seine Lustspiele.* Wien und Leipzig, 1897.
Dragosh Protopopesco. *Un Classique Moderne William Congreve Sa Vie, Son Oeuvre.* Paris, 1924.
D. Crane Taylor. *William Congreve.* London, 1931.
John C. Hodges. *William Congreve the Man.* New York and London, 1941.
Kathleen M. Lynch. *A Congreve Gallery.* Cambridge: Harvard University Press, 1951.

IV. OTHER STUDIES—CHIEFLY CRITICAL

Samuel Johnson. "Congreve," in *Lives of the English Poets* (1781). Edited by George Birkbeck Hill, II, 212-234. Oxford, 1905.
William Hazlitt. *Lectures on the English Comic Dramatists.* London, 1819.
Charles Lamb. "On the Artificial Comedy of the Last Century," in *Essays of Elia* (1823-1835). Edited by Homer E. Woodbridge, pp. 211-220. New York: Macmillan, 1927.
Thomas Babington Macaulay. "Leigh Hunt: Comic Dramatists of the Restoration," in the *Edinburgh Review* for January, 1941. Edited by F. C. Montague in *Critical and Historical Essays,* III, 3-48. London, 1903.
William Makepeace Thackeray. "Congreve and Addison," in *The English Humourists of the Eighteenth Century,* pp. 55-104. London, 1853.
George Meredith. *An Essay on Comedy and the Uses of the Comic Spirit* (1877). Edited by Lane Cooper. New York, 1918.
John Palmer. *The Comedy of Manners.* London, 1913.
Allardyce Nicoll. *A History of Restoration Drama.* London, 1923.
Bonamy Dobrée. *Restoration Comedy 1660-1720.* Oxford, 1924.
Joseph Wood Krutch. *Comedy and Conscience after the Restoration.* New York: Columbia University Press, 1924. Revised, 1949.
Henry Ten Eyck Perry. *The Comic Spirit in Restoration Drama.* New Haven: Yale University Press, 1925.
Kathleen M. Lynch. *The Social Mode of Restoration Comedy.* University of Michigan Publications, III. New York: Macmillan, 1926.
Emmett L. Avery. *Congreve's Plays on the Eighteenth-Century Stage.* New York: Modern Language Association, 1951.
Thomas H. Fujimura. *The Restoration Comedy of Wit.* Princeton: Princeton University Press, 1952.
John C. Hodges. *The Library of William Congreve.* New York: The New York Public Library, 1955.
Paul and Miriam Mueschke. *A New View of Congreve's Way of the World.* Ann Arbor: The University of Michigan Press, 1958.
Norman N. Holland. *The First Modern Comedies.* Cambridge: Harvard University Press, 1959.

INDEX

All references are to pages. C = Congreve, the dramatist.

INDEX

293

Porter, Mrs. Frances (Bracegirdle): sister of
    Anne Bracegirdle, 7, 12; confused
    with Mary Porter, the actress, 7; C's
    letters to her, 15-16, 71-72; making
    shirts for Keally, 63-64, 65, 66; hopes
    to meet Keally at Bath, 68; C wishes
    her a Happy New Year, 69; her sick-
    ness, 71-72; is remembered in C's
    will, 254, 256; mentioned, 15, 49
Porter, Mary, the actress, confused with
    Frances Porter, 7
Portland, Duchess of, 269
Portland, Duke of, impeached, 23
Portlock, Ben, 103
Portsmouth, Duchess of, 47
Portugal, 11, 25
Powel, Martha: sister of Col. Ralph Con-
    greve, 141; her daughter, 140; her
    husband, 141
Powell, George, 112
Prior, Matthew, 59, 77
Protopopesco, Dragosh, 52
Public Record Office, 83, 153
Purcell, Daniel, his music for C's masque, 20-
    22
Purcell, Henry, 21, 204
Pyrgopolinices, in *Miles Gloriosus*, 181
Pythics, of Pindar, 218

Queen's gardens, at St. James's, 26
Queen's Theatre. *See* Haymarket Theatre
Quillet, Claude, 228
Quintilian, 215, 219

Rabble Club, 192-193, 194
Radcliffe, Edward, second Earl of Derwent-
    water, Dryden's letter to, 89-90
Radcliffe, Dr. John, 147
Rehearsal, The: C's copy, 160; Addison's ref-
    erence to, 211
Reinagle, Philip, 136
Revolution in Sweden, The, by Catharine
    Trotter Cockburn, 199, 212-213
Revolution, of 1688, 74, 78
Reynardson, Jacob, 51
Rhine, 206
Riccoboni, Louis: visits C, 157; his comment
    on C, 245
Rich, Christopher: outwitted, 43-44; his com-
    plaint against Vanbrugh and C, 111-
    112
Richmond, Charles Lennox, first Duke of, 46-
    47
Richmond, near London: C likes spa water
    there, 56; ladies there value C, 239
Rivers, Richard Savage, Earl of, 57
Robinson, Dr. Tancred, 71-72
Rob, or Robin. *See* Fitzgerald, Robert
Rochester, second Earl of. *See* Wilmot, John
Rome, 22, 189, 194
Rome, Church of, 226
Rooke, Mrs. Deborah, 244, 254, 256
Rosenberg, Albert, 193

Rotterdam, C's letter from, 14, 15
Rous, Robert, 258
Routh, Cuthbert, 135
Rouen, France, 193
Rowe, Nicholas: his tragedy, 18-19; his farce,
    34-35; Swift's assistance to, 134;
    poems dedicated to his memory, 156,
    227-228; C's opinion of his work,
    228
Royal College of Physicians, 92
Royal Society, 242
Royal Society of Literature, Transactions of,
    199
Rymer, Thomas, 148
Ryswick, Treaty of, 4, 10

Sacheverell, Dr. Henry, 226
Sailor Ben, Doggett as, 112
St. Bartholomew, Feast of, 189
St. Cecilia's Day, C's poem for, 13
St. Clement Danes, 118, 131, 137, 254, 257
Saint Evremond, 77
St. James's, Court at, 111
St. James's Palace, 26
St. James's Park, 26-27
St. James's Street or Square, 22, 39, 248, 269,
    271
St. John, Henry, first Viscount Bolingbroke,
    64, 222
Saint-Malo, France: C fears Keally a prisoner
    there, 4, 9-10; Keally's letters to, 31
St. Margaret, Parish of, 256
St. Omer, France, 14
St. Patrick's, 9, 151
Salisbury, 8
Saltash, 195
Sanford, for Sansom, 37-38
Sansom, John: sends C a mare, 19-20; and
    C's usquebaugh, 47; C sorry for, 37-
    38, 51
Sapho, C's dog, 16, 18, 24, 25
Sappho, 198
Scarsdale, third Earl of. *See* Leke, Robert
Schmid, Erasmus, 218-219
Scipio, 208, 209
Scotch, 48
Scotland, 40, 48, 247, 252
*Secret History of Henrada Maria Teresa,
    The*, 251, 252, 259, 272-279
"Selinda Pious," C's poem, 248
Semele, C's masque, 13
Senock, for Seven Oaks, 91-92
Seven Oaks, 92
Seymour, Sir Edward, 29-30
Shakespeare, Rowe's edition of, 229
Shannon, Viscount. *See* Boyle, Richard
Sheffield, John, Duke of Buckinghamshire,
    130
Sherburn, George, 223, 227, 229, 231, 232,
    234, 239, 244-245
Shovel, Sir Clowdisley, in storm, 27-28
Shrewsbury, 91
Sign of the Cock, in Bow Street, 114